WESTERN
HIGH SPOTS

WESTERN
HIGH SPOTS

Reading and Collecting Guides

BY JEFF C. DYKES

foreword by Leland D. Case

NORTHLAND PRESS

FIRST EDITION
ISBN 0–87358–162–8
Library of Congress Catalog Card Number 76–52539
Composed and Printed in the United States of America

FOR THE WESTERNERS

Of all the organizations of which I am a member, the Westerners continue to give me the most pleasure.

Table of Contents

List of Illustrations

Foreword

"YOU DON'T NEED an oil well to begin collecting western art" was the *Buckskin Bulletin* headline announcing the Northland Press publication of Jeff Dykes's *Fifty Great Western Illustrators*.

A sly asterisk, however, lured the reading eye to a puckish footnote: "But it could come in mighty handy!"

True. Canvases by Charlie Russell, the one-time Montana cowboy, have zoomed into the "Old Masters" bracket. Frederic Remington's *Turn Him Loose, Bill* fetched $175,000 at a Sotheby auction. Originals by any of Jeff's "greats" bring fancy figures, with bidders throwing punches backed by dollars in banks from Sarasota to Seattle and from Frankfort to Tokyo. Collecting western art is "in."

But there's a joker in the deck, and it's wild. The little guy with peanuts to spend after taxes can have just as much fun as the proud possessor of an oil well. It comes as he searches for his favorite artist's illustration in new or old books, ancient magazines, or even giveaway calendars. Santa Claus at an orphanage couldn't have a greater spinal tingle than thrills the beginner who spots a goodie on a dusty shelf at a Salvation Army resale shop or rescues one from a pile of basement rubbish just ahead of the garbageman!

All would-be collectors are instinctively followers of Flaubert, the shrewd French novelist, who affirmed that "if one has a determined purpose, it is surprising how often he is aided by chance."

Stephen Leacock, Canadian economist and humorist, had the same idea saying, "Yes, I'm a great believer in luck. I've noticed, though, that the harder I work the more I have of it."

Ben Franklin put it even pithier: "Diligence is the mother of good luck."

If these quotes compose a "creed for collectors," Jefferson Chenowth Dykes could sound a booming "Amen!" It's the gospel he has been preaching twenty-eight years, two months and nine days, he recently told me. That means he started long before 1965, when he hung his professional laurels as a United States conservation expert to become a bookseller in partnership with his wife, Martha. Now every room of their home — 4511 Guilford Road, College Park, Maryland, just over the District of Columbia line — bulges with books. They're even stacked in bathrooms.

At the Portland Hilton last October during a lull in the yearly conference of the Western History Association, Jeff was, as usual, effervescing conversationally on joys of finding, swapping, or selling Westerniana — thereby subtly persuading listeners through osmosis of suggestion to go and do likewise. "Start 'em young," he was saying. "My mother got me on track at age twelve with *The Boy Captive of the Texas Mier Expedition*. See that handsome buckaroo over there, tall enough to be a Texan? He's Bill Reese, now the very able assistant to Archie Hanna, top honcho of Beneicke Library at Yale University and sheriff of the New Haven Corral. But Bill was only sixteen when he came to our house with an 'I want' list. He bought over $1,000 worth that day and many more over the years."

Jeff's eyes twinkled and his Falstaffian figure rumpled with a mellow chuckle. Jeff is ever the Texan. He 'lowed that he found as much human nature in moving books as our late and mutual friend "Doc" Ben Green did in hoss tradin'.

"At least," he went on, "that's the idea running through talks I made over the years to Westerners. Now they're to be chapters in the book you're to do the foreword for. But remember, some readers don't know how Westerners organize and operate, so you'd better tuck in an explanation of who they are and why."

That part of the assignment is easy because I can crib from an article, "The Westerners: Twenty-five Years of Riding the Range," in the first issue of *The Western Historical Quarterly* for January, 1970:

"Westerners are bunches of males mostly, who meet monthly, usually, to chomp and chat — then after a speech on western history to haze or praise the speaker. . . . Dubbed 'a unique fellowship,' The Westerners fit into the organizational spectrum somewhere between a scholarly historical society and a Lion's Club, with attributes of both. . . . They ride with an easy rein."

Our first local unit, Chicago, named itself a "corral" when it organized back in 1944. Now the tally sheet shows nearly 100, including 16 outside the USA — Denmark, England, France, Japan, Mexico, Norway and Sweden. Each corral is autonomous, governed largely by "old traditions" which — and this *is* our most ancient "old tradition" — may be started any time at the drop of a big hat. Some organizational agglutination is provided by the WI (Westerners International) "home ranch" at Tucson, Arizona.

Actually, local corrals are somewhat like jackrabbits, for their programs tend to take on environmental coloration. In England or France or Washington, D.C., Westerners delve into whatever topics they fancy — but I hope someday, somewhere, a bold innovator will read a paper paralleling Caesar's Tenth Legion with Custer's Seventh Cavalry. Another might relate Wyoming's Sheridan to Italy's Florence of the Medici epoch; both having economics linked to wool.

In the USA westward from the Mississippi, however, monthly roundups usually deal with regional or local lore and history. Perhaps this is as it should be, for in an era when such centrifugal forces as television tug minds outwardly, we may need the centripetal to alert us to values that mark mature scholarship and provide perspective.

Refreshing variants also abound. Fort Worth Westerners heard a professor's heavily researched dissertation on fictional Sherlock Holmes and his synthetic American West. A research chemist told the new Arizona Corral at Scottsdale about pemmican, the dessicated meat that enabled Geronimo's warriors to play tag with the United States Cavalry — and the later, more sophisticated pemmican which provisioned the moonbound astronauts. South Dakota Westerners at Hot Springs (population 5,000) located and marked for the first time intrepid Jedediah Smith's 1823 trail through the Black Hills.

Humor and whimsy mingle with remuda aromas, too. Corrals lucky enough to own sun-bleached bison skulls pay ceremonial obeisance to "Old Joe, You Buffalo!" Probably Mari Sandoz, the late Nebraska author marooned in New York, was the first "sidesaddler," but female members now abound. At Oklahoma City there's even an "all gal" corral!

Many corrals publish and cherish periodicals. Especially noteworthy ones are mailed from Billings, Spokane, San Diego, Los Angeles, Tucson, Denver and Chicago. As you read on you'll see that Jeff gives High Spot ratings to several annual hardbacks. So prolific are writers, the *Buckskin Bulletin* finds space only for brief "Blinks at Books by Westerners."

"Scratch a Westerner," runs our folklore, "and a book collector bleeds." Jeff wouldn't fault that except to add that most collectors start as random book "accumulators." Only when they become discriminating and selective do they merit the proud title of "collectors." As such they earnestly but joyously seek everything worthwhile in their specific fields.

Categories abound. Under events, places, and people the list is endless — Custer's bash, Indians good and bad, or just the Sioux, or Navajo blankets, mountain men, California missions, and on ad infinitum. Personalities are popular, especially badmen or artists and authors. Jeff rates Mark Twain high and might even agree with Ernest Hemingway who pontificated, "All modern American literature comes from one book by Mark Twain called *Huckleberry Finn* . . . There was nothing before. There has been nothing as good since."

Fortunately, scholarly but readable bibliographies, such as J. Leonard Jennewein's *Black Hills Book Trails,* exist for countless categories. Why, Paul Galleher, a Los Angeles Westerner, has even done a *Mini-Bibliography* of corral-published "Westerner-iana!"

Specialize is the key word. Jeff's Emersonesque advice is to push on through the amorphous "I-like-it" phases to more celestial levels of collectordom.

In the Ozarks they tell of a hillsman who arrived late for a political rally, and was asked if he'd talked to the orator of the day. "We've howdied," he 'lowed, "but we ain't yet shook." Jeff Dykes wants accumulators to step right to to shake — and thereafter be card carrying members of the global fraternity of collectors!

LELAND D. CASE
President emeritus of
Westerners International and
Keeper of the Pitchfork
Tucson, Arizona

My Sport

"MY SPORT is bookhunting. I look upon it as a game, a game requiring skill, some money, and some luck." I don't know the author of that quotation, but it nearly expresses my feelings about collecting. Our Registrar of Marks and Brands, Hal Taylor, put it up to me this way, "Could you write an article — on how to go about starting a Western Americana book collection? I have the feeling that lots of us would like to get started on a collection, but have no idea where to begin."

Before taking up my sport perhaps it would be wise to ask yourself a one-word question. Why?

There are a number of sound reasons for becoming a collector. In my own case, my long-time friend and associate, Louis P. Merrill, now a successful Angus breeder at Midlothian, Texas, pointed out to me that the money I was spending for books was adding little or nothing to my estate. I protested that I bought only the books I wanted to read. Louis countered by saying that I was learning a very little about a wide range of subjects and that if I persisted in my reading habits I might be a widely read man but not very well informed on any one subject.

Finally, I decided to stop being a book accumulator and become a collector. Looking back over the years, I think Louis was motivated by selfish reasons — he wanted a close neighbor to whom he could show his acquisitions, brag on occasion, and confess his mistakes on others. In the six years we were together in Fort Worth we lived within a few blocks of each other. We exchanged much information on books and dealers, traded catalogs and occasionally books, and each helped the other.

Whatever his motive in persuading me to become a collector, I will always be grateful — collecting opened new vistas to me. So far the major dividend has been the numerous friends throughout the country among the Western bookmen, dealers, writers, illustrators, and fellow collectors.

If you want to be an authority on or to write on a western subject, you will be wise to collect the major references on that subject. For example, it would have been impossible for me to have compiled *Billy the Kid: The Bibliography of a Legend* (Albuquerque, 1952), if I had not had most of the items listed in my own collection. If you want to be more articulate about the glorious history of our West, or if you can say you feel that collecting some Western Americana will make you a better Westerner, you have satisfactorily answered that one-word question, "Why?"

"Why" having been disposed of, you will probably find the guidelines that follow of some use.

My recommendation is that first you do some reading about the books about the West. Fortunately, there are a number of good ones available now — this was not the case when I started many years ago. Number one on my list for reading is J. Frank Dobie's *Guide to Life and Literature of the Southwest* (Dallas, 1952). This book is a reprint, "revised and enlarged in both knowledge and wisdom," of an Austin (1943) issue and of numerous mimeographed lists used in his classes at the University of Texas that preceded the printed book. J. Frank Dobie, teacher, folklorist, historian, critic, storyteller, hunter, explorer, cowman, and top all-around Westerner, appraises the books about the Southwest in this volume. A collector has been described as one who collects everything—worthy and unworthy — on his subject. Frank's pithy comments have guided my buying of the worthy for many years, though I confess to having erred on more than one purchase.

Lawrence Clark Powell, former Dean of the School of Library Science, University of California at Los Angeles, writes beautifully about books. Among the numerous articles and volumes of his that I have found helpful are: *Heart of the Southwest* (Los Angeles, 1955), *A Southwest Century* (Van Nuys, California, 1958) and *Land of Fiction* (Pasadena, 1952).

Other books that will introduce you to the various phases of the vast literature of the West are *Southwest Heritage* (Albuquerque, 1938) by Mabel Major, Rebecca Smith and T. M. Pearce; *The Literature of the Rocky Mountain West, 1803–1903* (Caldwell, Idaho, 1939) by L. J. Davidson and P. Bostick; and *The American Historical Novel* (Norman, 1950) by Ernest E. Leisy. There are many others.

Before you make your final choice of a collecting field or subject it might also be wise to read one general book on book collecting. My own favorite is Herbert Faulkner West's *Modern Book Collecting for the Impecunious Amateur*. Herb West is Professor of Comparative Literature at Dartmouth. He is a writer, a collector, a book-seller, an artist, and a campus rebel. His thoughts are presented with wit and wisdom.

The reading done, some talks with collectors and booksellers may help you decide on your collecting field. My advice is to keep it narrow in the beginning. I started by collecting books on the Texas Rangers and for a number of years confined my purchases to books about them. After you have gained some experience you can spread out into related fields more intelligently. Books about a state may be either a satisfactory field (North Dakota or Idaho) or entirely too broad (Texas or California). You may want to collect books by a particular Western writer or books illustrated by your favorite Western artist. There are collectors who seek imprints by a particular publisher or printer — I compete with a number of others in trying to maintain my status as the premier collector of the books designed or printed by Carl Hertzog of El Paso, the great Texas typographer. There are many phases of western literature and numerous collectors working the field. The cowboy and cattle collectors are quite numerous and the outlaw-gunmen collectors rival them in number. Each of these broad fields can be broken down to size for beginners.

How to Begin

In all instances possible, your first book to buy is the best bibliography that covers your field. For example, if you decide to collect books about South Dakota, the Black Hills, or Deadwood by all means start with J. Leonard Jennewein's *Black Hills Booktrails* (Mitchell, South Dakota, 1962). *An Arizona Gathering* (Tucson, 1960), compiled by Donald M. Powell, will be helpful to all those collecting modern books about Arizona. E. I. Edwards's *Desert Voices* (Los Angeles, 1958) is an excellent descriptive bibliography and will guide those interested in any phase of the history of California deserts. Some so-called bibliographies are mere lists of books and are too general to be helpful — if the "bibliography" is not annotated, save your money!

The one mark of the true collector is a "Want List." This may be handwritten, typed, or merely strongly remembered. A good bibliography is very helpful in developing a want list, and that is one of the main reasons for spending some money early on a good bibliography, should there be a worthy one available. If there is no suitable bibliography, you can compile a want list from other sources. When I started collecting books about the Texas Rangers there was no bibliography on that particular subject and there is not today. My first want list consisted of eleven items — all that were

included under that heading in J. Frank Dobie's 1936 mimeographed *Life and Literature of the Southwest*. The last book on that list was Walter Prescott Webb's *The Texas Rangers* (Boston, 1935) with a typical Dobie comment, "The beginning, end, and middle of the whole subject." One word followed this description — "Bibliography." I had to have Dr. Webb's book for two reasons — it was the best book about Texas Rangers then (and still is), and it contained a list of the sources he used in writing it. I bought a copy of the first trade edition at once. My first catalog purchase was from that genial Georgian who has graced the Chicago book world for so many years, Wright Howes, and it was no. 184 of the limited, signed edition of 205 copies of Dr. Webb's *The Texas Rangers*. My want list grew as I saw other ranger items on the shelves of book dealers or listed in catalogs. Perhaps you may wonder why I didn't immediately buy these items — frankly, some of them I couldn't afford at the time and in other instances the condition was unsatisfactory, or they were reprints, or priced too high. Other items were added to my want list as I visited libraries and other collectors.

With a good want list compiled the next step is some judicious buying. The best book hunting of all is in the book stores — there is no thrill equal to spotting an item on your want list on the shelf — if it happens to be priced below the market, there is the added thrill of having found a bargain. There will be some frustrations, of course — the book may be priced over the market, incomplete, soiled, or battered, and you will return it to its place on the shelf and hunt again.

Catalog reading is one of the most pleasant ways of book hunting, but it often leads to heartaches. You find a book on your want list, priced right, and described as being in very good condition, so you order. Ten days later your check comes back and the single word "Sold" is written across your order. I have tried airmail, telegrams, and telephone in my attempts to beat out my fellow collectors for books on my want list — with some success and with many disappointments.

Most dealers do a satisfactory job of describing the books they list in their catalogs. Some do make honest mistakes, and some get careless on occasion, but these are minor crosses to be borne. Catalogs greatly extend your buying opportunities and each collector should be on the mailing list of those dealers in this country and in England who issue "cats" listing items in their particular fields. Each year *Antiquarian Bookman,* the weekly magazine of the trade, issues *The AB Bookman's Yearbook.* It always includes a "Reference Directory of Specialist and Antiquarian Booksellers" that provides valuable tips on the dealers to contact. Unfortunately, the *Yearbook* does not indicate the dealers who issued catalogs, and it is necessary to inquire by mail.

In both bookstore and catalog buying, be patient. Do not buy an inferior copy or one priced too high for fear that you will never have another chance. The failure of another copy to appear on the market has occurred less than a half dozen times in my book hunting experiences extending over a quarter of a century. Patience may be a necessity, as it was in my own case, since I never had any great amount of money to spend on books at any one time. I did set aside a little money each month for books, and I did and do buy regularly both in the shops and from "cats." My sport does require some money. The skills in appraising condition, values, and editions will come with experience as will your skill in spotting a wanted book on a cluttered table or a crowded upper shelf. I have had my share of luck — all collectors do. However, you make a lot of your collecting luck by establishing the right contacts with specialist booksellers in your collecting field. Most of them are grand folks.

One final bit of advice — card your buys. Plain three by five index cards will serve nicely. You can make your records as elaborate as you like but as a minimum set down the author, title, place of publication, date of issue, the bookseller's name, and the price you paid. As your collection grows you will find this information very helpful in avoiding duplicate buying, in ordering from catalogs, and in getting a certain satisfaction from comparing the prices you paid with the market level as books go out-of-print (OP) and become scarcer.

A lot of fun in my sport — bookhunting — is the same as in other hunting sports — showing off trophies. I like to see my books, to handle them, and to read them. But my greatest pleasure is in showing them to my fellow collectors. If you take up my sport, my wish for you is good hunting — bookhunting, that is!

CHAPTER I

Collecting Modern Western Americana

A FEW YEARS AGO I had the privilege of spending a couple of days in the little cow town of Ekalaka, Montana. My interest in Western local history led me to inquire about the town's birth and this is the story I was told — Claude Carter, a buffalo hunter turned bartender, was on his way to another location with a load of logs and whiskey when his wagon got stuck in a mudhole. Since he had to unload anyway to get the wagon out he was credited with stating, "Hell, any place in Montana is a good place to build a saloon." He built it right there; and Puptown grew up around it. The numerous prairie dogs in the vicinity were adequate justification for its first name. However, the citizens gladly changed it to Ekalaka to honor the bride of the first white homesteader there. She was a Sioux princess, and the niece of Sitting Bull. The Sioux meaning Ekalaka is "swift one" — I was there on a Saturday night and the name seems appropriate.

All this leads to a paraphrase of Carter's homily — *Hell, any time is a good time to start a Western Americana Collection!* As a matter of fact, the past few years have been particularly rich in worthwhile Western non-fiction.

It will be impossible for me to discuss in this article all the good Western books that have been published in the past dec-

ade or two or even in the last two years. However, I believe two or three examples will drive home my point.

Range Life

As a professional conservationist I know something about the importance of grass as a land builder, as a preventer of wind and water erosion. I appreciate its importance in our Western economy — two-thirds of the farm and ranch land in our seventeen Western states is covered with grass and the livestock fed wholly or in part by it provide fifty percent of the agricultural income of these same states. Grass built the West and is still the solid foundation on which rests the prosperity of well over half of the land area of our country.

The range livestock industry, which developed quite naturally because there was grass, is one of the most thoroughly documented segments of our economy over the last seventy-five years. Surely, think you, there was nothing left to say about cowboys and cattle, range life and wars when January 1, 1954, rolled around.

Let's take a look at the record — Wayne Gard wrote a great book about a famous "drove road." *The Chisholm Trail* (University of Oklahoma Press, 1954, $4.50). Dr. Walker D. Wyman's

Nothing but Prairie and Sky (University of Oklahoma Press, 1954, $3.75) is as excellent on Dakota ranching as is E. F. Hagell's *When the Grass was Free* (Bourgey & Curl, 1954, $2.50) on Canadian range life. Fabriola Cabeza de Baca's *We Fed Them Cactus* (University of New Mexico, 1954, $3.50) is a poetic saga of Mexican ranching on the Llano Estacado, of eastern New Mexico. Jim and Ann Counselor's *Wild, Wooly, and Wonderful* (Vantage, 1954, $3.75) is about ranching in another part of New Mexico, the Navajo country, where they combined sheep raising with keeping a trading post. Stanford C. Yoder in *Horse Trails Along the Desert* (Herald Press, Scottsdale, Pennsylvania, $2.50) tells about range life in the Northwest half a century ago.

Histories of two great cowmen organizations appeared in the last two years — Maurice Frink's *Cow Country Cavalcade* (Old West Publishing Co., 1954, $4.50) is the story of eighty years of the Wyoming Stock Growers Association. Lewis Nordyke's *Great Roundup* (Morrow, 1955, $5.00) covers the nearly as long history of the Texas and Southwestern Cattle Raisers Association.

Edmund Randolph's *Hell Among the Yearlings* (Norton, 1955, $3.75) is a rollicking tale of the Montana range thirty years ago. Dean Krakel's *The Saga of Tom Horn* (Powder River Publishers, 1954, $4.50) is on the other hand a truthful if grim account of some of the doings on the Wyoming range a few years earlier.

S. Omar Barker's *Songs of the Saddlemen* (Sage, 1954, $2.75) will be appreciated by all who love horses, cattle, grass and blue skies. Duncan Emrick's *The Cowboy's Own Brand Book* (Crowell, 1954, $1.50) is informative and delightful reading for all boys from seven to seventy.

Colonel Eddie Wentworth and his cousin, Charles Wayland Towne, have just issued an entertaining volume *Cattle and Men* (University of Oklahoma Press, 1955, $4.00). Clifford F. Westermeir's *Trailing the Cowboy* (Caxton, 1955, $5.00) is a new venture in cowboy storytelling since he has done a magnificent job in digging up the original material from the pens of frontier journalists who lived and wrote when the cowboy news was hot.

Dr. Frank Goodwyn's *Lone Star Land* (Knopf, 1955, $5.00) is a vivid, balanced word picture of present-day Texas. The present has its roots in the past and Frank has provided chapters on "The Longhorns," "The Cowboy" and "New Horizons on the Range." There is even a photograph of whitefaces being rounded up by helicopter on the Waggoner Ranch in Wilbarger County.

Of a more technical nature there is *Breeding Beef Cattle for Unfavorable Environments* (University of Texas Press, 1955, $4.75) edited by Albert O. Rhoad, a report of a symposium held to commemorate the one hundredth anniversary of the famous King Ranch of Texas. This was an international conference of breeders and scientists that considered the problems of cattle raising in the intense heat on the arid range common to many parts of the world. Of more general interest was Bob Kleberg's paper on the development of the Santa Gertrudis, the great new breed of American cattle, the first that we can claim as our own. This book has world-wide value.

This isn't the complete list of good books about range life but perhaps it will serve to indicate that now is a good time to start a cowboy and cattle collection.

Guns, Gunmen, and Outlaws

If you prefer to think about the West in terms of guns, gunmen, and outlaws instead of grass, you can also start.

Ramon F. Adams's *Sixguns and Saddle Leather* (University of Oklahoma Press, 1954, $12.50) is the first comprehensive bibliography of western gunmen and outlaws. It would be the cornerstone on which to build a collection. Many of the rarities described in my friend Ramon's bibliography are extremely expensive and some are practically impossible to obtain. Fortunately, new reprints are putting many of these rarities within pocket range of us all. Savoie Lottinville of the University of Oklahoma Press is one of our benefactors — three of the rarest of the outlaw books are included in "The Western Frontier Library," issued at $2.00 each by his distinguished regional press; A. S. Mercer's *The Banditti of the Plains* (1954), the classic of the Johnson County (Wyoming) War, with a foreword full of history and brightened with the wit of Bill Kittrell; Pat F. Garrett's *The Authentic Life of Billy the Kid* (1954), likewise for the Lincoln County War, with an introduction by your writer that shows it to be not so authentic; Ridge's *The Life and Adventures of Joaquin Murieta* (1955) with a debunking intro-

duction by the late beloved Joe Jackson, literary editor of the San Francisco *Chronicle* for a quarter of a century. Also recommended is Charles Lee Martin's *Sam Bass* with an introduction by Ramon Adams.

Ed Bartholomew of the Frontier Press of Houston, Texas, is our other benefactor. He has reissued W. M. Walton's *Life and Adventures of Ben Thompson* (1954, $3.95); O. S. Clark's *Life of Clay Allison* (1954, $1.25); J. W. Bridwell's *Life and Adventures of Robert McKimie, "Little Reddie From Texas"* (he wasn't) (1955, $1.50); *Life of Cole Younger,* by himself (1955, $3.00); and, in 1954, *Belle Starr* and *Cherokee Bill* by S. W. Harmon at $1.50 each.

Ed is a student, researcher and writer, and from his pen and press we also have *Cullen Baker* (1954, $3.00); *Life of Black Jack Ketchem* (1955, $2.50); and *Life of Jesse Evans* (1955, $1.50). All the Frontier Press books are issued in strictly limited editions and are sure to be collector's items in the not too distant future.

There were also some great originals issued after January 1, 1954: *Pictorial History of the Wild West* (Crown, 1954, $5.95), a big, extremely well-illustrated volume that calls the roll in words and pictures of all the notorious and a few of the minor gunmen in the post Civil War period; John M. Myers's *Doc Holliday* (Little, Brown, 1955, $4.50), the first biography of the soft-spoken Georgia dentist who went west to die of TB and finally did just that — despite half a hundred knife and gun fights; and finally Sonnichsen and Morrison's *Alias Billy the Kid* (University of New Mexico Press, 1955, $4.00), perhaps the most entertaining and surely the most contro-versial Western book of 1955.

Yes, if you have a yen for the wild bunch, now is a good time to start col-lecting material about its members.

Western Illustrators

On the other hand, if you believe as I do that our good Western illustrators are just as truly historians as our writers and you have a yen for books illustrated by that great cowboy artist and storyteller, Charlie Russell of Montana, or by the famous Frederic Remington, you can start a "Not-in-Yost" or "Not-in-Mc-Cracken" collection.

Among the books enhanced by Rus-sell illustrations in 1954–55 are: Mary Joan Boyer's *The Old Gravois Coal Dig-gings* (privately printed, 1954, $3.50); Amanda E. Ellis's *Legends and Tales of the Rockies* (Dentan Printing Co., Colo-rado Springs, 1954, $1.00); Nordyke's *Great Roundup;* Frank Gilbert Roe's *The Indian and the Horse* (University of Oklahoma Press, 1955, $5.00); *Year's Pictorial History of America* (Lear, 1954, $9.95); Elmer Keith's *Sixguns* (Stockpole, 1955, $10.00); and several reprints from the *Montana Magazine of History* plus new well-illustrated cata-logues of the collections at Helena and at Great Falls.

The "Not-in-McCracken" or Reming-ton list includes: Roe's *The Indian and the Horse;* Harold McCracken's *The Beast That Walks Like Man* (Hanover House, 1955, $4.50); *Year's Pictorial History of America;* Horan & Samm's *Pictorial History of the Wild West;* Har-old McCracken's *A Catalogue of the Frederic Remington Memorial Collec-*

tion (Gallery Press, 1954, $5.00); *The Denver Brand Book* edited by Maurice Frink (The Westerners, 1954, $7.00); Mari Sandoz's *The Buffalo Hunters* (Hastings, 1954, $4.50); *Profile of Amer-ica* edited by Emily Davie (Crowell, 1954, $8.50); L. A. Deywall's *The Story of Monument Hill* (La Grange Journal, 1955, $1.50); and *Westward the Way* edited by Perry T. Rathbone (City Art Museum of Saint Louis, 1954, $3.75). Perhaps I missed a few in running my cards but that gives you an idea.

Harold Bugbee illustrated Barker's *Songs of the Saddlemen* and John Mc-Carthy's *Adobe Wall Bride* (Naylor, 1955, $3.50). Ross Santee's *Dog Days* (Scribner, $3.95) is illustrated by the au-thor. Lew Larkin's *Bingham; Fighting Artist* (State Publishing Co., 1955, $4.00) contains several illustrations by the bat-tling Missourian. Laura Bickerstaff's *Pi-oneer Artists of Taos* (Sage, 1955, $3.00) contains biographies of, and illustrations by, the first six Taos painters — Oscar E. Berninghaus, Ernest L. Blumenschein, E. Irving Couse, W. Herbert (Buck) Dunton, Bert G. Phillips, and John Henry Sharp, each richly deserving the recognition accorded him.

Yes, if you have a yen for Western il-lustrators you can start now.

Western Fiction

I have used three examples—enough? Almost as good a case can be made for Indians, overland travel, exploration, and western railroads. A list fully as long as the above can be made for Western fiction, although here due care must be exercised since much of it does not mea-sure up.

For example, a Western written by a New York lady in 1954 opens with *three* cowboys driving a Texas trail herd to Abilene. One night the three bed down in a *cowhouse* conveniently located by the side of the trail for the comfort of tired cowboys. Three buffalo hunters steal the herd while our heroes sleep. The herd has a five-hour start but it takes the cowboys *two days* of hard fast riding to catch up with it. The buffalo hunters are all asleep so our heroes get the drop on them. However, the chief villain *bellers like a bull* and stampedes the herd. The rest of the book isn't quite that bad but it will find no favor with Westerners anywhere.

If you want your history mild and in painless, even enjoyable, doses get these 1954 Westerns: Alan LeMay's *The Searchers* (Harper, $3.00); Ford Logan's *Fire in the Desert* (Ballantine, cloth $2.00, wraps 35¢); Milton Lott's *The Last Hunt* (Houghton Mifflin, $3.95); Wayne Overholser's *The Violent Land* (Macmillan, $2.95); Ernest Haycox's *The Adventurers* (Little, Brown, $3.95); and John Prescott's *Journey by the River* (Random House, $3.00). The best of 1955 are all plenty good and I am glad to recommend Red Reeder's *The Mackenzie Raid* (Ballantine, cloth $2.00, wraps 35¢); Rutherford G. Montgomery's *Black Powder Empire* (Little, Brown, $2.75); Will Henry's *Who Rides With Wyatt* (Random House, $3.00); Brad Ward's *Six Gun Heritage* (Dutton, $2.50); William Colt MacDonald's *Destination, Danger* (Lippincott, $2.75); Lucas Todd's *Showdown Creek* (Macmillan, $2.75), and Sigman Byrd and John Sutherland's *The Valiant* (Jason Press, $3.25). That's a baker's dozen for a start.

For a general guide to the great books of Western Americana in the last decade I refer you to the publications of the Chicago Westerners. Nine consecutive times beginning in 1946 they have chosen the Best Ten Western Books of the Year. The composite list of ninety is by far the best buying guide available to the beginning collector.

So I say, again — Hell, anytime is a good time to start a Western Americana collection!

CHAPTER II

Western Movement — Its Literature

THE LITERATURE of the western movement in this country is so varied and so vast that in the space allotted for this article, we can only hit the High Spots. In trying to find a way to limit the discussion to a manageable segment, serious consideration was given to mentioning only those books that *influenced* the movement. To have done so would have eliminated some of the best of the literature — in fact, practically all the books written in the last one hundred years. The influence of the literature on the movement has received considerable thought on the selections that follow, but has not been limiting.

Numerous events and situations were of great historical significance in the westward movement. Among those of particular importance, I have listed: The Louisiana Purchase; the Lewis and Clark Expedition; the fur trade; the Santa Fe market; the annexation of Texas followed by the Mexican War and the Gadsden Purchase; the opening of the Oregon Trail, followed by the settling of the United States–Canada boundary dispute; the railroad surveys and other official exploring expeditions; the persecution of the Mormons in Missouri and Illinois; the discovery of gold in California; the growth of the Texas Longhorn herds during the Civil War;

the completion of the transcontinental railroad; the Battle of Palo Duro Canyon and General A. Miles's winter campaign following the Battle of the Little Big Horn. Please note that only a few of the important happenings listed occurred after 1850. The early writings about the pre-1850 events and situations nearly all had some influence on the westward movement.

The Beginnings

It is here recognized that the westward movement really began with the first moves inland from the sea coast colonial settlements and that the further expansion from the Appalachians to the Mississippi was another important step on the way to the Pacific. However, only a few books on the beginnings will be mentioned here as our emphasis is on the West from the Mississippi. In 1817, Morris Birkbeck's *Notes on a Journey in America . . . to the Territory of Illinois* was issued in Philadelphia. It includes the first description known to me of the true or tallgrass prairie — probably the greatest natural grassland area in the world, stretching from Lake Winnipeg in Canada to the Gulf of Mexico. Birkbeck was an English land scout who led a band of English settlers to their new homes in Illinois. His book was reprinted several times in England and Ireland, there was a German edition in 1818, and a Dutch printing in 1820. In 1822, Birkbeck issued *An Address to the Farmers of Great Britain, with an Essay on the Prairies of the Western Country* in London, an expansion of his description of the prairie in his 1817 book.

Theodore Roosevelt's four-volume set, *Winning the West* (New York, 1889–1894–1896), is entirely devoted to the Appalachian to Mississippi frontier. It was the first segment of a planned set that was to have covered the entire western movement — the author's duties after 1896 did not permit him to finish the job.

Lewis and Clark

The first important event in the expansion across the Mississippi was the purchase of Louisiana — making the exploration of the new territory a matter of extreme urgency. The literature of the first of the expeditions — by Lewis and Clark — is extensive indeed. Patrick Gass was a member of the party, and his book was the earliest firsthand account of the expedition. It was issued in Pittsburg in 1807 with the title, *Journal of Voyages and Travels.* The first British edition came out in 1808 and Wright Howes in *U.S.iana* (New York, 1962) calls it the "best" and claims that the map included in the French edition of 1810 was the "best of the Lewis and Clark route done up to this date." The authorized report was issued in Philadelphia in 1814 and was reprinted many times, the most scholarly being that of 1893. President Jefferson's message to Congress in 1806, *Communicating Dis-coveries—By Captains Lewis and Clark, Dr. Sibley and Mr. Dunbar,* was issued by both the House (believed to be the earlier) and the Senate. The message does not include much on the Lewis and Clark Expedition but is important for the information on the Louisiana-Texas frontier and the southern portion of the Louisiana Purchase.

The Mountain Men

The Canadians dominated the fur trade prior to the Louisiana Purchase — however, the Yankees challenged almost immediately. A party of trappers en route to fur country met Lewis and Clark on their return trip. John Colter decided to forego the hero's welcome awaiting the Lewis and Clark party in the East to return to the mountains to trap. During the period 1805–1845 the mountain men wrote much history on the land if not on paper. They trapped and traded to be sure, but they explored, found mountain passes, blazed trails, produced maps, served as scouts and guides to official exploring parties and later the army. They were the forerunners of the western settlers. Much has been written about Jed Smith, Hugh Glass, Old Bill Williams, Joe Walker, Ewing Young, Kit Carson, Jim Bridger, Broken Hand Fitzpatrick, and others of that valiant band. If they found little time to write they had their Boswells. Washington Irving's *The Rocky Mountains — Adventures in the Far West* (Philadelphia, 1837) was based on Captain Bonneville's papers and other sources. So far as I know all of the numerous reprints used the title, *Adventures of Captain Bonneville.* The previous year (1836) Irving's *Astoria* was released at Philadelphia. It is the story of the 1811 American attempt at settlement on the Pacific coast to bolster our claim to Oregon. Many years later Hiram M. Chittenden's *The American Fur Trade of the Far West* (New York, 1902) was issued in three volumes — it must be regarded as the classic on the subject. I freely confess, however, that I find some still later books more readable including *The Travels of Jedediah Smith* (Santa Ana, California, 1934), edited by Maurice S. Sullivan and printing for the first time Jed's own journals; Dr. LeRoy Hafen's *Broken Hand* (Denver, 1931), a biography of Thomas Fitzpatrick, and Walter S. Campbell's (writing as Stanley Vestal) biographies of *Joe Meek* (Caldwell, Idaho, 1952) and *Kit Carson* (Boston, 1928).

The Santa Fe Trail

Rumors trickled back to the States that there was a ready market for American goods in Santa Fe. It was only eight hundred miles from Independence on the Missouri to Santa Fe so naturally the American merchants set out to supply the market despite the dangers of the trail which included attacks by the Comanches. Much of the literature on the trail and on Santa Fe is superb. Josiah Gregg's two-volume account, *Commerce on the Prairies* (New York, 1844) is a classic. R. L. Duffus's *The Santa Fe Trail* (New York, 1930) is a top job as is *El Gringo,* or *New Mexico and Her People* (New York, 1857) by William W. H. Davis. Willa Cather's *Death Comes for the Archbishop* (New York, 1927) is a moving piece of writing with

a historical base. I can particularly recommend to you *Southwest on the Turquoise Trail: The First Diaries on the Road to Santa Fe* (Denver, 1933), edited, with bibliographical résumé, 1810–1825, by Archer Butler Hulbert.

The Mexican War

In the meantime, much else was happening in the Southwest. The annexation of Texas in 1845 made war with Mexico almost a certainty since the United States adopted the Texas position in the still hot boundary dispute. When the war was over, the Southwest, including California, was a part of the United States. The Gadsden Purchase ended the United States–Mexico boundary dispute and the road was clear for further westward expansion. John R. Bartlett's *Personal Narrative of Explorations — In Texas, New Mexico, California, Etc. — With the United States and Mexican Boundary Commission* (New York, 1854) is a nicely illustrated two-volume set that tells all about marking the boundary from the Texas line to the Pacific.

Many visitors from the States and Europe came to Texas during the days of the republic and the early days of statehood. Much was printed about the resources of Texas, and those who did not write books spread the news by letter or word of mouth. Among the books, Mary Austin Holley's *Texas* (Baltimore, 1833) seems to have been written to encourage emigration to the colony of her cousin, Stephen F. Austin. It was rewritten and reissued in Lexington, Kentucky, in 1836 with the primary purpose of seeking recognition of the infant republic by the United States. Jacob De Cordova's *Texas: Her Resources and Her Public Men* (Philadelphia, 1858) was another emigration pitch. De Cordova owned much land script that he was anxious to market — despite the obvious profit motive, it is a good book. Not all the promotional books on Texas were published in this country — Dr. Ferdinand von Roemer's *Texas* was issued in German in Bonn in 1849 and included the first geological map of the state. Roemer, a paleontologist, came to Texas in 1845 and spent two years gathering material for his book, not printed in English until 1935.

A number of excellent books were issued about the Mexican War. My favorites are *Sketches of the Campaign in Northern Mexico* (New York, 1835), probably by Major Luther P. Giddings, but also attributed to M. E. Curwen; Captain W. S. Henry's *Campaign Sketches of the War with Mexico* (New York, 1847) and *The Scouting Expeditions of McCulloch's Texas Rangers* (Philadelphia, 1847) by Samuel G. Reid, Jr., a Louisiana lawyer who served with McCulloch in Mexico. Justin H. Smith's two-volume set, *The War with Mexico, 1846–48* (New York, 1919), is very good formal history.

The Mormon Trek

The Mormon trek and the settling of Utah was a dramatic episode in the westward movement. Many of those who went to other parts of the West were seeking a quick fortune with the thought of returning to their homes in the East. The Mormons, driven out of Missouri and later out of Illinois, sought asylum

and a permanent place to establish their homes. They actively sought new members and thus new citizens for the West, in this country and in Western Europe primarily through tracts and missionaries. My favorite book on the subject is Vardis Fisher's *Children of God* (New York, 1939). It comes nearer than any book I know of to covering the entire history of the Mormons up to 1890. A drier history is *The Rocky Mountain Saints: A Full and Complete History of the Mormons* (New York, 1873) by T. B. H. Stenhouse.

The California and Oregon Trail

The boundary problem with Canada was settled by treaty while the Mexican War was in progress. Long before this, however, a number of Americans had made their way overland via the Oregon Trail to settle in the Willamette Valley — a few others made the trip around the Horn by boat. The Hudson's Bay Company factor at Fort Vancouver on the north bank of the Columbia, Dr. John McLoughlin, did his best to hold Oregon for England. Stripping the country south of the Columbia of furs was the strategy used by Dr. McLoughlin to discourage the Americans. However, these Americans were interested in land and homes rather than furs, and the strategy failed. A number of the mountain men, including Ewing Young and Joe Meek, gave up their traps to settle in the rich valley. When Dr. McLoughlin refused to sell cows to the settlers, Ewing Young led a party south to Mexican California to buy some. The story of the 1837 trail drive from California is well told in Col. Phillip I. Edwards's *California in 1837*

(Sacramento, 1890). Richard Henry Dana's *Two Years Before the Mast* (New York, 1840) has something to say about ranching in Mexican California and has long been considered the classic on the hide and tallow trade. My favorite books about ranching in Spanish and later Mexican California were both written by Stewart Edward White: *Ranchero* (Garden City, 1933) and *Folded Hills* (Garden City, 1934). In these carefully researched novels the author continues the saga of Mountain Man Andy Burnett's personal westward trek that he started in *The Long Rifle* (Garden City, 1932).

I suppose it would be considered treason to ignore Francis Parkman's *The California and Oregon Trail* (New York, 1849) and beginning with the fourth edition in 1872, shortened to *The Oregon Trail*. I am inclined to agree with my old friend J. Frank Dobie who commented in his *Guide to Life and Literature of the Southwest* (Austin, 1943): "A good book, but not so good as fifty others in these lists." I do admire the 1892 edition with the handsome Frederic Remington illustrations.

California Gold

The discovery of gold in California early in 1848 turned a trickle of emigrants to the new territory into a torrent. Gold lured them to California but many of them became permanent residents. Gold was the single greatest stimulant to emigration in the history of the West. Samuel Clemens or, if you prefer, Mark Twain, was there during most of the exciting doings, and, in my opinion, *Roughing It* (Hartford, 1872) is the single best book about the gold era. Twain told it like it was. It has been a personal favorite for well over sixty years and it seems unlikely that it will ever be replaced. Bayard Taylor's *El Dorado* (New York, 1850) is a classic by a distinguished writer, world traveler and competent artist that appeared twenty-two years before *Roughing It*. Doubtless it had more influence on the westward movement, but Taylor was a reporter covering a news story while Twain lived it. William M'Ilvaine's *Sketches of Scenery and Notes of Personal Adventure in California and Mexico* (Philadelphia, 1850) is nearly as good as *El Dorado,* and the illustrations are better. M'Ilvaine had a Master of Arts degree from the University of Pennsylvania and had studied art in Europe before trying his luck in the gold fields. He soon decided that the life in the mining camps was too rough for him, but before he left for home, he made numerous on-the-spot sketches of Sacramento and San Francisco — seventeen of them were used to illustrate his book. Merle Johnson in his *High Spots of American Literature* (New York, 1929) included Stewart Edward White's California trilogy: *Gold* (Garden City, 1913), *The Gray Dawn* (Garden City, 1915) and *The Rose Dawn* (Garden City, 1920). *Gold* deals with the days of '49; *The Gray Dawn* with the struggle to establish law and order, including the vigilantes, and *The Rose Dawn* with the widespread agricultural development of the state. All are very good, indeed.

The discovery of gold and the rush of settlers to California gave further emphasis to the need for a railroad link between the two coasts. Both the government and the railroads had survey parties in the field to determine the most practical routes. *Reports of Explorations and Surveys to Ascertain the Most Practical and Economic Route for a Railroad from the Mississippi River to the Pacific Ocean* (commonly called *The Railroad Surveys*) was issued by the government, volume by volume, 1855 to 1861 — the set with the atlas totaled twelve volumes and Volume Twelve was issued in two parts. In this set the whole of the West was mapped and pictured rather adequately for the first time. John Mix Stanley, a very good artist who had been west several times before was responsible for many of the illustrations, and he had competent assistants. A. B. Gray's *Survey of a Route for the Southern Pacific on 32nd Parallel* (Cincinnati, 1856) was privately issued, and I chose the second edition because the plates are vastly superior — some of the best ever made of southwestern scenes.

THE CATTLE TRADE

The Civil War slowed the westward movement materially, but when it was over, the rush started again. The railroads were building westward, and a good many Southerners could not abide the Scalawag-Carpetbagger rule during reconstruction and took their families to the West. While many of the Confederate soldiers went home to hopeless situations, such was not the case in Texas. While the Texans were away fighting, their Longhorn herds had continued to grow — the old men and boys who were left at home had been unable to brand them, and only a few had reached the market. The Texans had the meat on hoof; the North wanted the meat and had the money to pay for it. Fortunately, the Longhorn was ideal for trail driving and the solution was easy — let meat and money come together at some halfway point, usually at some railroad town in Kansas. It was an exciting period. Population mushroomed at the cattle shipping centers, and a huge time was had by all. The books on the trail-cowtown days are numerous, and I suppose it is only fair to mention first *Historic Sketches of the Cattle Trade* (Kansas City, 1874) by Joseph G. McCoy. It was McCoy who conceived and built the the shipping pens and other facilities for marketing and handling trail herds at Abilene, Kansas. Andy Adams's *The Log of a Cowboy* (Boston, 1903) is my favorite on trail driving. Sam P. Riding's *The Chisholm Trail* (Guthrie, 1936) and Wayne Gard's *The Chisholm Trail* (Norman, 1954) are tops on the most important of the trails. I regard Floyd B. Streeter's *Prairie Trails & Cow Towns* (Boston, 1936) as the classic on the Kansas cow towns, and for the critters there is nothing that will even approach J. Frank Dobie's *The Longhorns* (Boston, 1941).

The Railroads Promote the Plains

The driving of the last spike that connected the Union Pacific and the Central Pacific at Promontory, Utah, on May 10, 1869, was certainly a high spot in the westward movement. However, long before it was driven the railroads were keenly aware of the need for freight revenues if the lines were to be made to pay. The Union Pacific also faced the problem of dealing with the myth of The Great American Desert. The area between the Missouri and the Rockies as far south as the Red and its tributaries and with an average width of five or six hundred miles was labeled "The Great American Desert" on most of the maps in histories, atlases, and geographies published in the period 1820–1850. The Stephen H. Long expedition of 1819–20 was responsible for the maps but not the myth — that was started by Coronado nearly three centuries before and perpetuated by nearly every explorer and visitor to the Plains thereafter. The story and map appear in *Account of an Expedition . . . to the Rockies* (Philadelphia, 1823) edited by Edwin James. In the book Major Long says of the great desert at the base of the Rocky Mountains: "In regard to this extensive section of country, I do not hesitate in giving the opinion that it is almost wholly unfit for cultivation, and of course uninhabitable by a people depending upon agriculture for their subsistence." Yes, the Union Pacific had problems — and a man to deal with them. Hiram Latham was the resident doctor at the Union Pacific Hospital at Laramie and an enthusiastic rancher on the Laramie Plains. He wrote a series of letters to the *Omaha Herald,* and they were published as a pamphlet with the title *Trans-Missouri Stock Raising: The Pasture Lands of North America: Winter Grazing* (Omaha, 1870) with the prediction in the subtitle; *The Sources of the Future Beef and Wool Supply of the United States.* The Union Pacific distributed thousands of copies of Dr. Latham's pamphlet to promote the growth of population along their lines. Dr. La-

tham's *Account* was the *first* general appraisal of any important segment of our great cow country. While McCoy's *Historic Sketches of the Cattle Trade* has long been regarded as the first of the great books about the range livestock industry, it was issued three years after the Latham. Only twelve copies of the Latham pamphlet are known today — all in institutional libraries. By 1881 the Union Pacific needed a new promotional piece and they persuaded General James S. Brisbin to lend his name to a rewrite of Latham's pamphlet. It was published by the J. B. Lippincott & Co. of Philadelphia with the title *The Beef Bonanza; or, How to Get Rich on the Plains.* Brisbin's book is credited with helping promote the great cattle boom of the early eighties and with leading the British capitalists to invest considerable sums in the cattle industry in the West.

The Indians Surrender

The Indians were off their reservations in great numbers in the spring and summer of 1874 in the southern plains. They raided in Texas and southern Colorado and were beaten off when they attacked a group of buffalo hide hunters at Adobe Walls in the Texas Panhandle. As winter approached the Comanches, Kiowas, Cheyennes and Arapahoes gathered on the floor of Palo Duro Canyon, a deep gash in the Llano Estacado. This was one of the last strongholds of the Indians and a favorite spot to winter. At dawn on September 28, 1874, Colonel Ranald Mackenzie and eight troops of the Fourth Cavalry surprised and routed the Indians. It was not quite a bloodless battle as the Indians may have lost as

Well-known western illustrator Harold Dow Bugbee created this watercolor for the author

many as fifty to sixty warriors while the Cavalry's losses were negligible. However, Mackenzie struck the Indians two fatal blows — he captured and destroyed their horse herd and chopped up and burned the lodges, buffalo robes and the winter food supply — the Indians were forced to return to their reservations. The victory at Palo Duro opened the South Plains and the Panhandle of Texas to settlement. Within months Charles Goodnight moved a cow herd into the Palo Duro to begin ranching operations. Captain Robert G. Carter's *On the Border with Mackenzie* (Washington, D.C., 1935) is excellent on the battle. Rupert Norval Richardson's *The Comanche Barrier to South Plains Settlement* is just as good on the events leading up to the battle.

After the standoff on the Rosebud and the disaster at the Little Big Horn in 1876, the army was strongly reinforced but was unable to find the Sioux and their allies. However, General Nelson A. Miles conducted an amazing campaign in the winter of 1876–77 that brought the Sioux to their knees and sent them back to their reservations. Miles operated from a post at the mouth of the Tongue River (near the present site of Miles City, Montana), and he searched out and destroyed the winter camps of the Indians. The Indians did not like to fight in the cold and snow of winter, and Miles kept the pressure on with his surprise attacks and artillery. By the summer of 1877 the fighting was all but over — Sitting Bull fled to Canada but occasionally crossed the border into Montana in search of food and loot and was closely watched by Miles until

he surrendered in 1881. The Northern Plains were finally open for settlement. General Miles's own book, *Personal Recollections and Observations* (New York, 1896), is almost surely the best evidence on the winter campaign.

The Open Range

Someone, perhaps J. Frank Dobie, paraphrased the old saying "Civilization follows the plow" with "Civilization follows the Longhorns" and this was certainly true in the Great Plains. The Longhorns moved into the southern plains in 1875 and into northern plains late in the summer of 1877. The great era of the open range cattle industry was beginning. Many great books were written about that period in our peopling of the West. Granville Stuart's two-volume account, *Forty Years on the Frontier* (Cleveland, 1925) is great on Montana. John Clay's *My Life on the Range* (Chicago, 1924) is just as good on Wyoming. Not all cattle that stocked the Montana and Wyoming ranges came up the trail from Texas — some herds of Oregon and Washington cattle were driven east to cross with the Longhorns. Charles J. Steedman's *Bucking the Sagebrush* (New York, 1904) is good on the eastbound drives and is enhanced with brilliant illustrations in color by Charles M. Russell.

Far to the south, J. Evetts Haley memorialized the greatest range man of them all in *Charles Goodnight, Cowman and Plainsman* (Boston, 1936). In my opinion, this is the best biography of a cowman ever written, and it may be the best biography ever written of any Westerner.

More Comprehensive Histories

In addition to the books dealing with important events and significant aspects of the westward movement, a number of our competent historians, amateur and professional, have summarized and editorialized on major segments of the movement as a whole. Among those overall books that impressed me the most are — *The Westward March of American Settlement* (Chicago, 1927) by Hamlin Garland; *The Far Western Frontier* (New York, 1956) by Ray A. Billington; *America's Frontier Story* (New York etc., 1969) edited by Martin Ridge and Ray A. Billington; *The Early Far West* (New York, 1931) by W. J. Ghent; *America Moves West* (New York, 1930) by Robert E. Riegel and *The Westward Movement* (New York, 1939) by Ina Fay Woestemeyer with the editorial collaboration of J. Montgomery Gambrill. I have saved until the last three of my favorite books — each about a major area of our great West — *The Southwest, Old and New* (New York, 1961) by W. Eugene Hollon; *Frontiers of the Northwest* (New York, London, 1940) by Harold E. Briggs, and *The Great Plains* (Boston, 1931) by Walter Prescott Webb. Hollon and Briggs did beautiful jobs on their regions and I believe *The Great Plains* is the best by far of all the books on any major area of the West. Webb was my favorite historian and a good friend. However, it was another friend, Bernard De Voto, in his finely edited and interpreted *The Journals of Lewis and Clark* (Boston, 1953) who used the words that describe us best — "a westering Nation." And we have the literature to prove it.

CHAPTER III

My Ten Most Outstanding Books on the West

BOOKS, STARTING WITH 10 BOOKS and ending up with 145 and more, were the subject matter for Westerners at the meeting held on Monday, September 27, 1954, at the Old Corral, Ireland's. There I began to speak on the subject, "My Ten Most Outstanding Books on the West," as follows:

I may as well confess that I tried very hard to cheat on this assignment. I played games with myself rather than settling down to serious work on it. First I played the "Desert Island Game" whereby I chose ten Western books from my own collection to go into isolation with me. You may be interested in the list because on examining it I found that the books included were, without exception, those I had read several to many times with pleasure and will likely continue to read as long as my tired old eyes hold out:

1. Dana's *Two Years Before the Mast* (New York, 1840) — except that I figured that I would take the 1911 Houghton Mifflin edition with the E. Boyd Smith illustrations, including eight in color.

2. Duval's *The Adventures of Big Foot Wallace* (Philadelphia, 1871). Bigfoot was my boyhood hero and this is, by far, the most entertaining, and best book, about him.

3. Gillett's *Six Years with the Texas Rangers* (Austin, 1921). I heard Captain Gillett tell this story, and it reads like he talked — you simply live those six years over with him.

4. Siringo's *A Texas Cowboy* (Chicago, 1885) — except that I substituted the 1950 Sloane edition with the J. Frank Dobie introduction and the Tom Lea illustrations.

5. Dearing's (editor) *The Best Novels and Stories of Eugene Manlove Rhodes* (Boston, 1949). Not because I could not choose my favorite Gene Rhodes story, I would just get more of him in this book. In addition, it contains an excellent essay on Gene by Dobie.

6. Fisher's *Children of God* (New York, 1939). A great novel about the Mormon trek and the settling of Utah.

7. Jennings's *A Texas Ranger* (New York, 1899). Again I would take the 1930 Southwest Press edition with the Dobie introduction rather than the first. Wonderful reading.

8. Dobie's *A Vaquero of the Brush Country* (Dallas, 1929). Long a favorite.

9. Adams's *The Log of a Cowboy* (Boston and New York, 1903). None better on trail driving.

10. Russell's *Trails Plowed Under* (Garden City, New York, 1927) "Rawhide Rawlings Stories" plus. Russell, the

great cowboy artist, was one of our really fine storytellers.

Starting Over Game

Then I played the "Starting Over Game," which simply meant that I could keep only ten of my 6,000-odd volumes as the nucleus of a new collection. At once the major consideration became the probable difficulty of replacing the volumes. With the element of comparative rarity dominant, I ended up with this list of ten:

1. Lee's *Three Years Among the Camanches* (Albany, 1859) — mighty rare and a fine narration of a Texas Ranger who was captured by the Comanches.

2. Wister's *The Virginian* (New York, 1911) — the limited edition of 100 copies signed by the author and illustrated by Russell and Remington.

3. Siringo's *A Texas Cowboy* (Chicago, 1885). The first, this time, since, as J. Frank Dobie says, it is "now scarcer than hen's teeth."

4. Haley's *The XIT Ranch* (Chicago, 1929)—beautifully printed at The Lakeside Press and made rare almost as soon as issued by another citizen of Chicago — a federal judge.

5. Tucker and Coates's *Riding the High Country* (Caldwell, Idaho, 1933). Is this one rare? Indeed, yes. I own no. 4 of a beautiful, gilt decorated limited and signed edition of 25 copies, bound in morocco. This limited edition is practically unknown to even the most ardent Russell collectors. It is "not in Yost." In addition, it is fine on Russell by an old friend.

6. Lea's *Calendar of Twelve Travelers Through the Pass of the North* (El Paso,

Texas, 1946). This is one of the finest books produced by that master printer, Carl Hertzog. The first printing was a limited edition of 365 copies and was selling at $45 a copy within three months of the issue date. It was catalogued this summer by a New York dealer at $100.

7. Webb's *The Texas Rangers* (Boston and New York, 1935). One of the limited, signed edition of 205 copies to which I am much attached since it was my first catalogue purchase as a collector — the dealer was Wright Howes.

8. Steedman's *Bucking the Sage Brush* (New York and London, 1904). At least it should be rated as scarce and my copy is from the library of Charley Russell, who illustrated the book. It could not be replaced.

9. Remington's *Done in the Open* (New York, 1902). This is the issue with the "Frederic(k)" spelled with a "k" on the front cover — it may have been a trial binding. To say the least not many reached the trade with this glaring error.

10. Dobie's *The Mustangs* (Boston, 1952). The Pinto Edition of 100 copies, signed by the author and illustrator and with one original drawing by the illustrator, bound in Pinto horsehide with the hair side out.

It was hard to pass up the limited edition of Dobie's *The Longhorns* (Boston, 1941) but after all it consisted of 265 copies, more than doubling my chances of securing another copy. The Pinto Edition failed to go around among the dedicated Dobie collectors. You had to "know" a dealer to get a copy and the casual Dobie collectors are simply out of luck on this beautiful issue of *The Mustangs*.

The Briefcase Game

Another game I played was based on Charlie Everitt's enchanting book, *The Adventures of a Treasure Hunter* (Boston, 1951), in which he makes the point, over and over again, that precious things come in small packages. So I picked out ten Western items in wraps that would fit comfortably into a small briefcase. Perhaps you will also find this list interesting as the dollar value may equal or exceed that of the ten rarities listed above:

1. Shaw's *Pioneering in Texas and Wyoming* (privately printed, Orin [Cheyenne], Wyoming, 1931). Herb Brayer reprinted this one with a dandy introduction as *North from Texas* (Chicago, 1952). If my memory is correct, Herb told me that the original edition was less than one hundred copies.

2. Latham's *Trans-Missouri Stock Raising: The Pasture Lands of North America: Winter Grazing* (Omaha, Nebraska, 1871). This pamphlet of 88 pages was issued three years before McCoy, and it was really the first survey of the range cattle industry. I believe it is much rarer than the first edition of McCoy.

3. Siringo's *Two Evil Isms* (Chicago, 1915). My friend Ramon Adams of Dallas in his excellent bibliography, *Six-Guns and Saddle Leather* (Norman, Oklahoma, 1954), calls this an "exceedingly rare" item and explains why.

4. Macomb's *Rules and Regulations for the Government of the Mounted Rangers* (Washington, D.C., 1832). My great, great uncle raised a company in Arkansas and was its C. O. at Fort Gibson, Indian Territory, in 1832. It would

be great if I could say that his own copy came down to me through family channels for my collection, but such is not the case. My copy is from the library of the Military Service Institution of the United States via Eddie Eberstadt. I'm told that the Military Service Institution was the predecessor of our present War College. These rangers were assured of a place in our literature by the fact that a well-known journalist accompanied them on *A Tour on the Prairie* (Philadelphia, 1835). The journalist was, of course, Washington Irving.

5. Biggers's *From Cattle Range to Cotton Patch* (Abilene, Texas, nd, but probably issued about 1910). Louis P. Merrill calls this an exceedingly rare item in his "Aristocrats of the Cow Country," *The Cattleman* (November, 1946). It is prime source material on the West Texas frontier, cattle, buffalo hunting, Indian fighting, etc.

6. *The Adventures and Recollections of General Walter P. Lane, a San Jacinto Veteran. Containing Sketches of the Texian, Mexican and Late Wars with Several Indian Fights Thrown In* (Marshall, Texas, 1887). Lane was a fighter and he told his story well in this very rare little pamphlet.

7. Marlows's *Life of the Marlows* (Ouray, Colorado, 1892) — mighty difficult to come by.

8. Lewis's *The True Life of Billy the Kid* (Wide Awake Library, no. 451, New York, 1881) — three copies only have been located.

9. Reid's *The Scouting Expeditions of McCulloch's Texas Rangers* (Philadelphia, 1847) — particularly hard to find in the original printed stiff wraps, but

any first printing in decent condition is a "buy."

10. Sivell's *Voices from the Range* (Toronto and Winnipeg, 1911). This little book of verse from the Canadian cow country has a frontispiece and a front cover illustration by Remington and one illustration by Russell. Yet it is "not in McCracken" and "not in Yost" as the dealers love to say in their catalogues. It is in my little house on Guilford Road.

More Serious Considerations

With the three lists before me it seemed that I should be able to pick out the ten most outstanding books on the West. I struggled with various combinations for some days only to come to these conclusions: 1) I had included too many recent books, published in this century, that have not stood the test of time. 2) The Texas Rangers, important as they were in the development of my home state, had been overemphasized. 3) My love for the works of our great western artists and my sincere belief that they are also highly important western historians had led me into the error of including several books primarily because of their illustrations. 4) Rarity is not a measuring stick for determining whether or not a book is outstanding. 5) That I'd better go to work on this assignment since there was no easy way to solve the problem.

Perhaps my games were necessary to developing a work plan. At least, during the process of playing and trying to analyze the results certain concepts developed. The West was and is, after all, made up of *people, events,* and *places*

and a consideration of the historical importance of each is necessary to an appraisal of western literature.

My first step in analysis was to list the people, events, and places. The second step was to determine their relative importance in the development of the West. The third and final step was the selection of the outstanding book about the people, events, and places of greatest historical significance. At this point, I decided that with the mass of written material on the West that if I was to avoid the mistakes I had made in developing the lists already discussed I would have to establish some definite selection criteria. After much weighing of factors, primarily by trial and error, i.e., listing and discarding, the following selection factors for determing the most outstanding books evolved: 1) Readability — reader appeal is, of course, only one factor to consider but a book cannot be outstanding that is dull and dry and, therefore, not readable. All the books on the first list I discussed passed this test. 2) Longevity — outstanding books will stand the test of time and be read almost as eagerly by each new generation as they were by those of the book's youth. 3) Historical significance and integrity — there have been some great books written about unimportant people and events but they cannot be considered for a place on a limited list of ten. To be outstanding, a book, whether fact or fiction, must truthfully portray the times, events, ways of life, and the people of the period covered in it.

Please note that *rarity, condition,* and *edition* so dear to the hearts of dealer-cataloguers have no place in my final list of three factors. To be sure, the first editions of some of the books on my final list are of great rarity and much sought by collectors, such as myself, but there is often a better edition available. A clean, crisp copy is, of course, desired by most book-buyers. With a list such as this, however, unless purchased new, the books are likely to have been read, read more than once, and read by a number of people and, therefore, not in mint condition.

I am including, here, only a few of the events that are important in the development and history of the West. This is by no means the complete list that I used in my study, but the short version illustrates the point: The Louisiana Purchase, The Lewis and Clark Expedition; The Fall of the Alamo; The Battle of San Jacinto; The Annexation of Texas; The War with Mexico; The Discovery of Gold in California and the Gold Rush; The Mormon Trek and the Settling of Utah; Cattle Roundups and Trail Drives; The Lincoln County War; Custer's Last Stand; and the San Francisco Earthquake.

I made a list of important, newsworthy individuals but in the end I discarded this entire list and developed one which I headed simply "Westerners" to connote types who were important in winning the West. Here are a few: explorers; mountain men, i.e., trappers and fur traders; Plains or Horse Indians; Pueblo Indians; Texas (California and Arizona) Rangers; cowboys, trail drivers, and ranchers; gunmen and outlaws; sheriffs and marshals; miners; mustangers; Pony Express riders; hide hunters; pioneer women; and homesteaders.

Our big, broad, beautiful and sometimes terrifying West provides just about any kind of stage, for any event, for any set of actors. My list of places of historical importance was long, but here is a sample from it: Oregon Trail; Santa Fe Trail; Chisholm Trail; Sutter's Fort; Donner Lake; Great Salt Lake; Llano Estacado; Grand Canyon; Yellowstone Park; Dodge City (and other cow towns); Deadwood; Cripple Creek, Pike's Peak; and the White Sands.

You will note, I'm sure, that I've left out *animals* (and the West has some rather distinctive ones in the longhorn, the mustang, the buffalo, the grizzly and the coyote); *plants* (grass, Redwoods, cacti, mesquite, etc.), and *things* (cowboy gear, guns, etc.) in my study. To be sure, animals, plants and things often have an important role in books about people, places and events and are, therefore, not entirely ignored. But, I do not believe that books devoted primarily to them, as important as they were in the West, can be considered in a limited list of most outstanding books.

THE BOOKS

1. Biddle's *History of the Expedition Under the Command of Captains Lewis and Clark, to the Sources of the Missouri, Thence Across the Rocky Mountains and Down the River Columbia to the Pacific Ocean* (Philadelphia, 1814). The purchase of Louisiana was the first and most important step in the westward expansion of our country across the Mississippi. While President Thomas Jefferson had made tentative plans for the exploration of the Missouri River country prior to the purchase, the expe-

dition became one of extraordinary urgency after it was consummated. This is, then, the history of the most important exploration of North America made by our own country. Biddle's *History* was based on the journals of the members of the party, and he had the personal assistance of at least one of the members. Somewhere I have seen the statement that at least twenty-four editions were issued by various publishers, and it is generally agreed that the Harper edition (New York, 1893) is by far the best since it contains much information not in previous issues. I will not quarrel too violently with those who believe that the *Original Journals of the Lewis and Clark Expedition, 1804–1806* (New York, 1904–5) should be substituted for Biddle's *History*. Without a doubt the *Journals* are a western classic, but I believe they contain far too much scientific information in the entries to make smooth reading. DeVoto's *The Journals of Lewis and Clark* (Boston, 1953) corrects that, and I can truthfully say I enjoyed reading the *Journals* for the first time in this extremely well-edited issue. Wheeler's *The Trail of Lewis and Clark, 1804–1904* (New York and London, 1904) is well worthwhile and contains over 200 illustrations including 3 (1 in color) by Charlie Russell.

2. Reid's *The Scouting Expeditions of McCulloch's Texas Rangers; or the Summer and Fall Campaign of the Army of the United States in Mexico — 1846* (Philadelphia, 1847). The Texas Revolution, including such dramatic events as the fall of the Alamo, the Run-a-way Scrape and the battle of San Jacinto, paved the way for further west-

ward expansion through the annexation of Texas. Mexico was ambitious to reconquer Texas, and when Texas became a state in 1845, after ten years as a republic, war became almost a certainty since the United States adopted the Texas position in the still-hot boundary dispute. When the war was over, the Southwest, including California, was a part of the United States, although we paid Mexico $15,000,000 to forestall any additional Mexican claims to the area. Reid provides a highly entertaining eyewitness account, based on his field diary, of the activities of General Taylor's army. Mc-Culloch's Texas Rangers were the eyes and ears of Taylor and the intelligence they provided had much to do with his successes. They also fought well in each of the battles. In addition to the vivid picture it provides of the war with Mexico, the book sketches the lives of Ben McCullogh, Jack Hayes, and Samuel Walker (of Colt revolver fame), three of the most famous Rangers during the days of the republic. The book has been reprinted many times, and while the first edition is definitely rare, particularly in the original wraps, a copy of one of the reprints can usually be had at a reasonable price. It was reprinted as late as 1936.

Note: As the fate of the Northwest, including Oregon, Washington, and Idaho, was settled during the Mexican War (1846) by treaty with Great Britain, we are now ready to consider the events that led to the rapid development of the West. I believe the most important of these events were the trek of the Mormons and their settling of Utah in 1847 and the discovery of gold in California in January, 1848. Perhaps more important than either of these events was a plant, a living thing to be sure, *grass*.

3. Fisher's *Children of God* (New York, 1939). The Mormon trek and the settling of Utah is a dramatic episode of much historical importance to our West. Many of the people who went to California, Oregon, and the Southwest were seeking a quick fortune with the thought of returning East to live once riches were theirs. While many of them fell in love with the West and became permanent residents, they were not home-seekers. The Mormons, driven out of Missouri and driven out of Illinois in what we must regard as a dark, dark spot on our national honor, had one purpose only and that was to find asylum and establish homes. This historical novel comes nearer than any book I know of covering the entire history of the Mormons — their strange beginnings, the growth of the church, the persecutions, and their most unbelievable trek to the Great Salt Lake. It gives most of the history of the "Saints" up to 1890 and in such readable form that you are unaware of the history lesson you get. It was Harpers's 1939–40 prize novel and has enjoyed steady sales ever since. Fisher was raised in the church but backslid. The Mormons do not care for the book although many will privately admit that it is the best history yet of the "Saints." Some of the Utah gentiles feel that Fisher has given the Mormons far too much the better of it in his presentation. Mormon literature, of which I have read quite a little, can be divided into two classes: *Pro* — dogmatic and with a blindness engendered by the church that prevents objec-

tivity, and *Anti* — prejudiced and often bitter, with far too much emphasis on polygamy. Fisher, sharp and analytical, drives down the middle road. This is, by far, the "youngest" book on my list — long shot. I believe that it is the best in its field.

4. Clemens's (Mark Twain) *Roughing It* (Hartford, 1872). This was a boyhood favorite primarily because it was entertaining. It is still a favorite, still entertaining, but much more than that I believe it is the best thing written on the miners, mining, and all the people of Early American California and Nevada. Some will perhaps quibble over the bold and sometimes brash reporting as well as the frontier journalistic style. But as far as I am concerned, these are minor faults, if you can call them faults at all. It is sad that the list is so limited that it cannot include Taylor's *Eldorado* (New York, 1850). It is a classic by a distinguished writer and artist who recorded all he saw and heard in California. He didn't miss much but to me he was the outsider looking at frontier life while Twain was of the frontier, not just a reporter of it. White's *Gold* (Garden City, New York, 1913) is one of Merle Johnson's high spots of American literature and fine reading.

5. McCoy's *Historic Sketches of the Cattle Trade of the West and Southwest* (Kansas City, 1874). The first comprehensive history of the range livestock industry, preceded only by Latham's brief account, this is a foundation book in any cowboy or cattle collection. McCoy established the first market for Texas cattle at Abilene, Kansas, and he knew the cowmen, the trail drivers, the buyers, the

trail-end-town hangers-on and the long-horn. He put them all in his book. Abilene was at the end of the Chisholm Trail, which was one of the three important places in the development of the West. The Glendale, California, edition of 1940, edited by Ralph Breber, is the preferred McCoy since it has a long and extremely well-done introduction. Cox's *The Cattle Industry of Texas and Adjacent Territory* (short title) (Saint Louis, 1895) and Freeman's *Prose and Poetry of the Livestock Industry of the United States* (Denver and Kansas City, 1905) are two of the really great books on the range. Unfortunately, their reading public is small — both were issued in small editions, neither was ever reprinted, and now both are classed as very to extremely rare. By their very exclusiveness they eliminate themselves from my list. Kelly's *The Range Men* (Toronto, 1913) is a fine, big volume on the Canadian cowmen. Wellman's *The Trampling Herd* (Garden City, New York, 1939); Osgood's *The Day of the Cattleman* (Minneapolis, 1929), and Nimmo's *The Range and Ranch Traffic in the Western States and Territories* (Washington, 1885) are all fine books but in the end, I always come back to McCoy.

6. Siringo's *A Texas Cowboy* (Chicago, 1885). The first autobiography of a cowboy and first in the hearts of many a range rider — it was virtually the cowboy's "bible" for nearly half a century. Siringo claimed that a million copies were sold during his lifetime. It was the first book I ever read on the cowboy and ranks along with Gillett among my reading favorites. Siringo's book assured Billy the Kid of his spot near the top of the ladder as a notorious outlaw and killer. In it Siringo followed the Garrett version of the Lincoln County War, one of the bloodiest range wars of all time, and of the career of the Kid. Much of the Garrett (and Upson) material quoted by Siringo is now known to be highly exaggerated (to be as kind as possible). In nearly every other respect Siringo's book is factual and the facts are presented with such vividness and strength that the book is a must for the cowboy and cattle collector. It was the forerunner of a large number of highly entertaining and useful reminiscences by cowboys, trail drivers and cowmen. We might say that it was the sire of a noble set of sons and a few daughters. There comes to mind Teddy Blue's (Abbott's) *We Pointed Them North* (New York, 1939); Bratt's *Trails of Yesterday* (Chicago, 1921). Clay's *My Life on the Range* (Chicago, 1924); McCauley's *A Stove-Up Cowboy's Story* (Austin, 1943). Agnes Morley Cleaveland's *No Life for a Lady* (Boston, 1941) is in the Siringo tradition and the best of all range life reminiscences from a woman's point of view. It is shocking to recognize that in a limited list such as this that the contribution of the pioneer women to the building of the West can be mentioned only in this left-handed way.

7. Adams's *The Log of a Cowboy* (Boston and New York, 1903). This is another one of my boyhood favorites, and it has been the favorite of many a boy and many a man for the past fifty years. But let J. Frank Dobie tell the story, and I quote from his *Life and Literature of the Southwest* (Dallas, 1952) — "if all the other books on trail driving

were destroyed, a reader could still get a just and authentic conception of trail men, trail work, range cattle, cow horses and the cow country in general from *The Log of a Cowboy*. It is a novel without a plot, a woman, character development, or sustained dramatic incident; yet it is the classic of the occupation." If any of you are prone to discount the importance of trail driving in the development of the West, permit me to remind you that trail herds provided beef for a meat-hungry North following the Civil War, built great packing centers at Kansas City, Omaha, and Chicago, provided much needed freight to the new and struggling railroads, populated Montana, Wyoming, Nebraska, and the Dakotas with cows and people, and greatly speeded the economic recovery of Texas and Kansas from the effects of the war. This is by no means a complete listing of the reasons trail driving is important, but it should suffice. There are other great books on trails, trail herds, and trail drivers — Ridings's *The Chisholm Trail* (Guthrie, Oklahoma, 1936); Rollinson's *Wyoming Cattle Trails* (Caldwell, Idaho, 1948); Streeter's *Prairie Trails and Cow Towns* (Boston, 1936), and that little gem by the Brayers, *American Cattle Trails, 1540–1900* (Bayside, New York, 1952). Then, there is that great compilation, edited by J. Marvin Hunter, *The Trail Drivers of Texas* (two volumes, Bandera, Texas, 1920 and 1923, and reprinted at Nashville, Tennessee, in one volume in 1925). Only this summer my good friend, Wayne Gard, of the Dallas *Morning News,* brought out a fine new book, *The Chisholm Trail* (Norman, Oklahoma, 1954), and

I predict there will be others. I also predict that *The Log of a Cowboy* will always top the list.

Note: I am sure at this point you feel that I have reverted to the early days of my preparation of this paper — my game-playing days — only that this time I am over-emphasizing the cowboy and the range instead of the Texas Rangers. Please remember that in including McCoy, Siringo, and Adams in my final list of ten that I am really emphasizing the importance of grass in the development of the West. "All flesh is grass," Isaiah says in the *Bible* and of all the families of plants, grass is the one most essential to man's existence. As a practicing conservationist I know something about the importance of grass as a land builder, as a preventer of wind and water erosion, as a guardian of the water supply of our cities, as an aid in flood prevention, and of its importance in our whole economy. Within the month I received and read Hagell's *When the Grass was Free* (New York, 1954), a book of stories and articles founded on fact about ranching in southern Alberta. Hagell is an artist and illustrated his own book, but it was the first lines of the first chapter that told me that he wrote with understanding and therefore probably had something to say: "It was grass that built the West. It powered the hay-burners of freighting trails, the railway construction machinery, the first farms and ranches. The explorer, the early trader, the plainsman, the first settler, the railway labor gangs, the soldier — all depended for meat upon the old plains monarch, the (grass eating) buffalo." Hagell did have something to say. I recommend his book. The importance of grass in building the West cannot be overemphasized, and for that matter, its importance today is indicated by these bare facts — two-thirds of the farm and ranch land in the seventeen western states is covered with grass. The livestock fed wholly or in part by it provides fifty percent of the agricultural income in these same states. I rest my case for grass and for McCoy, Siringo and Adams.

8. Gregg's *Commerce of the Prairies* (New York, 1844). The Santa Fe Trail ranks with the Chisholm Trail in its historical importance as a place in the West, and Gregg is the classic of that trail and the commerce on it. This book (two volumes) is authentic, entertaining, and natural. It was written by a man who spent nine years as a Santa Fe trader and who knew the trail, the varmints and plants along it, the Indians, and his Mexican customers. He kept a diary, and his carefully recorded notes were before him as he wrote the book. It has been source material for all the other books on the Santa Fe Trail and trade. After several printings it was allowed to go out-of-print about forty years ago, but it was too good a book to "just fade away." It was reissued this month by the University of Oklahoma Press with a fine biographical essay and truly great index by Max L. Moorhead of the university faculty.

9. Parkman's *The California and Oregon Trail* (New York, 1849). The third of the great trails in our western history was the Oregon Trail — its importance for emigrants parallels that of the Chisholm Trail for cattle and of the Santa Fe Trail for commerce with Mex-

ico. Parkman's book is usually referred to (and the later editions carry the title) as *The Oregon Trail*. It is based on his own exploration and trip over a part of the trail. Perhaps others saw as much as Parkman but did not have the talent to write that he possessed. It has been reprinted many, many times and after 105 years it still sells well. In my opinion, the 1892 Little, Brown & Co. edition, illustrated by Frederic Remington, is the best. The Wyeth-Remington edition of 975 numbered copies issued by the same publisher in 1925 is very good, as is the issue by the Limited Editions Club (New York, 1943) illustrated in color by Maynard Dixon.

10. Grinnell's *The Fighting Cheyennes* (New York, 1915). This book was expanded into two volumes and reissued with the title *The Cheyenne Indians* (New Haven, 1923). This is the better edition. The Plains Indian loved freedom enough to fight for it. It was superior numbers and fire power plus the destruction of their food supply (the buffalo) that finally broke the hold of these superb horsemen and fighters on the Plains. Grinnell was a scholar and a plainsman who collected his material on the ground. This is an excellent book that towers over a number of others written about the Horse Indians. McLaughlin's *My Friend the Indian* (Boston, 1910) is good on the Sioux, Nez Perces, and the Cheyennes. Schultz's *My Life as an Indian* (Boston, 1907) is on his life with the Blackfeet. Richardson's *The Comanche Barrier to the South Plains* (Glendale, California, 1933) and *The Comanches: Lords of the South Plains* (Norman, Oklahoma, 1952), by Wal-

lace and Hoebel are both factual and entertaining. And there are many others. The Apaches and the Navajos of the Southwest are close kin to the Plains Indian in their love of freedom and their fierce resistance to the white man's ways. Bourke's *On the Border with Crook* (New York, 1891) is excellent on the Apaches and on the campaigns against them. Coolidge's *The Navajo Indians* (Boston, 1930) is adequate as is Lockwood's *The Apache Indians* (New York, 1938). Also close kin spiritually to the Plains tribes were the Nez Perces who produced some of the great warrior-leaders of all Indian history. Caxton at Caldwell, Idaho, issued McWhorter's *Hear Me, My Chiefs* in 1952 that tells their story very well indeed. It was one of our "Ten Best" for 1952. With the possible exception of the Bourke, I believe the Grinnell has the best chance of all those mentioned to survive and become a classic in its field.

I am sorry that in a list of ten it was impossible to include one of the many fine books available about the mountain men. And there should be a place for Dobie's *The Long Horns* and his *The Mustangs,* previously mentioned; for Haley's *Charles Goodnight* (Boston, 1936) which I regard as the best biography of a cowman written to date; for Conrad Richter's *The Sea of Grass* (New York, 1937), an absolute classic that I have furnished to many friends, and many more. However, I'll stick with my ten as named above. I've read and scanned over one hundred books in the last three months in deciding on the ones to name — more time would not help. I've had my say — the task was an impossible one. Perhaps most of you would agree that my ten should be included in any list of one hundred most outstanding books on the West but it would be expecting too much for there to be substantial agreement on a list of ten. In fact, it would be "the most unheard of thing I ever heard of." I yield.

CHAPTER IV

High Spots of Western Fiction: 1902-1952

WESTERN FICTION as used in the title is defined as the novels and short stories concerned with the conquest of, and life in, that part of the United States west of the Mississippi River. This definition eliminates folk tales and the whole general field of folklore. This may be a grievous error since it bars such great books as J. Frank Dobie's tales of lost mines and buried treasure; Dobie's and Applegate's Mexican and Indian folklore; and Linderman's Indian folk tales. It also bars from consideration some fine Mexican novels including Tom Lea's *The Brave Bulls* (Little, Brown, 1949); such great Alaskan novels as Jack London's *The Call of the Wild* (Macmillan, 1903) and Rex Beach's *The Spoilers* (Harper, 1906); and some mighty fine Canadian fiction including the novels and short stories about one of the really great organizations of peace officers — The Canadian Northwest Mounted.

I also want to roughly define the term High Spots as used in the title. I borrowed it from Merle Johnson's solid bibliographic check list *High Spots of American Literature* (Bennett, 1929). As I have used it, a High Spot is a novel or book of short stories that for one reason or other stands out in my memory from the mass of western fiction I have read. One real good test that I have used

consistently is the desire to save the book to read again from time to time. I am sure that in the list I am presenting there are books I have read a dozen times, many more a half dozen times, and nearly all of them twice, once within the past three months. (I have been on a reading binge.)

One other question with regard to the title may be in your mind — why the period 1902–1952? It has been said after Wister's *The Virginian* (Macmillan, 1902), the deluge! In other words, the recognized date of the beginning of the period of immense popularity of westerns was 1902. Fifty years seemed a good round number and there had to be some cut-off date to give me a chance to catch up on my reading. However, this cut-off date eliminated some very good recent novels, for example, Alan LeMay's *The Searchers* (Harper, 1954) and Milton Lott's *The Last Hunt* (Houghton, Mifflin, 1954).

I want to make it clear that the list presented is my own. I do want to acknowledge the cooperation of Hoffman Birney, western historian, western novelist, and *New York Times* western fiction critic; Dr. Lawrence Clark Powell, bibliographer in the field of western fiction; Dr. C. L. Sonnichsen, western historian, bibliographer and teacher of a course in Southwest Literature at Texas Western College; W. H. Hutchison, publisher, author, and book reviewer of Chico, California; and Merrell Kitchen, western fiction collector and critic, long-time member of the Los Angeles Westerners, and now librarian of the Pioneer Museum at Stockton, California. I sent each of these experts (and I do consider each of them an expert, and collectively a panel whose judgment on western fiction commands respect in any company) a copy of my preliminary list and asked them to do two things — 1) to question any book they did not consider a High Spot, and 2) to suggest other High Spots. I promised them only one thing — that I would read or reread each book questioned or suggested as an addition. Therefore, do not blame them for errors of omission or commission — the responsibility is mine and mine alone. I do appreciate the guidance they gave.

I could not have attempted this presentation if practically all the books had not been in my own collection. They did not get there by accident. A collector has been characterized as an individual who tries to get everything, worthy and unworthy, in his particular field. Since I am not a collector of western fiction but of Western Americana who has used western fiction as a supplement to the Americana and for my own reading pleasure, I have tried to buy, primarily, *the worthy*. To the extent that I have succeeded I am indebted to J. Frank Dobie's *Guide to Life and Literature of the Southwest* (University of Texas Press, 1943 and SMU Press, 1952); Leisy's *The American Historical Novel* (University of Oklahoma Press, 1950); Hoffman Birney's

"Western Roundup," a column that has appeared regularly in the Sunday Book Review Section of the *New York Times* for many years; Dr. Lawrence Clark Powell's *Heart of the Southwest* (Dawson, 1955); Dr. Douglas Branch's *The Cowboy and His Interpreters* (Appleton, 1926); Merle Johnson's *High Spots of American Literature* (Bennett, 1929); and to the other state and regional bibliographers who have wisely recognized the place of fiction in the literature of their areas.

I also want to pay tribute to the Western Writers of America, a relatively new organization dedicated to the improvement of western fiction. This group of free-lance western novelists (they also have magazine and associate members — they honor me by permitting me to be one) is banded together in an earnest attempt by each and every member to lift the standard of their product in the eyes of the reading public and to gain for the western novel more effective and widespread promotion and publicity. *The Roundup,* the official organ of WWA, is issued monthly and is full of ideas for the guidance of western fiction writers.

Hoffman Birney in the *New York Times,* December 23, 1951, points out that "just blazing guns won't make a western good." The books on my list are not bang-bang pot boilers although there is plenty of action in most of them. The late Joe Jackson, great book editor of the San Francisco *Chronicle* for many years, insisted that a western did not have to be literary but that it *must tell a story.* I agree, although several of the books I have included are certainly literature — and the literature of the West is the only truly original American form. Joyce Cary, the English novelist, writing in the *New York Times,* said that the public mind rates novels in two chief kinds, the formal work of art and *the slice of life.* I believe that practically all the fiction I have included is of the latter, *the slice of life,* kind.

In 1953, W. H. Hutchinson in The Huntington Library *Quarterly* characterizes those westerns of the cowboy-free range-horseback complex as being primarily concerned with the three V's — Virgins, Villains and Varmints. My list includes fiction about the whole of Bernard DeVoto's "theme of wonder" —exploration, fur trade, overland travel, Indian wars, the gold rush, the Mormons, as well as cowboys, cattle, trail drivers, bad men, peace officers, missionaries, homesteaders, etc.

In "Owen Wister's West" in *The Atlantic,* for May, 1958, edited by Fanny Kemble Wister, it is claimed that *The Virginian* set the tradition of the western permanently — "the cowboy hero defends justice and his girl's honor, and shoots it out with the villain. Owen Wister created this pattern." With such a conclusion, I cannot agree — the dime novelists and their forerunners were using that formula before Wister was born. Wister put it in hard covers and his success encouraged others to use the formula and to expand and improve it.

Wister, however, rather satisfactorily answers another question you may want to ask — are the books you list historical fiction? If you accept his statement, "Any narrative which presents faithfully a day and a generation is of necessity historical," ("To the Reader," *The Virgin-*

ian) the answer is "yes." You see, in the end I used the same measuring stick on the High Spots that I did in selecting My Ten Most Outstanding Books on the West (see previous chapter): 1) Readability; 2) Longevity (of course, I am gambling on the more recent issues); 3) Historical significance and integrity.

Perhaps you will recall that I stated that to be outstanding a book, whether fact or fiction, must truthfully portray the times, events, ways of life, and the people of the period covered in it. Hoffman Birney asks it this way, "Could this have happened?" I believe that the High Spots I have selected are concerned with people who *could* have lived in our fabulous West and that the fictional events in which they had a part *could* have taken place. For the most part, I have no quarrel with the geography of the authors or with their use of the historical characters and events appearing in the background of these long and short stories. It is one man's opinion that these are the High Spots of western fiction.

THE NOVELS

Concerning the Lewis and Clark Expedition, I have chosen Eva Emery Dye's *The Conquest* (McClurg, 1902) — actually the author also covers the migration to and early development of Oregon; Emerson Hough's *The Magnificent Adventure* (Appleton, 1916) which provides some background of the diplomatic questions involved as well as a good pen portrait of Sacajawea; and Ethel Hueston's *Star of the West* (Bobbs-Merrill, 1935), perhaps the soundest of the lot from a historical standpoint.

The fight for Texas turned out to be a fight for the entire Southwest including California. Moncure Lyne's *The Grito* (Neale, 1904) and Eugene P. Lyle's *The Lone Star* (Doubleday, Page, 1907) are good Texas Revolution novels but must yield first place to Laura Krey's *On the Long Tide* (Houghton, Mifflin, 1940). The best biographical novel about one of the heroes of the Texas Revolution is Paul Wellman's *The Iron Mistress* (Doubleday, 1951), based on the life of Jim Bowie, a martyr of the Alamo, and on his famous knife. Elithe Hamilton Kirkland's *Divine Average* (Little, Brown, 1952) is a fine novel on the violent Texas years, 1838–1858. The Mexican War was a continuation of the fight for Texas and the Mexican viewpoint is ably set forth in Herbert Gorman's *The Wine of San Lorenzo* (Farrar and Rinehart, 1945).

The conquest of Santa Fe is covered in Hoffman Birney's *Eagle in the Sun* (Putnam, A Minton Balch Book, 1935) and the march on Los Angeles, guided by Kit Carson, is the subject of Scott O'Dell's *Hill of the Hawk* (Bobbs-Merrill, 1947). For my money the California events are best set forth in Stewart Edward White's *Folded Hills* (Doubleday, Doran, 1934), the third Andy Burnett book. While the Mexican War was underway the Oregon question was settled by treaty, and while some of you will dissent, I believe the settling of our differences with Great Britain over such an important segment of our great West should be included, even if the major actions did take place in Washington, D.C., rather than Washington State. I like Emerson Hough's *54–40 or Fight*

(Bobbs-Merrill, 1909) on this subject.

Much later Hough wrote his good *The Covered Wagon* (Appleton, 1922) about travel on the Oregon Trail. A much more recent book, A. B. Guthrie's *The Way West* (Sloane, 1949), is also a much better one on the same subject. Early Astoria is the focal point of John Jennings's *River to the West* (Doubleday, 1948) and of the earlier Gilbert Gabriel novel, *I, James Lewis* (Doubleday, Doran, 1932), both good. Nard Jones's *Swift Flows the River* (Dodd, Mead, 1940) is a dandy tale of the beginnings of steamboating on the Columbia River. H. L. Davis's *Honey in the Horn* (Harper, 1935) is a vigorous exposé of early twentieth-century pioneering in Oregon that won a Pulitzer Prize for the author.

The Mormon Trek and the settlement of Utah were events of much historical importance. The great novel about these events is Vardis Fisher's *Children of God* (Harper, 1939). Maurine Whipple's *The Giant Joshua* (Houghton, Mifflin, 1942) is a good novel of the later fortunes of the Mormons in expanding their settlements to Southern Utah. In Zane Grey's *Riders of the Purple Sage* (Harper, 1912) the Mormons are the villains. This is the only one of Grey's novels that will be mentioned as a High Spot here. Zane's horses and the gunman hero, Lassiter, a former Texas Ranger, are certainly memorable as is the climax — the rolling of the balance rock to close the narrow pass in the very teeth of the pursuing Mormons. Dr. Powell calls this "perhaps the finest moment in all western fiction." Hoffman Birney's *Ann Carmeny* (Putnam, 1941) reveals the villainy of the gang of Mormon toughs who were terrorizing the California-bound wagon trains. It is one of the two novels I recall that deals with the Montana Vigilante movement.

R. L. Duffus's *Jornada* (Covici, Friede, 1935) is a good novel of a caravan of the Santa Fe Trail in 1846.

The Gold Rush and the Americanization of California stories are best told in a trilogy by Stewart Edward White — *Gold* (1913), *The Gray Dawn* (1915), and *The Rose Dawn* (1920), all published by Doubleday, Page & Co. Long ago I heard this little jingle, "If you want to learn to write, read Stewart Edward White." I do and I have. That I haven't learned is not the fault of the master. His second Andy Burnett story, *Ranchero* (Doubleday, Doran, 1933), is the best I have come across on the 1840s in California. *Stampede* (Doubleday, Doran, 1942) is the fourth and last in the Andy Burnett series and deals with the bitter struggle between the native Californians and the newcomer Americans over land rights. In inscribing a copy to me the author wrote, "Just to let Andy settle down for good." One of the real tragic episodes in the migration to California was the fate of the Donner party in 1846. Of the numerous novels dealing with this tragedy, my choice is Hoffman Birney's *Grim Journey* (Minton Balch, 1934).

Close on the heels of the western explorers were the mountain men, fur trappers and traders. Some great novels have been written about them — perhaps the most widely acclaimed is A. B. Guthrie's *The Big Sky* (Sloane, 1947). It is a High Spot, yet J. Frank Dobie thinks

Harvey Ferguson's *Wolf Song* (Knopf, 1927) is better. I agree that Ferguson's book is also a High Spot but my number one choice is the first of the Andy Burnett series, Stewart Edward White's *The Long Rifle* (Doubleday, Doran, 1932). The two novels by Frank Bird Linderman, *Lige Mount, Free Trapper* (Scribner, 1922 and retitled *Morning Light* in 1930) and *Beyond Law* (John Day, 1933), are the only other mountain men tales I know worthy of mention as being close to the top three.

Harvey Ferguson's *Grant of Kingdom* (Morrow, 1950) has an ex-mountain man and Taos trader as a hero but is noteworthy primarily because it is the best novel I am familiar with based on the fabled Maxwell Land Grant.

Just as I chose three books out of ten on the range cattle industry in my paper of last September, I am long in High Spots on range life. I trust that it is not necessary for me to again emphasize the importance of grass and range livestock in the development of the West to justify the number I have named. Our starting point novel, Owen Wister's *The Virginian* (Macmillan, 1902) has become an American classic and is still selling after more than fifty years.

Andy Adams's *The Log of a Cowboy* (Houghton, Mifflin, 1903) is the greatest novel ever written about any phase of the range livestock industry and it is quite likely second to *The Virginian* in sales over the past half century. *The Log* is not only the best novel but the best book ever written on trail driving.

Emerson Hough's *North of 36* (Appleton, 1923) is a good trail driving novel that stirred up the critics in the mid-twenties. Lewis B. Miller's *Saddles and Lariats* (Dana Estes, 1912) is one of the very few, if not the only novel about a trail drive from Texas to California. His *A Crooked Trail* (Axtel-Rush, 1908) is a Merrill Aristocrat, much sought by cowboy and cattle collectors.

Two of the famous fictional brands were the Bar 20 and the Flying U. Clarence E. Mulford's *Bar 20* (Outing, 1907) and *Hopalong Cassidy* (McClurg, 1910) seem to me to be the High Spots in the lengthy Bar 20 series. Bertha M. Sinclair-Cowan, using the pen name B. M. Bower, wrote the Flying U series—*Chip of the Flying U* (Street & Smith, 1905) illustrated by Charles M. Russell, is my High Spot in this series. It has been said that Russell was Chip. Unfortunately, the author of the stories about the third of the great fictional brands, the Bar Cross (it was a real one, too), was not nearly so prolific as Mulford or Bower. I say unfortunately because he has been my favorite cow-country novelist for more than forty years. I am referring, of course, to Eugene Manlove Rhodes — all of his novels are good but some are better than others, for example, *Good Men and True* (Holt, 1910), *Bransford in Arcadia* (Holt, 1914), *West is West* (Fly, 1917) and *The Trusty Knaves* (Houghton, Mifflin, 1933).

Henry Herbert Knibbs, widely acknowledged to be one of the best of the western verse writers, was also a competent western novelist. His *Overland Red* (1914) and *Sundown Slim* (1915) are dandy tales that were followed by his greatest novel, *The Ridin' Kid from Powder River* (1919), all published by Houghton, Mifflin.

Ross Santee, novelist and illustrator, knows his West firsthand — my Santee High Spots, all illustrated by the author, are *Cowboy* (Cosmopolitan, 1928); *The Bubbling Spring* (Scribner, 1949); and *Hardrock and Silver Sage* (Scribner, 1951). His friend, Will James, another writer-illustrator, also knew his West. J. Frank Dobie puts it this way, "Will James knew his frijoles, but burned them up before he died, in 1942." His first two books, *Cowboys North and South* (Scribner, 1924) and *The Drifting Cowboy* (Scribner, 1925) are High Spots for my money, along with his third book which will be mentioned later.

Conrad Richter's *The Sea of Grass* (Knopf, 1937) is an absolute cow country classic, Dr. Will Lillibridge's *Ben Blair* (McClurg, 1905) belongs, as does James Boyd's *Bitter Creek* (Scribner, 1939). Walter Van Tilberg Clark's *The Ox-Bow Incident* (Random, 1940) is great. Harry Leon Wilson's *Ruggles of Red Cap* (Doubleday, Page, 1915) is an amusing tale of an English butler on a western ranch. Alice MacGowan and Grace MacGowan Cooke wrote *Huldah* (Bobbs-Merrill, 1904), one of the few out-of-print books on this list, a much sought-for novel about a range boarding house. The triumph of the newcomer, often the subject of a western, is well done in W. H. B. Kent's entertaining *The Tenderfoot* (Macmillan, 1942). Jack Shaefer's *Shane* (Houghton, Mifflin, 1949) is good on the pressure the big cattlemen put on the homesteaders, and the gunfight climax will be long remembered.

There have been some great cow horse

stories written. Louis P. Merrill in his "Aristocrats of the Cow Country" in *The Cattleman* (November, 1946) called John H. Burns's *Memoirs of a Cow Pony* (Eastern, 1906) the *Black Beauty* of the range. It's that good. Merrill also named Will James's *Smoky* (Scribner, 1926) an "Aristocrat" — here it is just a High Spot. There also appeared that year Hal G. Evarts's worthy *The Painted Stallion* (Little, Brown, 1926).

Luke D. Sweetman's *Gotch — The Story of a Cow Horse* (Caxton, 1936) is another good yarn where the author, as did Burns, let the horse tell the story. Owen Wister, in the preface, calls Charles Elliott Perkins's *The Pinto Horse* (Fisher & Skofield, 1937) the best horse story he ever read — it's good.

Shortly after the turn of the century President Teddy Roosevelt set aside many millions of acres, considered by ranchers to be open range for summer use, as national forests. This resulted in immediate difficulties (some of which are not settled to this day) between the newly created Forest Service and the ranchers. And to further complicate the situation, some of the lumber companies with their "clean cut — get out" policies also made trouble for the new agency. Some fine books were written about the early days of the Forest Service in the West — two of the best by writers who assisted the first Chief of the Forest Service, Gifford Pinchot, in starting the agency. They are Stewart Edward White's *The Rules of the Game* (Doubleday, Page, 1910) and Hamlin Garland's *Cavanagh, Forest Ranger* (Harper, 1910). White, in inscribing my copy of his book, proudly acknowledged his "small part" in getting the new forest conservation program underway. One of Henry Herbert Knibbs's best western novels, *Tang of Life* (Houghton Mifflin, 1918), is of some Forest Ranger interest. Tom Gill's *Red Earth* (Farrar & Rinehart, 1937), despite the title, is a good western with a Forest Ranger lending a hand in the undoing of an outlaw.

Many of our western outlaws were cowboys gone bad, for example, Billy the Kid. At least three westerns stand out that are based on some feature of the legendary career of The Kid — Eugene Cunningham's *Diamond River Man* (Houghton Mifflin, 1934); E. B. Mann's *Gamblin' Man* (Morrow, 1934); and Nelson Nye's *Pistols for Hire* (Macmillan, 1941). Edwin Corle's *Billy the Kid* (Duell, Sloan & Pearce and Little, Brown, 1953) is a year young for inclusion in this list but it is one of the best. Ernest Haycox's *The Wild Bunch* (Little, Brown, 1942) is considerably better than most of the novels in which the hero on vengeance bent cleans up an outlaw gang, in this case, a gang of cattle rustlers.

The western sheriff is the hero in three worthy novels — Cunningham's *Texas Sheriff* (Houghton Mifflin, 1934); Gene Rhodes's *The Proud Sheriff* (Houghton Mifflin, 1925); and Tom J. Hopkins's *Trouble in Tombstone* (Doubleday, 1951), based on the life of John Slaughter, one of Arizona's great sheriffs and cowmen. Rhodes's book, published after his death and with a fine tribute to Gene by Henry Herbert Knibbs as the preface, lacks the tight construction of most of his novels. But in adherence to the code of the West it bows to none —

the Proud Sheriff kills the villain, and in response to his friend's remarks on his giving the murderer the first shot, the Sheriff said, "I owed him that much chance." His *Once in the Saddle* (Houghton Mifflin, 1927) is made of two short novels or two long short stories, whichever you prefer, of which "Paso por Aqui," with Sheriff Pat Garrett in a minor but starring role, is considered by many to be Rhodes's greatest literary achievement.

Frank H. Spearman's *Whispering Smith* (Scribner, 1906) is one of the really great westerns — the exploits of the hero, a railroad troubleshooter, were based on the true experiences of Joe Lefors, the great Wyoming peace officer who trapped Tom Horn. Ernest Haycox's *Trouble Shooter* (Doubleday, Doran, 1937) is the best I have come across on the construction race of the Union Pacific against the Central Pacific to Salt Lake City.

The Texas Rangers are still one of the most written-about peace officer organizations that ever existed. Westerns about them are legion. My High Spots are Eugene Cunningham's *The Ranger Way* (1937) and *Spiderwebb Trail* (1940), both published by Houghton Mifflin; Clem Yore's *Ranger Bill* (Macauly, 1931); William MacLeod Raine's *The Damyank* (Houghton Mifflin, 1942); C. M. Beeler's *Rangers is Powerful Hard to Kill* (Doubleday, Doran, 1936) by Caddo Cameron (pseud.), the first of a series of rollicking, fighting tales about a Ranger team, Badger and Blizzard; and Tom Lea's *The Wonderful Country* (Little, Brown, 1952), which is much more than just a good Ranger yarn as is

Paul Wellman's *Jubal Troop* (Carrick & Evans, 1939). Not so well known are the short-lived Arizona Rangers. Fortunately, the late beloved Bill Raine was a friend of the Territorial Governor during their heyday, and Bill had permission to ride with them. As a result he had firsthand knowledge of their doings which he reported in two good westerns, *Bucky O'Connor* (1910) and *Brand Blotters* (1912), both issued by Dillingham. Dane Coolidge was an itinerant photographer who knew his West. His *The Fighting Fool* (Dutton, 1918) is a fictionalized biography of Capt. Harry Wheeler of the Arizona Rangers. That good novel about the California Rangers hasn't been written as yet.

Novels about the "Soldiers of the Lord" in the West are not as numerous but two stand out — Willa Cather's *Death Comes for the Archbishop* (Knopf, 1927) and Helen C. White's *Dust on the King's Highway* (Macmillan, 1947). *Lone Star Preacher* (Scribner, 1937) by the fighting Texas Marine, John W. Thomason, is a fine tale but some will probably quibble over my including it because part of the action takes place east of the river during the Civil War.

Thomason's *Gone to Texas* (Scribner, 1937) and Laura Krey's *And Tell of Time* (Houghton Mifflin, 1938), are High Spots of Reconstruction days in Texas — not as tough as in the border states but tough enough and plenty exciting.

The Indian barrier to the exploration and settling of the West and the conflicts with the Plains soldiers who finally conquered them are favorite subjects of the western fiction writers. Paul Horgan's *The Habit of Empire* (Rydal Press, 1938) is a brief classic of the Spanish conquest of the pueblos of New Mexico in 1604. The Apache wars have fathered an unusually large number of fine novels including Will Levington Comfort's *Apache* (Dutton, 1930), by far his best and great by any standard; Fred D. Glidden's *Ambush* (Houghton Mifflin, 1950) by Luke Short (pseud.); Paul Wellman's *Broncho Apache* (Macmillan, 1936); Elliott Arnold's *Blood Brother* (Duell, Sloan and Pearce, 1947), perhaps a little wordy but sound; Ernest Haycox's *Border Trumpet* (Little, Brown, 1939) tops on Army life in Arizona, and Edwin Corle's *Fig Tree John* (Liveright, 1935), perhaps his best novel. If it isn't, then his *People on the Earth* (Random, 1937) is, a great novel on the Navajos. Ranking with Corle's novel is Oliver La Farge's *Laughing Boy* (Houghton Mifflin, 1929), another powerful Navajo story. Laura Adams Armer's *Dark Circle of Branches* (Longman Green, 1933) is by far the best of the sparse fiction concerning the roundup of the Navajos by Kit Carson and the "Long Walk" from Canyon de Chelly to Fort Sumner on the Pecos in 1862.

By comparison, the northern tribes have inspired much less great fiction but there are some High Spots. Perhaps the greatest of all Indian novels is Frederic Remington's *The Way of an Indian* (Fox Duffield, 1906). This simply told, powerful tale of the Cheyennes is also a Merle Johnson High Spot who comments, "Perhaps the only successful attempt to give the psychology of the western Indian in his war and love-life." The illustrations by the author enhance the book. Remington's *John Ermine of the Yellowstone* (Macmillan, 1902) suffers by comparison with his later novel but is still a High Spot. The Crows and their Indian enemies as well as the Plains Soldiers have important roles. The novel became a Broadway play.

Alan LeMay's *Painted Ponies* (Doubleday, Doran, 1929) is his best novel and he uses the suicidal flight of the Cheyennes from the reservation in Indian Territory to their home range very effectively in it. Despite the numerous novels about the Battle of the Little Big Horn the High Spots are few and far between. My choice is Ernest Haycox's *Bugles in the Afternoon* (Little, Brown, 1955). James Willard Schultz wrote authoritatively of the Blackfeet (he married into the tribe and lived with them for many years). His *Sinopah, the Indian Boy* (Houghton Mifflin, 1913) will be classed as a juvenile by most critics but it is the best I know on the daily life and customs of the Blackfeet. John Joseph Mathews's *Sun Down* (Longman Green, 1934) is superb. The hero is a young Osage and Mathews knows the Osages—his grandmother was an Osage and the wife of Old Bill Williams, mountain man.

The settlers of the West had enemies other than Indians to conquer — drought, blizzards, wind, panics, distance from market, etc. Three great novels about farm pioneering in three different states come to mind — O. E. Rolvaag's *Giants in the Earth* (Harper, 1928), one of the truly great novels of immigrant life on the Dakota prairie, was written originally in Norwegian;

Vardis Fisher's *Toilers of the Hills* (Houghton Mifflin, 1928) deals realistically with a new dry-farming section of southern Idaho; and Ernest Haycox's *The Earthbreakers* (Little, Brown, 1952) is an Oregon masterpiece, revealing the versatility of the author. Dorothy Scarborough's *The Wind* (Harper, 1925) is strong enough to set West Texas Chambers of Commerce on their collective ears. Willa Cather's *My Antonia* (Houghton Mifflin, 1918) is a sensitive, strong novel of a courageous Bohemian girl and her struggles on a Nebraska prairie farm.

Edna Ferber's *Cimarron* (Doubleday, Doran, 1930) deals with the Oklahoma Run and early history but has a superman hero and too many coincidences. Despite these faults, a top saga. Edwin Lanham's *The Wind Blew West* (Longman Green, 1935) is good on the railroad promotion–land boom theme — a lusty, full-blooded novel. Conrad Richter's *Tacey Cromwell* (Knopf, 1942) is about a different kind of pioneering — the attempt of a former madame to achieve respectability as the wife of a gambler. Richter uses the right words to make his characters live. Many of us have known a *Hounddog Man* (Harper, 1949). Author Fred Gipson wrote some real social history of the Texas Hill Country in this book. George Sessions Perry's *Hold Autumn in Your Hand* (Viking, 1941) is also social history, and the hero is a courageous, skin-of-the-teeth, sharecropper. Wallace Stegner's *The Big Rock Candy Mountain* (Duell, Sloan & Pearce, 1943) is broad in its sweep, and, with a hero born fifty years too late, it is a good social history of some phases of life in our more modern-day West.

SHORT STORIES

Some of the most incisive and powerful fiction about the West has appeared in short story form. That is the reason that I chose to discuss *fiction* instead of *novels* in this paper. For example, "Last of the Troubadours" is a range classic — it appears in O. Henry's (William Sidney Porter) *Sixes and Sevens* (Doubleday, Page, 1911) along with a mixture of western and eastern tales. "The Caballero's Way" is almost as good, it appears in another O. Henry collection, *Heart of the West* (McClure, 1907) — in case you've forgotten this one. The Cisco Kid was the Caballero. "The Rawhide" in Stewart Edward White's *Arizona Nights* (McClure, 1907) is the standout in a collection of strong stories.

"Corazon," a horse story that is tops, appears in George Patullo's *The Untamed* (Desmond Fitzgerald, 1911). Ross Santee's *Men and Horses* (Appleton-Century, 1926) is chock full of good horse yarns including "The Rummy Kid." I don't think I'll ever forget "In Line of Duty" in Jack Weadock's good collection, *Dust of the Desert* (Appleton-Century, 1936). Edwin Corle's *Mojave* (Liveright, 1934) is a book of good stories including "The Ghost of Billy the Kid." That particular story also appears in *Western Story Omnibus* (Tower, 1945) edited by William Targ, along with "The Caballero's Way," "The Rummy Kid" and sixteen others. Targ's *The American West* (World, 1946) is another great anthology including, for one, "Corazon."

Alfred Henry Lewis's *Wolfville* (Stokes, 1897) is a mite old for this list but fortunately it was but the beginning of a series of books filled with stories of the old cattleman. Of those eligible by age, I have chosen his *Wolfville Folks* (Appleton, 1908). There are some sharp pictures of range life in Andy Adams's *Cattle Brands* (Houghton Mifflin, 1906). Will C. Barnes's *Tales from the X Bar Horse Camp* (Breeder's Gazette, 1920) is a series of plain tales by a man who had been there.

Many do not know that in addition to being a great illustrator, artist, and sculptor, Charles M. Russell was a superb storyteller. His *Rawhide Rawlins Stories* (Montana Newspapers, 1921) is a grand collection of tales told with humor and fidelity. All but one of the stories in this book, plus many others, are included in *Trails Plowed Under* (Doubleday, Page, 1927). Henry Wallace Phillips's *Red Saunders' Pets and Other Critters* (McClure Phillips, 1906) is full of the undated humor of the range — good yesterday, today and tomorrow.

Eugene Manlove Rhodes's *The Little World Waddies* (privately printed for W. H. Hutchinson, by master printer Carl Hertzog of El Paso, 1946) is a collector's item all the way. Hutch selected and edited the stories, published, promoted, and distributed the 1,000 copies. There is a fine introduction by J. Frank Dobie and the book is illustrated by Harold Bugbee. Did I forget to say that the stories, tied together by a salty Rhodes's hero, Aforesaid Bates, are excellent? Three other books of western short stories insist on intruding on my memory — Morley Robert's *Painted Rock* (Lippincott, 1907), stories by an educated Englishman who knew the western range; Dr. Will Lillibridge's *A Breath of Prairie* (McClurg, 1911); and Ernest Haycox's *By Rope and Lead* (Little, Brown, 1951). I'll have to admit that I had somehow missed Haycox's short stories prior to buying this volume — that is my misfortune because, if anything, his short stories are better than his best novels and that is very good indeed.

In Closing

I know that the reading of fiction is for pleasure and that if knowledge be increased, there is an unearned increment. I think I am safe in promising that if you read the High Spots I have named you will enjoy them and in addition, you will have had the most painless history course on record.

CHAPTER V

High Spots of Western Illustrating

TO BEGIN, a definition is in order. *Illustrating* as used in this paper refers to the pictorial presentations in books in whatever forms they occur. The original picture may have been an oil painting, a watercolor, a pen and ink drawing, a pencil sketch, a cartoon, or a photograph. The making of book illustrations from the originals is a technical matter in which great progress has been made in the last century and need not concern us. Suffice it to say that reproduction was a costly process up to 1850 — most publishers had to be content with a few woodcuts since sales would not justify anything more. Steel engravings were far too expensive and only the federal government was willing to pay for lithography. Many of the early books about the West were not illustrated — even Washington Irving's *Astoria,* 1836, and *The Rocky Mountains,* 1837, with an assured popularity and sale, fell into this class.

In choosing the High Spots from the great number of illustrated books about the American West, I have ignored the original prices at which they were issued. Some of my High Spots were given away free — some were issued in limited editions and were costly. To be sure, practically all the early illustrated books about the West are now rated as scarce

to extremely rare and are priced accordingly. I have not given serious consideration to the text in choosing my High Spots. In a few, but only a few, cases I feel that the text is less than adequate — most publishers assured themselves of a good to excellent text and then sought capable illustrators to finish the job. My High Spots include books from many literary fields — juvenile, fiction, poetry, biography, personal narratives, history, travel, and on and on through government reports to the so-called picture books. My High Spots, then, are books about the country, people and events, west of the Mississippi River with distinctly above average to outstanding illustrations.

I have rather arbitrarily divided the last one hundred twenty-five years into three periods for ease of discussion of the artist-illustrators and their books. In addition, it seems less confusing to consider the books illustrated with photos separately.

THE DOCUMENTARY YEARS

The period 1836–1887 in western illustrating was dominated by the government artists — artists employed to accompany the various governmental expeditions into the West. Their jobs were to record or document and for that reason I have dubbed this period, *The Documentary Years*. High Spot 1 is the famous three-volume set, *History of the Indian Tribes of North America,* by Thomas L. McKenney and James Hall and issued in 1836, 1838 and 1844. The set was illustrated with 120 excellent portraits and the lithography and color are superb. The portraits were selected from those in the Indian Gallery in the War Department, established in 1821. A majority of the portraits were by Charles Bird King, a skillful artist, who painted the chiefs while they were in Washington on various occasions to confer with the Great White Father. James Otto Lewis had rushed his *Aboriginal Portfolio* into print in 1835, obviously to get it on the market ahead of the McKenney and Hall set. It was issued in ten parts and is very rare and costly but practically worthless as the illustrations failed to provide even historical documentation of the Indians he painted. Lewis had been commissioned by the U.S. Indian Department "to attend the different Indian Councils, for the purpose of taking portraits of the distinguished chiefs." He was at Prairie du Chien (now Wisconsin) in 1825 and later he attended Councils at Fon du Lac, Fort Wayne and other outposts. Lewis had the opportunities, under government auspices, but he could not deliver.

High Spot 2 is Maximilian of Wied's *Reise in das Innere Nord — America* published in German at Coblenz in 1839. It was beautifully illustrated by Karl (also known as Charles) Bodmer, a Swiss artist who had studied in Paris. The Prince was a noted scientist and his travels in 1833–34 took him far up the Missouri to the edge of the Blackfoot country. The Prince took Bodmer along to record scientific information and what a choice the young Swiss turned out to be! He was extremely accurate, a fine draftsman and had an excellent eye for color. There are eighty-one beautifully engraved, hand-colored plates in this book. It was translated into English in 1843 and has been reprinted several times, but no issue has quite matched the 1839 Coblenz edition.

A year before Bodmer accompanied Maximilian on his travels, an American artist, George Catlin, had covered much the same ground and painted many of the same tribes. In 1834 he was at Fort Gibson (now Oklahoma) painting the Southwestern tribes, and the following year he painted the Eastern Sioux on the Upper Mississippi. In 1836 he visited and painted the Indians in the country of the upper Great Lakes, and the following year he painted the captive Seminoles in South Carolina. He produced a tremendous number of good paintings, and while his art has been criticized by some, it has been freely admitted that a Catlin Crow was a Crow and a Catlin Mandan a Mandan. After a number of showings of his pictures in this country and disappointed over his failure to interest Congress in their purchase, he took his collection abroad. In London in 1841, he issued his first book, *Letters and Notes — on American Indians.* It was profusely illustrated with crude outline drawings from his paintings and is my High Spot 3. Catlin was our first real painter of the West, but by only the margin of the year was he ahead of Bodmer. Catlin, beset by financial difficulties, lived in London for some years and while he made several sketching and painting trips to the Americas, the first editions of his books were all issued in London. His *North American Indian Portfolio,* an album of twenty-five lithographed prints, was issued in 1844 and is my High Spot 4. In 1861, Catlin issued *Life Among the Indians,* High Spot 13; and in 1867 two of his books were released — *O-Kee-Pa,* High Spot 16, and *Last Rambles Among the Indians of the Rocky Mountains and the Andes,* High Spot 17.

While George Catlin was in self-imposed exile another American artist, John Mix Stanley, was painting the American Indians. He was at Fort Snelling in 1839 and at Fort Gibson and Tahlequah, capital of the Cherokee Nation, in 1842 and 1843. In 1846, he joined the Magoffin trading expedition for a trip over the Santa Fe Trail. The Mexican War caught Stanley in Santa Fe and he signed on as a draftsman with Colonel Emory for an exploratory trip across mountains and deserts to San Diego. Stanley had some thrilling experiences on this tough trip but found time to sketch. My High Spot 5 is L. Col. William Helmsley Emory's *Notes of a Military Reconnaissance from Fort Leavenworth, in Missouri, to San Diego, in California.* This government report was issued in Washington in 1848 and was illustrated with lithographs after drawings by Stanley, some of them unsurpassed today. Stanley also had an important hand in illustrating my High Spot 10, the great twelve-volume set, *Reports of Explorations and Surveys to Ascertain the Most Practicable and Economic Route for a Railroad from the Mississippi River to the Pacific Ocean.* It was issued in Washington, volume by volume, from 1855 to 1861. It is said that Stanley's signature appears on more plates in this set than that of any other artist. Stanley's pay as an artist, doubling as a photographer, was one dollar per day. The whole of the West was rather adequately pictured for the first time in this set, and John Mix Stanley was in no small measure responsible. A set of the surveys for a Pacific railroad is a much-sought item by Western Americana collectors for both the words and pictures.

William M'Ilvaine, Jr., was a graduate of the University of Pennsylvania with a degree of Master of Arts, and he had studied art in Europe. He was a Forty-Niner but was soon discouraged by the rough life on the mining frontier. He made a number of on-the-spot sketches of San Francisco and Sacramento, and he used seventeen of them to illustrate his book, *Sketches of Scenery and Notes of Personal Adventure in California and Mexico.* It was issued after his return to Philadelphia, via Mexico, in 1850 and is my High Spot 6. It was reprinted by Grabhorn in San Francisco in 1951 with sixteen plates.

In 1847, Congress authorized the Bureau of Indian Affairs to collect and prepare for publication all available information about the Indians of the United States. Henry R. Schoolcraft was placed in charge of this project and the Bureau borrowed Capt. Seth Eastman from the Army to serve as illustrator. The resulting six large quarto volumes, *Historical and Statistical Information Respecting the History, Conditions and Prospects of the Indian Tribes of the United States* is my High Spot 7. The set was printed in Philadelphia and issued, volume by volume, in 1851 to 1857. Captain Eastman's illustrations are regarded as well above average. Seth Eastman received most of his art training at West Point and later taught art there. He served at Fort Snelling and at various other frontier posts, and he was experienced in western art forms long before he was drafted to help Schoolcraft. His wife, Mary Henderson Eastman, was a rather talented writer and they collaborated on a number of books. *Romance of Indian Life* issued in Philadelphia in 1852 is my High Spot 8 and my 9 is their *The American Aboriginal Portfolio,* Philadelphia, 1853.

At the same time that the government studies were underway, the railroads were busy on their own surveys. I selected A. B. Gray's *Survey of a Route for the Southern Pacific Railroad on 32nd Parallel,* Cincinnati, 1856, as my High Spot 11. Please note the date and let me point out that this is one of the few times that a second edition has been named. The reason is simple, the plates in the 1856 edition are vastly superior — some of the best ever made of southwestern scenes.

Paul Kane was an Irish lad whose parents brought him to Canada at an early age. While most of his work was done in Canada, and he was one of the best known of the Canadian artists, he was at Fort Snelling, Saint Louis and on numerous occasions visited and painted in the Northern Lake States and the far Northwest. It seems appropriate to include as my High Spot 12 his own book, *Wanderings of an Artist Among the In-*

dians of North America, London, 1859. Kane was good and this book includes reproductions of some of his best early pictures.

My High Spot 14 is another government issue, Joseph C. Ives's *Report Upon the Colorado River of the West,* Washington, 1861. The leading artist on this exploring expedition was Heinrich Baldwin Möllhausen, a German who made at least two other trips to the West. F. W. von Egloffstein, a Bavarian topographer, was a member of the party and shared the illustrating duties with Möllhausen. There are differences of opinion on the quality of the illustrations by Möllhausen but those in this report seem to me to be his best and the von Egloffstein's panoramic views are outstanding. Interestingly enough, Möllhausen became a prolific writer of western fiction for the German youth of his day. He died in 1905.

Alfred E. Mathews was born in England but his father brought the family to Ohio when Alfred was two. He served the Union during the Civil War and made a number of sketches that were later lithographed. He earned the praise of General U. S. Grant for his *Siege of Vicksburg.* Mathews was not satisfied to settle down at the close of the war; in 1865 he was in Nebraska, and in the fall of that year continued west to Denver. His *Pencil Sketches of Colorado,* New York, 1866, is my High Spot 15. It contained 36 lithographs and sold for $30 at the time of issue. It is not quite that cheap today. Mathews continued his exploration of the West but remained a resident of Colorado. He did three other books, and I selected his *Pencil Sketches of Montana,* New York, 1868, both as the best of them and as my High Spot 18.

The geological surveys under the direction of F. V. Hayden maintained the domination of government artists in the last of the documentary years. My High Spot 19 is *The Yellowstone National Park, and the Mountain Regions of Idaho, Nevada, Colorado and Montana,* Boston, 1876, with illustrations by Thomas Moran and others and with descriptions by Professor Hayden. Moran made the sketches on this trip for his famous painting *The Grand Canyon of the Yellowstone* that Congress bought for the Capitol for $10,000. Moran was also along and shared the illustrating with W. H. Holmes of the book that is my High Spot 20, Clarence E. Dutton's *Tertiary History of the Grand Canyon District, with Atlas,* Washington, 1882. This book has been called by some the most beautiful of all the governmental survey reports. I am not quite willing to go that far, remembering *Emory,* High Spot 5, and one or two volumes of *The Pacific Railroad Surveys,* High Spot 10, but I do agree that it is outstanding and a definite High Spot. The title discouraged many Western Americana collectors but this has been offset by the intensive search for this volume by the scientists, so it is an expensive book today.

Only Catlin, M'Ilvaine, Mathews and Kane were on their own in their trips to the West to sketch and paint. To be sure, Bodmer was employed by Maximilian rather than by the government but he was essentially a documentary artist at this stage in his career — later he was a well-known member of the Barbizon School. Catlin was definitely a docu-mentary artist during the 1830s when he visited the various western tribes to record for posterity their features, every-day life, dances and ceremonies. McIlvaine and Mathews, in their drawings, were recording with fidelity. This leaves Kane. I hesitate to call Kane a documentary artist — an examination of his work, however, indicates that his early pictures, such as those used in High Spot 12, were free of much of the romanticism present in some of his later paintings.

Let me make this abundantly clear, documentary art was not bad art. It was good art and highly essential to our knowing how things were in the old days. Photography was in its infancy during the first part of this period and there were still technical problems to be solved in turning a photographic print into a magazine or book illustration. These documentary artists also served, and the best of Karl Bodmer, John Mix Stanley, and Captain Seth Eastman are unsurpassed today.

The Golden Age

In my opinion, the years 1888 through 1938 were The Golden Age of western illustrating. Two great artists, Frederic Remington and Charles Marion Russell, share the credit for making it so, but they were joined by a great number of other competent illustrators and artists. My own collection of books illustrated by the artists of this period totals more than 2,500 volumes, and it is by no means complete. Many of the technical reproduction problems were solved just prior to and in the early years of The Golden Age, making it financially possible for publishers to use black and white and color illustrations in their books and still put them on the market at prices within the reach of all. During the Golden Age, the publishers were just as generous as they had been frugal during The Documentary Years. While we are not considering the illustrated magazines, it is well to remember that many of the artists got their starts by drawing for *Scribners, Harper's, Leslie's* or *Century*. The book publishers learned much from the magazines about the knack of economical illustrating, so we do owe the mags a debt of gratitude.

Theodore Roosevelt's *Ranch Life and the Hunting Trail,* my High Spot 21, was issued in 1888 with eighty-three drawings by Frederic Remington and was an immediate success. Remington was a New Yorker by birth and, except for a brief interlude on a Kansas ranch and a briefer one as a partner in a Kansas City saloon, lived his adult years in or near New York City. However, Remington made many trips to the West, and he must be considered one of our foremost western illustrators and artists. He accepted several magazine illustrating commissions early in his career, and when the editors found that he also was an adequate reporter he received assignments, including those covering the waning days of the Indian Wars, for both the words and pictures. He tried his hand at fiction and one of his novels, *The Way of an Indian,* High Spot 37, has been widely praised. In 1892 he illustrated Francis Parkman's *The Oregon Trail,* High Spot 23, and five of his illustrations were retained in the limited edition of this book illustrated in color by N. C. Wyeth and issued in 1925, High

Spot 46. The Remington illustrations were not used in the trade edition of the 1925 issue.

In 1895 Remington's *Pony Tracks,* High Spot 24, was issued. This was a gathering of his illustrated magazine articles and is one of his best books. *Drawings,* High Spot 25, was issued in 1897; *Frontier Sketches,* High Spot 26, in 1898; and *Done in the Open,* High Spot 30, in 1902. There is a point on the first printing of *Done in the Open* that it is wise to keep in mind — Frederic on the front cover is spelled with a "k." The addition of that one letter makes several dollars difference in the cost of this big picture book, considered by many to be Remington's best.

A number of portfolios of prints of Remington's paintings were issued but despite their general excellence you will not find them among my High Spots — I do not consider them to be books. This does not mean that you should turn down a set of *A Bunch of Buckskins,* i.e., if offered cheap.

Remington died in 1909, a victim of the lack of adequate medical knowledge of appendicitis. The publishers did not stop using his art after his death. For example, my High Spot 45 is Hamlin Garland's *The Book of the American Indian,* New York, 1923, beautifully illustrated with carefully selected Remington drawings and oils. It is interesting to note that Garland was not particularly fond of Remington, a one-time fellow member of a New York City club. He thought Remington drank too much and found him surly in his cups. When his publisher suggested the use of Remington's illustrations he objected but was told firmly by the publisher that they were the best available. Garland was fair, later he admitted that the publisher was right — the book was reprinted several times and he gave the Remington illustrations much of the credit.

The other leader in The Golden Age, Charlie Russell, was born in Saint Louis and at sixteen was sent to Montana by his father to cure him of his youthful yen for cowboy life. Charlie fooled his father and everyone else — he stayed. Today his statue stands in one of the two niches reserved for the State of Montana in the Hall of Fame in the rotunda of the Capitol in Washington. Charlie's first job was sheep herding, but he didn't like the woolies. He spent the winter with a trapper and in the spring got a job as a horse wrangler. He spent his early years in Montana as a roaming cowboy but was no expert. The reason was simple, he was far too busy sketching the range life he was living, or modeling in clay the animals he saw, to become a top hand. His first book, *Studies of Western Life,* New York, 1890, is my High Spot 22. His *Pen Sketches,* Great Falls, Montana, 1899, is my High Spot 28. The illustrations in these two books lack the finish of his art of later years, but each plate tells its story with power, and both belong.

Russell was commissioned to do the illustrations for many books. There isn't a bad one in the lot, but with the help of my longtime associate and friend, Fred Renner, former sheriff of the Potomac Corral, *The Westerners,* and top Russell art expert, I have selected the best. My High Spot 34 is Charles J. Steedman's *Bucking the Sage Brush,* New York,

1904. It is an important range book as it is one of the few narratives of a west to east trail drive, Oregon to Montana. High Spot 39 is Carrie Adele Strahorn's *Fifteen Thousand Miles by Stage,* New York, London, 1911. It is enhanced with 55 Russell drawings. There was a second edition in 1915 with one additional Russell illustration.

Frank B. Linderman's *Indian Why Stories,* New York, 1915, is my High Spot 41. The fine color plates are some of Russell's best, showing his understanding of the Indians and their legends. He lived with Indians for awhile and visited their camps and ceremonies on every possible occasion.

After Russell's death in 1926 his best stories (he was a great storyteller) were issued as *Trails Plowed Under,* New York, 1927, with some fine Russell illustrations. It is my High Spot 50. *Good Medicine,* Garden City, New York, 1929, is High Spot 52 and is a book of illustrated Russell letters. In writing to his friends Charlie usually decorated his letters with one or more small and delightfully appropriate watercolor or pen drawings. Mrs. Russell borrowed the letters from Charlie's friends and they were reproduced in full. The 1929 edition was limited to 134 copies and is now very scarce indeed. A trade edition was issued in 1930, and the first trade copies did not last long. It has been reprinted many times.

Remington and Russell each left behind an estimated 3,000 originals — pen and ink drawings, watercolors, oils and bronzes. Their leadership was not based on quantity but quality. Of course, the fact that a quality illustration by a name artist was available to fill just about any need of a publisher didn't hurt their causes (or pocketbooks). Despite the terrific output of the two leaders the demand for western art for book illustrations was so great that at least forty other competent to outstanding artists devoted a major part or all of their time to western illustrating during The Golden Age. Some used their magazines and book illustrating assignments as stepping stones to full-time painting careers. Just a quarter of a century ago Theodore Bolton's *American Book Illustrators,* New York, 1938, appeared. While some effort had been made previously to prepare a bibliography of the illustrators of juveniles, Bolton pioneered the field. As a young (at least, a new) collector, I applauded the appearance of Bolton's book, yet I found it very disappointing — he had included only nine of the some forty western illustrators I was trying to collect. And the lists for the nine he did include were quite incomplete. This situation inspired me, or perhaps it would be more accurate to say gigged me, to action. My black book (a la Wright Howes) was fortunately loose-leaf in type and grew mightily over the years. It is now published as *Fifty Great Western Illustrators* (Northland, 1975).

Ernest L. Blumenschien, Ed Borein, Will Crawford, Edwin Willard Deming, Maynard Dixon, Harvey Dunn, W. Herbert (Buck) Dunton, R. Farrington Elwell, Thomas Fogarty, Philip Goodwin, Will James, Frank Tenney Johnson, Arthur I. Keller, W. H. D. Koerner, William R. Leigh, Fernand Lungren, J. N. Marchand, Clarence Rowe, Frank E. Schoonover, E. Boyd Smith, Charles Schreyvogel and Stanley Wood are among The Golden Age artists who contributed mightily to the great illustrating of this period. To be sure, not all the artists listed above have their names on a High Spot and a few artists who rarely turned their attention to the western scene did make it.

Edwin Willard Deming devoted most of his adult life to painting the American Indians. One of his early books, text by Mrs. Deming, *Indian Child Life,* New York, 1899, is my High Spot 27. It was reprinted several times and the first edition is much superior. The first may be identified by the heavy calendared pages, 11⅜ by 8⅜ inches, used for the colored plates. In later editions, the plates are on lighter, glazed paper, size 11⅛ by 8⅛ inches.

In 1902 Owen Wister's *The Virginian* hit the American reading public with a terrific impact. It was the first of the great western novels and I selected it as my High Spot 1 in my paper, "High Spots of Western Fiction, 1902–1952," delivered before the Chicago Corral, *The Westerners,* some years ago. *The Virginian* became a best seller, was reprinted many times, and in time achieved the status of a minor American classic. The first edition was illustrated by Arthur I. Keller, a member of the American Academy and an illustrator of note. It is my High Spot 31. The 1911 edition is my High Spot 40. It was illustrated by Remington and Russell and there was a limited signed edition of 100 copies that is a High High Spot. This is the most sought for and expensive of all the numerous editions of *The Virginian.* Many years later the Limited Editions

Club brought out a beautifully printed edition with illustrations by William Moyers that almost made my list.

My High Spot 29, Charles Eastman's *Indian Boyhood,* New York, 1902, was illustrated by Ernest L. Blumenschein, one of the earliest and most talented of the Taos artists. He told me that he accepted no illustrating assignments after 1919 — this was so he could devote his full time to painting.

Mary Austin's *Land of Little Rain,* Boston, 1903, is my High Spot 32. It was illustrated by E. Boyd Smith. He illustrated a number of the books by Andy Adams and others for Mary Austin. He finally settled down in Connecticut and devoted his time to writing and illustrating a number of juveniles. He was known as the "Children's Artist" so popular were his illustrations with the small fry.

Fernand Lungren, talented California artist, illustrated a number of the books written by Stewart Edward White. I selected White's *The Mountains,* New York, 1904, as High Spot 35. A biography of Lungren, by John A. Berger, was issued in Santa Barbara in 1936 and is High Spot 55. It has a number of fine Lungren plates. High Spot 42, *Art in California,* San Francisco, 1916, by Bruce Porter and others, reproduces Lungren's *The Abyss. Art in California* contains 332 fine numbered plates that constitute, for all practical purposes, a history of illustrating in California. Maynard Dixon is represented in this book.

Dixon's own book, *Injun Babies,* New York, 1923, is my High Spot 44 and is comparable in nearly all respects with Deming's *Indian Child Life,* High Spot 27. At this point, permit me to comment on illustrated western fiction. Many of the publishers of westerns issued them with illustrations in color, sometimes only a frontispiece but more often with four color plates. There was a close working relationship between certain publishers and certain artists that spanned the years. For example, Dixon illustrated at least fourteen western novels for A. C. McClurg Co. of Chicago between 1902 and 1913. A similar tie-up seems to have existed between Frank Tenney Johnson and Charles Scribner's Sons.

Some publishers, on the other hand, used the illustrations of several artists to get those that best told the story. A good example of this practice, Cyrus Townsend Brady's *Indian Fights and Fighters,* New York, 1904, is my High Spot 33. It contains good illustrations by Blumenschein, Crawford, Deming, Elwell, Remington and Schreyvogel.

High Spot 36, Herbert Myrick's *Cache la Poudre,* New York, Chicago, 1905, is illustrated by Deming and Charles Schreyvogel and with photos. A limited edition of 500 copies in Indian-tanned buckskin is now scarce and expensive but a copy of the trade edition can still be found at a reasonable price.

Charles Schreyvogel's *My Bunkie and Others,* New York, 1909, is my High Spot 38. It features his famous prize-winning painting, *My Bunkie,* that was responsible for one of the most heartwarming true Horatio Alger stories. Schreyvogel was a fine artist and while he was by no means as productive as Remington, he was his equal on frontier military art.

Riders of the Purple Sage was the only novel by the prolific Zane Grey to make "My High Spots of Western Fiction" list. As High Spot 43 it is one of the few novels to make this list and the particular edition selected was beautifully illustrated with twelve color plates by Buck Dunton, another great Taos artist. It was issued in 1921 in the Illustrated Classics format.

My High Spot 47 is Ross Santee's *Men and Horses,* New York, 1926. J. Frank Dobie favors *Cowboy* as the best of the early books by Ross, but I am sure Frank had in mind Ross the writer rather than Ross the illustrator since he comments in his *Life and Literature of the Southwest,* Dallas, 1952, "Passages in *Cowboy* combine reality and elemental melody in a way that almost no range writer . . . has achieved." Few illustrators have the knack of doing so much with pen and ink as Ross. Incidentally, nearly all the other quotations from J. Frank Dobie in this paper are from the same book.

Will James was another writer-illustrator that utilized line drawings with good effect. He wrote and illustrated a number of books over about a twenty-year period. My High Spot 48 is James's *Cow Country,* New York, 1927. The pen and ink drawings in this book have power although some may lack the slick execution of his drawings in some of his later books.

There is a highly entertaining story to be told about High Spot 49, F. W. La Frentz's *Cowboy Stuff,* New York, 1927, but it is a little long to relate here. Suffice it to say that the 500 new copies of this book were never for sale yet resulted in raising over $100,000 for a girl's dormitory at a small southern college. It was illustrated by Henry Zeigler and all copies were signed by author, artist and publisher. Although poetry, it is a much sought for and expensive range book.

My High Spot 51, *Frontier Days,* Philadelphia, 1928, was compiled and edited by Oliver G. Swan for the younger readers. It contains many beautiful color plates plus other illustrations. Frank E. Schoonover is represented in this volume by four color plates — some of the best by this graduate of Howard Pyle's Chadd Ford School.

William R. Leigh's *The Western Pony,* New York, 1933, is "One of the most beautifully printed books on the West; beautiful illustrations . . ." according to J. Frank Dobie. It is my High Spot 53 and is quite expensive today. There was a second edition that doesn't quite match the expert printing and reproductions of the first.

Winold Reiss painted a wonderful series of portraits of the Blackfeet in the 1930s. The Great Northern Railroad issued them in 1935 in a book with the text by Frank B. Linderman. That book is High Spot 54 and to be prized if you own one. The going price in September, 1963, in New York was $15 for a single color plate from the book. The title — *Blackfeet Indians,* Saint Paul, 1935.

The year 1936 saw the first of several words-by-Haley – drawings-by-Bugbee books issued. It was J. Evetts Haley's *Charles Goodnight,* Boston, New York, 1936, and the greatest biography of a cowman written to date. I am inclined to go farther and rank it the greatest biography of a westerner written to date. The numerous drawings by Harold

Bugbee, my old college classmate, certainly enhance the book and it is my High Spot 56. Harold died last spring, but more of him later.

Dan Muller was an old Buffalo Bill hand and like Bob Elwell, Cody's Wyoming ranch manager, a good artist. Dan wrote and illustrated three books of which the limited edition of *Horses* is by far the most costly now. However, I selected his *Chico of the Crossup,* Chicago, 1938, written for the young horse lovers, as my High Spot 57. It has some really wonderful horse pictures.

My High Spot 58 is *This Was California,* New York, 1938. It was assembled and edited by A. Sheldon Pennoyer and reprints many rare magazine and book illustrations covering the whole of California history. There is a frontispiece by Frederic Remington and it seems appropriate that the last High Spot on my list for The Golden Age have one of his drawings — the first, High Spot 21, carried only his illustrations.

THE LAST QUARTER CENTURY

It has been impossible for me to find an appropriate term with which to characterize the fine illustrated books of the last quarter century. There has been a little bit of everything — some great young artist-illustrators appeared, illustrated biographies of the artists of both The Documentary Years and The Golden Age were issued, and several books of appraisal of western art were so well illustrated that they had to be included. Some of the greats of The Golden Age lived and worked some years after my cutoff date, 1938, and receive additional attention.

However, there was no indecision on my part in selecting High Spot 59, J. Frank Dobie's *Apache Gold and Yaqui Silver,* Boston, 1939. It was expertly illustrated by Tom Lea of El Paso. Frank said of Tom shortly after this book was issued, "Meanwhile Tom Lea of El Paso, muralist, illustrator and powerful picturer of America at war, is rising like the morning sun." The Sierra Madre edition, limited to 265 numbered and signed copies is always preferred. *The Longhorns,* Boston, 1941, by Dobie and also illustrated by Tom Lea is High Spot 62. This is one of the most important range books of all time and a copy of one of the limited edition of 265 copies, signed by Dobie and Lea, is the one you should strive for. Lea worked closely with his El Paso friend Carl Hertzog, the master typographer and printer, on many projects. While it was a close choice, my selection of their best collaboration is *Calendar of Twelve Travelers through the Pass of the North,* with words and drawings by Lea and handsomely printed by Hertzog in 1946. It is my High Spot 68. The edition was limited to 365 copies but it has been reprinted several times. Lea is an artist of many talents and in recent years has written both history and fiction of merit.

Fairfax Downey's *Indian-Fighting Army,* New York, 1941, is High Spot 63. It has illustrations by Remington, Schreyvogel, Leigh and others. I bought five copies at seventy cents each from a remainder table in a Fort Worth department store late in 1941. Thank goodness I had sense enough not to trade them all off — there is still a copy on the shelf in the little house on Guilford Road. Dealers don't bat an eye now when they ask you twenty to thirty times what I paid for a copy of this fine book.

J. Frank Dobie has this to say about my High Spot 60, Agnes Morley Cleaveland's *No Life for a Lady,* Boston, 1941: "Best book on range life from a woman's point of view ever published." It was illustrated by Ed Borein, the cowboy artist and etcher of California. Borein was a close friend of Charlie Russell and like him never a top hand — too interested in his art to become a good cowboy. Most of Borein's work was done during The Golden Age but its excellence was not really appreciated until after his death in 1947. Borein's friend, Edward S. Spaulding of Santa Barbara, assembled and edited two great memorial volumes: *Etching of the West,* Santa Barbara, 1950, my High Spot 77, and limited to 1,001 copies numbered and boxed, and *Borein's West,* Santa Barbara, 1952, my High Spot 82. Much to be desired is the Vaquero Edition limited to 300 copies since it carries nine vignettes in color that do not appear in the trade edition.

Spaulding also compiled *Adobe Days Along the Channel,* Santa Barbara, 1957, with some perfectly charming little watercolors by Luella P. Welch and with several Borein drawings and one color plate each by Borein, Borg and Lungren. It is my High Spot 89.

A reprint of *My Adventures in Zuni* by Frank Hamilton Cushing with delightful illustrations and decorations in color and black and white by Fanita Lanier is my High Spot 61. It was printed in a fine format by the Rydal Press at Santa Fe and in all respects is a joy to have and hold.

One of the remarkable phenomena of the late depression years was the Federal Writer's Project responsible for the highly useful American Guide Series. The Project was responsible for some fine books in addition to the state, county and municipal guides. One of the off-beat books written by Project workers is my High Spot 64. It is *Land of Nakoda,* Helena, Montana, 1942, the story of the Old Ones of the Assiniboines as told to James L. Long (First Boy) with many appropriate drawings by William Standing (Fire Bear), both members of the tribe. It was prepared under the supervision of Michael Kennedy, now Executive Secretary of the Montana Historical Society and responsible for the operation of the Russell Gallery in Helena. The edition was limited to 500 copies. It is now hard to find but worth the trouble. It was recently reprinted by the University of Oklahoma with a different title — *The Assiniboines.*

High Spot 65 is Robert Isaacson's *Frederic Remington, a Painter of American Life,* Brooklyn, 1943, with a minimum of text and a number of expertly reproduced plates.

An old friend appears on the list for the third time as High Spot 66, Francis Parkman's *The Oregon Trail,* New York, 1943. It was illustrated by Maynard Dixon for the Limited Editions Club and distributed to the members. Occasionally a copy comes on the market but usually at a substantial price. In 1945, there appeared *Maynard Dixon, Painter of the West,* Tucson, Arizona, 1945, with an informative introduction by Arthur Millier. This is my High Spot 67 and is a must for all Dixon collectors since it includes the best biographical sketch available of Dixon plus many fine Dixon plates. Dixon is also one of Ed Ainsworth's *Painters of the Desert,* Palm Desert, California, 1960, and my High Spot 95. There is a brief biographical sketch of each of the artists plus representative examples of their art, many in color. In addition to Dixon, the artists include Don Perceval, Nicolai Fechin, and Jimmy Swinnerton.

Bernard De Voto's *Across the Wide Missouri,* Boston, 1947, is well illustrated; every drawing and painting reproduced was over a hundred years old! Artists who illustrated my High Spot 69 were Alfred Jacob Miller, Charles (Karl) Bodmer and George Catlin.

Taos and Its Artists, New York, 1947, is my High Spot 70. It was written by the long-time resident of Taos, Mabel Dodge Luhan, a devotee of the arts. While she was personally acquainted with all the artists she did a really objective job on this book. In addition to biographical sketches, comments on their art, and some well-chosen illustrations of Blumenschein and Dunton, she covered others of the art colony not known for their illustrations.

Ross Santee is still active — my long-time friend has been doing some very striking watercolors for the past few years and just as couple of years ago he started to work with oils. However, outside the appearance of a number of watercolors in *Arizona Highways,* he has stuck to line drawings for his published illustrations. My High Spot 71 is his *Apache Land,* New York, 1947. It has been widely acclaimed for both the words and drawings.

The Los Angeles Corral, *The Westerners,* has issued a number of well-illustrated books but two of the lot are prime. My High Spot 72 is *The Westerners Brand Book, 1948,* with the text by Roscoe P. Conkling, *et al.* It has a double-page plate in color by Russell, a photo of Russell and a brief tribute to him by Homer E. Britzman plus several small Russell drawings. Two illustrations by Borein, seven by Clarence Ellsworth, one by Nicholas S. Firfires, and one by Remington plus several photos round out the art work. *The Westerners Brand Book, 1949,* is my High Spot 75 primarily because it contains "The West in Bronze" by Homer Britzman with photographs of eighty-three Charlie Russell bronzes by Lonnie Hull. In addition, "Edward Borein, Western Artist" by Carl S. Dentzel has ten Borein illustrations. Then toss in "The Art of Western America" by Don Perceval with illustrations by Dixon, Johnson, Blumenschein, Borg, and others. Perceval and Ellsworth also contribute illustrations. This is by far the most expensive of all the various brand books now and the hardest to find since the edition was limited to 400 (really 398) copies. I was tempted to include a third Los Angeles Corral *Brand Book,* their Number Eight. "A Maynard Dixon Sketch Book," by Don Perceval, occupies pp. 79 to 160 and is loaded with Dixon drawings as are the dw and the endsheets. There are also two Ellsworth illustrations and a number of historical photos.

The team of Haley and Bugbee continued the good work they started in The Golden Age. Of their team jobs in the last quarter century, my High Spot selections are 73 and 76, *Some South-western Trails,* El Paso, 1948, and *The Heraldry of the Range,* Canyon, 1949. Both were printed by Carl Hertzog. In addition, Bugbee illustrated the huge volume *America's Sheep Trails,* Ames, Iowa, 1948, by late Col. Edward N. Wentworth, a charter member of the Chicago Corral, *The Westerners.* This is not a great book despite its size but it has a fine lot of drawings plus many photos of sheep, a much-neglected subject in western illustrating, and is my High Spot 74.

Marvin C. Ross's *The West of Alfred Jacob Miller,* Norman, 1951, is my High Spot 78. It was long overdue since Miller was a contemporary of Bodmer, Catlin, Eastman, and Stanley. He accompanied William Drummond Stewart, the Scotch sportsman, on the hunting expedition to the West in 1937. A few of Miller's drawings appeared in color as lithographs in two of C. W. Webber's sporting books in the 1850s, but, with the exception of those in *Across the Wide Missouri,* this is our first real look at a cross section of Miller's art.

J. R. (Jim) Williams was our one great cow country cartoonist. I selected his *Cowboys Out Our Way,* New York, 1951, as my High Spot 79. There is a fine tribute to Jim in it by another range man, J. Frank Dobie. Jim is gone now but his cartoons continue to depict the way it was when you worked with cows and at the same time provides many chuckles. Ace Reid of Kerrville, Texas, is doing some very good cartoons now, but I do not feel that any of his books quite merit a High Spot rating.

In the past ten years Harold Mc-Cracken, Director of the Whitney Museum of Western Art at Cody, Wyoming, has been one of the most persistent of the commentators on western art and illustrating. The plates, many in color, in the following four books of his, have been expertly reproduced. His *Portrait of the Old West,* New York, Toronto, London, 1952, is High Spot 80. *The Charles M. Russell Book,* Garden City, New York, 1957, is High Spot 88 — the 250-copy limited edition was over-subscribed before publication and is a very expensive item now. *George Catlin and the Old Frontier,* New York, 1959, is High Spot 92 and High Spot 96 is *Frederic Remington's Own West,* New York, 1960.

New Mexico Artists, Albuquerque, 1952, was written by Walter Pach and others and is my High Spot 81. In addition to eleven illustrations by Blumenschein of Taos, Peter Hurd of San Patricio, pupil and son-in-law of N. C. Wyeth, earns high praise. The numerous illustrations include seventeen by Pete. As High Spot 87, I chose *The Peter Hurd Mural* as described in the 1957 issue of *The Museum Journal,* Lubbock, Texas, and edited by Frances M. Holden. The technical discussion on murals is outstanding, and so are the sixteen Hurd color plates.

The late Dr. Robert Taft of the faculty of the University of Kansas was one of the great scholars of western art. The series of articles that appears in the *Kansas Historical Quarterly* were made into a book with the title, *Artists and Illustrators of the Old West, 1850–1900,* New York, 1953, and it is High Spot 83. In addition to the critical analysis of the art of his chosen half century, there are ninety plates. Among the artists represented with illustrations are Stanley, Möllhausen, Mathews, Farny and Remington.

Albin Widen's *Carl Oscar Borg,* Stockholm, Sweden, 1953, is printed in Swedish — I don't read Swedish so good but the numerous illustrations come through loud and clear — it is my High Spot 84. Borg painted in California but made an annual pilgrimage to Arizona to paint the Navajos. *A Navajo Sketch Book,* Flagstaff, Arizona, 1962, with a descriptive text by Clay Lockett and with the sketches by Don Perceval complements Borg's work and is my High Spot 100. The limited, signed edition with an original drawing by the artist, beautifully bound and boxed, consists of fifty-five copies and is much to be desired.

Westward the Way, Saint Louis, 1954, by Percy T. Rathbone was well done indeed and is my High Spot 85. Despite the 224 plates, 4 of which were in color, the asking price was only $3.95. Among the artists represented by illustrations are Eastman, Wimar, Bodmer, Miller and Bingham.

John Francis McDermott's *George Caleb Bingham, River Portraitist,* Norman, 1959, finally gave Bingham his just dues. It is my High Spot 93. There have been other biographies of Bingham but not in the class with this one. No less than 79 plates and 112 sketches by Bingham are used in the book.

I want no quibbling about my High Spot 86 — it was chosen with much care from quite a number of book and art dealer catalogues in my collection. *A*

Distinguished Collection of Western Paintings, New York, 1956, is Catalogue 139 of Edward Eberstadt & Sons, the well-known Western Americana dealers. The illustrations just about call the roll — Borein, Deming, Dixon, Johnson, Leigh, Remington and Russell.

Interwoven, El Paso, 1958, is a great reprint of Sallie Reynolds Mathews's book about ranch life in West Texas, first issued in 1936. It was long OP and expensive. The reprint has something added — a series of fine drawings by another old college classmate of mine, E. M. (Buck) Schiwetz. It was designed and printed by Carl Hertzog and is my High Spot 90. For more of Buck's great drawings, a lot more, I strongly recommend *Buck Schiwetz's Texas,* Austin, 1960, my High Spot 97. Buck had high school history under the late Walter Prescott Webb and Dr. Webb wrote a revealing introduction for Buck's book.

The Limited Edition Club issue of *Ramona,* New York, 1959, by Helen Hunt Jackson is my High Spot 91. Like all the Club books it is handsomely done and the illustrations by Everett Gee Jackson seem most appropriate. As an extra incentive, J. Frank Dobie wrote the introduction for this edition.

Lewis Henry Morgan: The Indian Journals, 1859–1862, Ann Arbor, 1959, was edited for its book publication by Leslie A. White. It is profusely illustrated and is my High Spot 94. There are sixteen plates in full color by Catlin, King, Bodmer and Lewis.

The American Heritage Magazine features good writing and illustrating. The books the company issues utilize both, and the quality is usually tops. My

High Spots of western illustrating by Northland Press

High Spot 98 is *The American Heritage Book of Indians,* wisely edited by Alvin M. Josephy, Jr., of the New York Corral, *The Westerners.* The book is profusely illustrated with selections from the art of just about everyone who ever painted an Indian. Perhaps I am immodest in naming my High Spot 99 — Don Ward's *Cowboys and Cattle Country,* New York, 1961. It is a Junior Heritage book, one of a series, all illustrated in color, and it just happened that I was the consultant and wrote the introduction for this one. I say you can't beat the art of Remington and Russell and while not all their pictures reproduced well, this is it, old double nine.

It seems appropriate to close this section with a great Russell book, *Paper Talk,* Fort Worth, 1962, compiled and written by Fred Renner for the Amon Carter Museum of Western Art at Fort Worth. The exhibition on which it was based was of a large number of Charlie's letters, many illustrated with watercolors. Charlie claimed he was "lame with a pen" but this book proves that he was just modest. It is my High Spot 101.

PHOTOGRAPHY AND THE WESTERN SCENE

The title for this section was cribbed from my old friend Robert Taft's book, *Photography and the American Scene.* With the perfecting of the halftone process the use of photographs to illustrate good western books zoomed. In recent years it seems that every publisher has tried to hit the Christmas gift book market with a big handsome picture book. Some of these are High Spots, of course, but I have always been primarily concerned with the pioneer photographers

who with their heavy, clumsy equipment helped record the Old West in its last stages. Names like W. H. Jackson, L. A. Huffman, Arundel C. Hull, Stanley J. Morrow, Ragsdale of San Angelo and a little later Erwin Smith, Noah Rose, Dane Coolidge, and Charles Belden come to mind. These picture takers were artists with cameras.

My High Spot 102 is S. Nugent Townshend's *Our Indian Summer in the Far West,* London, 1880. It is a most unusual book. Townshend, *St. James of the Field,* English sporting magazine, brought along his own photographer, J. G. Hyde, and they solved their reproduction problem quite simply — the book contains sixty photographic prints mounted on heavy paper. Townshend and Hyde visited, wrote about and photographed Kansas farms and ranches, Fort Elliot, Texas and the famous JA Ranch and Charles Goodnight. Needless to say, it is a very scarce and costly collector's item today.

I am sorry that I cannot supply more bibliographic data about my High Spot 103, *A Souvenir of Cattle Scenes on the Range.* My copy was given to someone with the compliments of Gasmann & Dudley, a livestock commission firm at Omaha. It was probably printed there as most of the numerous advertisements are those of Omaha business firms. It is rare.

Ragsdale's *Views of San Angelo and Frontier Life in the Concho Country,* San Angelo, Texas, 1905, is my High Spot 104. About half the photos are of range scenes. It is very scarce.

The government started using photographers on its western expeditions as early as the 1850s and gradually the picture takers replaced the artist-illustrators. My High Spot 105 is *Guide Book of the Western United States, Part D. The Shasta Route and Coast Line,* Washington, 1915, by J. S. Diller and others. It is one of a long, nicely illustrated series, all good, issued by the Geological Survey, further enhanced with numerous geologic and topographic strip maps.

Badger Clark's *Grass Grown Trails,* Boston, 1917, illustrated with photos by L. A. Huffman of Miles City, Montana, is my High Spot 106. I am not sure whose idea it was to use photos to illustrate Badger's books of range verse. My collection includes a first edition of *Sun and Saddle Leather,* Boston, 1915, Badger's first book once owned by Huffman. Except for a portrait frontispiece it was not illustrated, but the second edition was—with Huffman photos. Huffman's pictures adorned the numerous reprints of *Sun and Saddle Leather* with the poems from *Grass Grown Trails* usually included. Two fine and much more recent books, both by Mark H. Brown and W. R. Felton, feature Huffman's photos — *The Frontier Years,* New York, 1955, my High Spot 126, and *Before Barbed Wire,* New York, 1956, my High Spot 128.

My High Spot 107 is *New Mexico,* Boston, 1920, by George Wharton James. Some of the photos are in color and this is one of a series of books about the southwestern states, all good.

My longtime friend, Frank Reeves, is the livestock reporter for the *Fort Worth Star-Telegram* and a fine photographer. My High Spots 108 and 109, *The Story of the Highlands,* Marfa, Texas, 1936,

and *Hacienda De Atotonilco,* Yerbanis, Durango, Mexico, 1936, are loaded with his fine ranch photos.

Dane Coolidge, sometimes historian and a better than average western novelist, was an itinerant photographer. He visited the roundups, camps, and ranches taking pictures everywhere. My High Spot 110 is his *Old California Cowboys,* New York, 1939, illustrated with his own photos. J. Frank Dobie said of his *Texas Cowboys,* "Thin but genuine" but added of the three Coolidge cowboy books, "All well illustrated by photographs...."

High Spot 111 is Oliver La Farge's *As Long As the Grass Shall Grow,* New York and Toronto, 1940, with numerous outstanding photos of our grasslands.

My High Spots 112, 113, and 116 are respectively, Charis W. and Edward Weston's *California and the West,* New York, 1940; Joseph Miller's *Arizona Pictorial,* Phoenix, 1944, and George Fitzpatrick's *Pictorial New Mexico,* Santa Fe, 1949, three great picture books.

The Callaghan, Encinal, Texas, 1945, is reputed to be the scarcest book by that one-time Kansas City reporter, Paul I. Wellman. It is good ranch history and the fine photos make it my High Spot 114. It was distributed free to the friends and customers of the ranch but now brings a very good price indeed when one does reach the market. John Bryson's *The Cowboy,* Garden City, New York, 1951, was issued in wraps to sell at $1.00. It has many good photos made on the Matador Ranch, a giant Texas spread recently broken up, by Leonard McCombe and is my High Spot 117. In addition to the photos there is one drawing by Harold Bugbee and one by Remington. If there is any prettier picture than white-faced cattle grazing on a green range, it has escaped me. *Cow Country, U.S.A.,* issued by the American Hereford Association in 1953 is my High Spot 121. The color photos by Charles Belden and others are outstanding.

Clarence S. Jackson writes well of his father in *Picture Maker of the Old West: William H. Jackson,* New York, London, 1947, but the real star was the old gentleman with his many great photos plus reproduction of a number of sketches he made as a young government photographer. It is High Spot 115.

J. Marvin Hunter, longtime editor and publisher of *Frontier Times,* and Noah H. Rose, itinerant photographer and collector of rare photographic plates, joined forces to produce *The Album of Gun-Fighters,* Bandera, Texas, 1951. The illustrations are remarkable considering the age and condition of many of the plates, and it is my High Spot 118. James D. Horan, former Sheriff, the New York Posse, *The Westerners,* and Paul Sann, editor of the *New York Post,* compiled the *Pictorial History of the Wild West,* New York, 1954, covering many of the same gun-fighters, and a good job, it is — good enough to be my High Spot 123.

My High Spot 119, *Trail Driving Days,* New York, 1952, was the joint effort of Dee Brown and Martin F. Schmitt. It has many excellent photographs, but good as it is, it can't match a book issued by the University of Texas Press at Austin the same year — *Life on the Texas Range.* Erwin Smith was a frustrated painter who became a master

with a camera. J. Evetts Haley did the text, and it is a collector's item all the way. As my 120 it gets the only High, High Spot rating among the books illustrated with photographs. Haley also wrote and selected the photos for my High Spot 130, *Focus on the Frontier,* Amarillo, 1957, printed by Carl Hertzog and with photos by Smith, Ragsdale and others.

Paul C. Henderson's *Landmarks on the Oregon Trail,* New York, 1953, was issued by the New York Posse, *The Westerners.* It is beautifully illustrated with thirty-two colored historic photographic views. The edition consisted of 300 copies. It is my High Spot 122.

Paul Griswold Howes's *The Giant Cactus Forest and Its World,* New York, 1954, My High Spot 124, features some spectacular plant photos. Another 1954 book, finely printed by the University of New Mexico Press is my High Spot 125: Bert Robinson's *The Basket Weavers of Arizona.* It has fourteen fine color plates in addition to the fifty-nine black and whites. Another book with some great photos of Indians is my High Spot 129 — Oliver La Farge's *A Pictorial History of the American Indian,* New York, 1956.

The trail ride is one of the popular pastimes of today's West. Neill C. Wilson's *Rancheros Vistadores,* Santa Barbara, 1955, High Spot 127, commemorates the fiftieth anniversary of the founding of the Santa Barbara riders. It is illustrated with many fine photos and with a number of drawings by Ed Borein, a member until his death in 1947.

So many big, handsome, well-illustrated books on the western railroads have been issued in recent years that I felt justified in seeking the advice of a real buff, my friend Fred Mazzulla, member of the Denver Posse, *The Westerners*. Fred and I agree that the *Pictorial Supplement to Denver South Park and Pacific,* issued by Rocky Mountain Railroad Club in Denver in 1959 is tops — and it is my High Spot 131. It was compiled by R. H. Kindig and others and many of the rare photos in the Mazzulla collection help make it great. In addition to the photos, eight drawings in color by Ronfor and Ward add to its value.

Dakota Panorama edited by J. Leonard Jennewein and Jane Boorman was issued by the Dakota Territory Centennial Commission in 1961. The well-selected photos depict just about every phase of South Dakota life in the past hundred years. The cover illustration is by Harvey T. Dunn, a Howard Pyle pupil and the best known of the South Dakota artists. It is my High Spot 132.

Jay Monaghan has already chided me for an Old Bookaroos review of my High Spot 133: John Rolfe Burroughs's *Where the Old West Stayed Young,* New York, 1962. Since his criticism was directed at us for not detecting some errors in the text, perhaps I will escape this time. The many pictures tell their own story — just the way it was.

John M. Slater's *El Morro: Inscription Rock, New Mexico,* is a handsome book, printed by the Marks at their Plantin Press. The date on the title page is 1961, but it was actually released in the spring of this year, 1963. As 134 it is almost a High, High Spot — the photographing of the inscriptions on El Morro must

have been a very difficult task involving many technical problems — the results are superb. As an extra added attraction there is a frontispiece in color from Lieutenant J. H. Simpson's *Journal of a Military Reconnaissance From Santa Fe to the Navaho Country,* Washington, 1850.

SINCE 1963

The period since I last talked to the Kansas City Westerners about western illustrators has been dominated by the large number of biographies of the artists. Since in practically all cases these books include comments on their art, it would probably be more accurate to say they are about the artists and their art.

My High Spot 135 is *Color and Light: The Southwest Canvases of Louis Akin* by Bruce E. Babbitt. Akin lived in Flagstaff, Arizona, for a number of years, so it seems quite in keeping that the book was published by the Northland Press of Flagstaff. Northland published more of my High Spots in the 1964–76 period than any other press. Fine design and expert printing characterize Northland books and the color reproductions are among the best. I learned about Northland in 1962 with the publication of my High Spot 100, *A Navajo Sketch Book* with illustrations by Don Perceval and text by Clay Lockett, and I have closely followed their publication program ever since. Akin lived across the street from the Locketts in Flagstaff, and Clay wrote the foreword for Babbitt's book — nicely illustrated including thirteen color plates by Akin.

Albert Bierstadt — Painter of the American West by Gordon Hendricks, my High Spot 136 was printed in Japan for the Amon Carter Museum and Abrams of New York — an expert job. *Edward Borein, Cowboy Artist,* High Spot 137, by Harold G. Davidson; *James Boren, A Study in Discipline* by Dean Krakel, High Spot 138, Northland; *George Elbert Burr, 1859–1939* by Louise Combes Seeber, High Spot 139, another Northland beauty; *José Cisneros at Paisano,* High Spot 140, by Al Lowman *et al.,* was designed by Bill Wittliff, the Encino Press publisher; *E. Irving Couse* by Nicholas Woloshuk, High Spot 141; *De Grazia, The Irreverent Angel* by William Reed, High Spot 142; *Maynard Dixon, Artist of the West* by Wesley M. Burnside, High Spot 143; *Maynard Dixon Sketch Book* edited by Don Perceval, High Spot 144, a Northland Press issue; *Will James, the Gilt Edged Cowboy,* High Spot 145, was written by Anthony Amaral and published by Westernlore Press in Los Angeles by Paul Bailey; *Eggenhofer: The Pulp Years* by John M. Carroll, with an introduction by your speaker, is High Spot 146 — Mike Koury's Old Army Press did a very good job on this one; *Clarence Arthur Ellsworth, Artist of the Old West, 1885–1964,* High Spot 147, was written and published by his Iowa patron, Otha D. Wearin, in an edition of 750 numbered and signed copies; *Nicolai Fechin* by Mary N. Balcomb is High Spot 148 and a Northland Press beauty; *Leon Gaspard* by Frank Waters, High Spot 149, is about another Taos artist and also from Northland — the de luxe edition of 500 numbered and signed copies especially bound and slipcased is the most desired; High Spot 150 is *The Great West in Painting* by Fred Harman; *Harry Jack-*

son by Frank Getlein is High Spot 151 — one of the 300 numbered signed copies in full leather with a signed etching by Jackson in a pocket inside the front cover, slipcased, is greately preferred; Harold McCracken's *The Frank Tenney Johnson Book,* High Spot 152, is especially desired in the limited, numbered and signed edition of 350 copies bound in full leather with a bronze medallion of Johnson by Glenna Goodacre and cast by Fenn Galleries, mounted in the front cover; *Paul Kane's Frontier* by J. Russell Harper, High Spot 153, was printed for the Amon Carter Museum by the University of Texas Press and includes a reprint of Kane's *Wandering of an Artist Among the Indians of North America,* my High Spot 12; *My Life with Sydney Laurence* by Jeanne Laurence, High Spot 154, is a beautiful book about the great Alaskan artist; the 1968 revised edition of *The West of Alfred Jacob Miller* with seventeen additional illustrations by Miller (nine in color) by Marvin C. Ross is High Spot 155 — the first edition is High Spot 78; *Al Nestler's Southwest,* another great Northland book with forty plates (twelve in color), is High Spot 156; *The Sketches of Tom Phillips* is High Spot 157 and of course, the limited of 250 copies each with an original drawing by Phillips, signed by him and Don Ornduff is much preferred — The Lowell Press ranks second in producing my High Spots and is responsible for many fine books — this is one of its best; *Sculptor in Buckskin,* the autobiography of Alexander Phimister Proctor, is High Spot 158 — it was issued by the University of Oklahoma Press in 1971; Ken Ralston's

Rhymes of a Cowboy is much more than a book of verse — it has a lot to say about his art and is High Spot 159; Dr. Franz Stenzel's scholarly study of *Cleveland Rockwell, Scientist and Artist, 1837–1907* is nicely illustrated, including eleven reproductions in color and is High Spot 160; *Tom Ryan, a Painter in Four Sixes Country* by Dean Krakel is High Spot 161 — a Northland "goodie" with fifteen reproductions in color among the numerous illustrations; *Texas' Buck Schiwetz* is High Spot 162 — it was issued as a catalog for Buck's exhibition at the Institute of Texan Cultures in San Antonio, December 4, 1971–January 15, 1972 — there is a fine tribute to Buck, one of my college classmates, by the late Henderson Shuffler, then director of the Institute; Buck's *The Schiwetz Legacy, an Artist's Tribute to Texas, 1910–1972* features ninety-six plates, many in color, and it is my High Spot 163; Philip G. Cole's *Montana in Miniature* is a pictorial history of Montana by O. C. Seltzer — it is High Spot 164, and the limited of 300 numbered copies bound in leather is much sought; James D. Horan's *The Life and Art of Charles Schreyvogel* is High Spot 165 — it has 160 illustrations, 36 in full color — preferred is the limited edition of 249 numbered and signed copies with 4 additional color plates; *Gus Shafer's West* is High Spot 166 — Don Bates lent a hand with the writings as well as the serving as publisher; *Gordon Snidow, Chronicler of the Contemporary West,* High Spot 167, is another Northland item — try for one of the 100 copies signed by Gordon with an original pencil drawing by him; *A Thomason Sketch Book* is High Spot 168 — it is

loaded with drawings by Thomason, there is a tribute to him by John Graves, and Arnold Rosenfeld wrote the foreword and served as editor; *Gunnar Widforss, Painter of the Grand Canyon,* my High Spot 169, was written by William, Jr., and Frances S. Belknap for the Museum of Northern Arizona at Flagstaff (designed and printed by Northland Press) and is enhanced with numerous illustrations by the artist. The number and quality of the books about the artists and their art in the last dozen years can be characterized as great and outstanding.

Another remarkable development in the western art world in recent years has been the increasing interest in the cowboy in art. The recent boom in western art prices with the works of cowboy artist Charlie Russell leading the way is partially responsible, I'm sure. However, the work of a dedicated group of our contemporary western artists operating as the Cowboy Artists of America with annual exhibitions and a great annual catalog certainly deserve part of the credit. Joe Beeler, Charlie Dye, George Phippen and John Hampton got the CAA started, and their first few annual shows were held at the Cowboy Hall of Fame in Oklahoma City. Northland Press got into the act with the printing of the Sixth Annual Exhibition Catalog in 1971 and of each year since then. Beginning with the eighth in 1973, the annual exhibition has been held at the Phoenix Art Museum. The show, sale, award dinner and art seminar each fall has become one of *the* social events in Phoenix and the Southwest. We had the privilege of attending the first of the Phoenix affairs, and it was great. All the catalogs of the CAA can be considered High Spots, but I have rather arbitrarily chosen the *Tenth Annual Exhibition (catalog), 1975,* as my High Spot 170 primarily because of the increase in use of color illustrations included — the limited edition of 150 copies signed by 17 of the artists is much more sought. For High Spot 171 I have picked Northland's *Ten Years with the Cowboy Artists of America,* especially the limited, numbered, signed, slipcased edition of 150 copies. Joe Beeler, a founding member and former president of the CAA, is responsible for two more of my High Spots — 172 is his *Cowboys and Indians* and 173 is *The Joe Beeler Sketch Book.* In addition Joe did the illustrations for Ben Green's delightful tale, *The Last Trail Drive Through Downtown Dallas,* published by Northland and my High Spot 174. Northland also published my High Spot 175, Ben Green's *The Color of Horses,* a serious study handsomely illustrated with thirty-four full-color plates by Darol Dickinson. There were limited editions of each of High Spot 172 through 175 and they are, of course, preferred. Another group, The Texas Cowboy Artists Association, illustrated *XIT — American Cowboy* by Caleb Pirtle, for Oxmoor House of Birmingham, Alabama — it is my High Spot 176 as these young artists did a fine job, but this is one case where you need not rush to your favorite book shop to assure yourself of a numbered signed copy — the edition is of 50,000 numbered copies, signed by author Pirtle.

Ed Ainsworth really started something with his *The Cowboy in Art,* my High Spot 177, published in 1968 in two bindings — 1,000 numbered copies in full leather (but Ed died before he had a chance to sign them) and a trade edition in pictorial cloth. Just about everyone who ever painted a cowboy is represented by one or more illustrations in Ed's overall look at cowboy art. John Meigs's *The Cowboy in American Prints* was issued by Swallow Press of Chicago in 1972 — it is my High Spot 178 — get the limited if you have the chance. Frank Harding's *A Livestock Heritage* issued in 1971 and my High Spot 179; John Galvin's *The Etchings of Edward Borein,* also 1971 and High Spot 180; Bart McDowell's *The American Cowboy in Life and Legend* issued in 1972 and High Spot 181; William H. Forbis's *The Cowboy* issued in 1973 and High Spot 182; Harold McCracken's *The American Cowboy* also 1973 and High Spot 183; Nicholas Woloshuk's *Edward Borein Volume II — The Cowboys* issued in 1974 and High Spot 184, and Royal B. Hassrick's *Cowboys* also 1974 and High Spot 185 all include fine illustrations, though there are some textual deficiencies in a few of them according to my range consultants. I have had nothing but praise, however, for my High Spot 186 — George F. Ellis's *Bell Ranch as I Knew It,* beautifully illustrated by Robert Lougheed and produced by Lowell Press — the limited is worth the difference. Lowell also did a great job on my old friend and fellow *Westerner* Byron Wolfe's *The Sketchbook of . . . ,* my High Spot 187.

A surprising number of good western artists received part or all of their training at Chadds Ford, Pennsylvania, and Wilmington, Delaware, from a master teacher, Howard Pyle. Three of Pyle's pupils became fine teachers and great illustrators — N. C. Wyeth, Harvey Dunn and Frank Schoonover. Henry Pitz's *The Brandywine Tradition,* published by Houghton Mifflin in 1969, is about Pyle and his followers, and the illustrations by Dunn, Peter Hurd, Schoonover, Wyeth *et al.* are very good indeed — it is my High Spot 188. Robert F. Karolevitz's *Where Your Heart Is: The Story of Harvey Dunn, Artist,* issued by the North Plains Press at Aberdeen, South Dakota, in 1970 is my High Spot 189. Walt Reed's *Harold Von Schmidt Draws and Paints the Old West* is a great Northland book, issued in 1972. Von, now "the dean" of western artists, is the best of the painters who studied with Dunn and for years taught in the Famous Artist School in Connecticut — the book is my High Spot 190. Unfortunately, the very handsome limited edition of 104 numbered copies signed by Reed and Von was issued jointly with Von's first bronze *The Startled Grizzly* at $900, pricing "the package" out of the market to many of my best customers. I've never liked package deals since I accumulated so much gin while trying to keep a little sour mash on the shelf during World War II — for my friends, of course. John M. Carroll's *Von Schmidt: The Complete Illustrator* is a nicely illustrated bibliography published by The Old Army Press — it is my High Spot 191. John F. Apgar, Jr., compiled and published *Frank Schoonover, Painter - Illustrator - A Bibliography* in 1969 — it is my High Spot 192 — one of the 50 copies signed by the author and Schoonover plus a photo of Schoon-

over is much preferred. Schoonover's son Cortlandt (Pat) edited his father's magazine articles on Canada for book publication in 1974 using the title *The Edge of the Wilderness* — it is handsomely illustrated and is my High Spot 193. Unfortunately, Pat did not live to see his biography of his father issued by Watson-Guptill — I am naming *Frank Schoonover* my High Spot 194. *The Wyeths,* my High Spot 195, is primarily the intimate correspondence of N. C. Wyeth and was edited by his daughter-in-law Betsy James (Mrs. Andrew) Wyeth — there are numerous illustrations by and of Wyeth. The following year, 1972, the Allens, Douglas, and Douglas, Jr., brought out *N. C. Wyeth,* also beautifully illustrated and my High Spot 196. Paul Horgan's *Peter Hurd: A Portrait Sketch from Life* my High Spot 197 issued by the Amon Carter Museum in 1965 is about the talented New Mexico artist who studied with Wyeth and married his maestro's daughter, Henriette. John Meigs edited *Peter Hurd, The Lithographs* for the Baker Gallery Press in Lubbock, Texas, in 1968 — it is my High Spot 198, and do try for one of the limited edition of 325 copies, each with an original lithograph signed by Pete. A number of catalogs of one-man shows by W. H. D. Koerner also steeped in the Brandywine Tradition have been issued in recent years — my choice for High Spot 199 is *W. H. D. Koerner, Illustrator of the West* issued for their 1968 show by the Los Angeles County Museum of Natural History, with 58 illustrations including 9 in color by Koerner and a photo of him.

I'm sure you will forgive "A Bit of

Braggin' About a Book" — a title that I borrowed except for one word from my friend J. Evetts Haley. My High Spot 200 is my own *Fifty Great Western Illustrators,* expertly produced by Northland. The bibliographic check lists include over 7,000 entries and 93 illustrations, 10 in color. It received The Wrangler Award for "Outstanding Western Non-Fiction Book, 1975–76" at the Cowboy Hall of Fame last April, so I feel I can include it without apology. Another highly useful reference book of pictorial merit is Walt Reed's *The Illustrator in America, 1900–1960s* issued by Reinhold in 1966 — it is my High Spot 201. The third reference volume that will serve collectors, dealers, librarians and researchers for years to come is the handsomely illustrated *Bronzes of the American West* by Patricia Janis Broder, issued by Abrams with 511 illustrations including 48 pages in full color — it is my High Spot 202. John C. Ewer's *Artists of the Old West* was first issued by Doubleday in 1965 and long scheduled to be my High Spot 203. However, Doubleday brought out an enlarged edition in 1973 with 194 illustrations including 44 in color and it became my High Spot 203. Paul A. Rossi and David C. Hunt's *The Art of the Old West* is based on the famed collection at the Gilcrease Institute in Tulsa — it was printed in Italy for Knopf, is beautifully illustrated, and includes many color plates — it is High Spot 204. Another beautiful Abrams book with 248 illustrations, including 119 in full color, is my High Spot 205, *The West of Buffalo Bill* by Don Hedgpeth, Dick Frost and Leo Platteter with an introduction by Harold McCracken

and based on the collections in the Buffalo Bill Historical Center at Cody, Wyoming.

The two giants of western art, Charles Marion Russell and Frederic Remington, who dominated my High Spots in The Golden Age, 1888–1938, were not neglected in the past dozen years. My longtime friend and associate Fred Renner, *the* Russell art expert, wrote *Charles M. Russell, Paintings, Drawings, and Sculpture in the Amon G. Carter Collection, a Descriptive Catalogue* in 1966 — it was published for the Amon Carter Museum by the University of Texas Press, and it is my High Spot 206 and the best book ever on Russell. Fred's book was reprinted for the Museum by Abrams in 1974 with 45 additional color plates, and thus became my High Spot 207. Fred also partnered Karl Yost in my High Spot 208 — *A Bibliography of the Published Works of Charles M. Russell* published by the University of Nebraska Press in 1971 with over 3,500 entries and 42 illustrations, including 19 in color. It is the finest bibliography ever issued of the published works of a western artist. Harold McCracken's *The Frederic Remington Book* was issued in 1966 by Doubleday — it is a beautiful book with numerous illustrations, including many in color, and is my High Spot 209. The de luxe edition of 500 numbered and signed copies in gilt decorated leather is much preferred. Don Hedgpeth's *The Art of Frederic Remington — An Exhibition Honoring Harold McCracken at the Whitney Gallery of Western Art* is the catalog of a spectacular Remington show at Cody in 1974 — there are 156 illustrations, including 16 in color — it is

High Spot 210. Peter H. Hassrick's *Frederic Remington,* based on the Amon Carter and Sid Richardson collections, was issued for the Amon Carter Museum by Abrams in 1973 with 94 illustrations, including 60 in color — it is High Spot 211, and in my opinion the best book yet on Remington.

Some books and exhibition catalogs of private collections have been outstanding in recent years. *The West and Walter Bimson* was published in 1971 by The University of Arizona Museum of Art at Tucson as a tribute to the former chairman of the board of the Valley National Bank of Arizona and an avid collector of western art — it was good to see reproductions of many of the items that I saw at the Valley Bank in Phoenix on my numerous visits over the years — it is my High Spot 212. Dorothy Harmsen's *Harmsen's Western Americana* features her family's private collection of one hundred western paintings with biographical profiles of the artists — the illustrations are all in full color and this Northland Press book is my High Spot 213. *The McKee Collection of Paintings* was designed by Carl Hertzog and issued by the El Paso Museum of Art in 1968 as a tribute to collectors Robert Eugene and Evelyn Woods McKee. It is nicely illustrated including twenty-five color plates of southwestern subjects and is my High Spot 214. *Edward Borein: The Katherine H. Haley Collection* is a fine catalog of the April 5–May 21, 1974, exhibition at the Phoenix Art Museum with fourteen illustrations, including five in color, by Borein plus photos of him and of Mrs. Haley with a part of her Borein Collection — it is High Spot 215.

The military collection of John M. Carroll, my friend and fellow Texan who now lives in New Brunswick, New Jersey, is particularly strong on the black troopers and Custer and the Seventh Cavalry. He has used reproductions from his collection to illustrate a number of his books. *The Black Military Experience in the American West* was compiled and edited by John and published by Liveright in New York — the illustrations from the Carroll Collection feature the drawings of Lorence Bjorklund, Harold Bugbee, José Cisneros, Nick Eggenhofer, Paul Rossi *et al.* — it is my High Spot 216. Carroll's *Buffalo Soldiers West* (The Old Army Press, 1971) features the same artists and is my High Spot 217 — the limited edition of fifty numbered copies each with an original drawing by Bjorklund is much desired.

In December 1969, we flew to San Antonio for the opening of the Tom Lea exhibition at the Institute of Texan Cultures. The catalog of the show, *Tom Lea, a Selection of Paintings and Drawings from the Nineteen-sixties,* prepared by Al Lowman *et al.,* is my High Spot 218. It was designed by Bill Wittliff of the Encino Press and includes 30 illustrations by Lea — the Rio Bravo Edition of 200 numbered and signed copies is preferred. My High Spot 219 is Tom's *A Picture Gallery,* issued in 1968 by Little, Brown in an autobiographical volume with numerous illustrations plus a portfolio of 35 prints including 12 in color enclosed in a single slipcase.

A number of exhibition and sales catalogs issued during the past dozen years are worthy additions to any collection of western illustrators. *Woolaroc Museum* is the catalog of the Bartlesville, Oklahoma, collection — it was issued in 1965 in both colored decorated boards and decorated wraps, and is handsomely illustrated — it is High Spot 220. We saw the exhibition *The West Remembered* at The Old Mint in San Francisco in September, 1973 — the beautifully illustrated catalog of the show compiled by Joseph A. Baird, Jr., is High Spot 221. *Walking Westward: An American Journey,* my High Spot 222 is the March, 1972, issue of *The Kennedy Quarterly* and includes illustrations by Johnson, Lungren, Miller, Remington, Russell, Schreyvogel *et al. American Masters in the West* (selections from the Anschutz Collection) was shown at The Boise Gallery of Art and at the Utah Museum of Fine Arts in 1974. The catalog was compiled by George Schriever and the forty-eight pages include many illustrations — it is High Spot 223.

David Dary's *The Buffalo Book* was published by the Swallow Press in 1974. There are numerous illustrations rather evenly divided between those from some great photos and from old prints plus drawings by John Mix Stanley, Catlin, Seton, Theodore R. Davis, Wimar, Darley, Remington, Russell *et al*. It is my High Spot 224 and the best of all the buffalo books to date.

Kenneth M. Chapman's *The Pottery of San Ildefonso Pueblo* was published for the School of American Research by the University of New Mexico Press. It is handsomely illustrated with line drawings and 174 color plates and is my High Spot 225.

A number of books illustrated only with photographs have been issued since 1963. In my opinion the outstanding book so illustrated is Don Hedgpeth's *Spurs Were a-Jinglin'* published by Northland in 1975 with great range photos by Charles J. Belden. It is my High Spot 226 — the limited, especially bound edition of fifty signed copies, each with a print of a Belden photo is preferred. *Season of the Elk,* my High Spot 227, was written by Dean Krakel II. The young author spent a year in Jackson Hole studying and photographing the elk herd. The book is illustrated with ninety-four of his full-color photographs and is another great Lowell issue. *An Honest Try* by Bob Scriver, another fine Lowell issue, ended up in this segment since most of its illustrations are photos of Bob's bronzes, featuring his excellent Rodeo series — it is my High Spot 228.

One of the great art bargains of the last thirteen years is *The Lure of the Great West* by Frank Getlein *et al*. and published by Country Beautiful at Waukesha, Michigan. It combines a sensitive text with 375 illustrations of which 150 are in color. It is my final choice at this time — my High Spot 229.

Looking over the number of good illustrated books on my shelves that I did not pick as High Spots, I am convinced that I could have added another twenty-five without getting down to skimmed milk. This is, of course, a sure sign that you would not have picked exactly the same ninety-five that I did. You are entitled to your choices, I've made mine.

THE DOCUMENTARY YEARS
1836–1887

1. M'Kenney, Thomas L. and Hall, James. *History of the Indian Tribes of*

North America (3 volumes). Philadelphia, 1836, 1838 and 1844.

2. Maximilian Prinz zu Wied-Neuwied. *Reise in das Innere Nord America.* Coblenz, Germany, 1839.

3. Catlin, George. *Letters and Notes . . . On American Indians.* London, 1841.

4. ———. *North American Portfolio.* London, 1844.

5. Emory, William Helmsley. *Notes of a Military Reconnaissance from Fort Leavenworth, in Missouri, to San Diego, in California.* Washington, 1848.

6. M'Ilvaine, William. *Sketches of Scenery and Notes of Personal Adventure in California and Mexico.* Philadelphia, 1850.

7. Schoolcraft, Henry R. *Historical and Statistical Information Respecting . . . the Indian Tribes of the United States* (6 volumes). Philadelphia, 1851–57.

8. Eastman, Mrs. Mary (Henderson). *Romance of Indian Life.* Philadelphia, 1852.

9. ———. *The American Aboriginal Portfolio.* Philadelphia, 1853.

10. *Reports of Explorations and Surveys to Ascertain the Most Practicable and Economic Route for a Railroad from the Missisisppi River to the Pacific Ocean* (12 volumes). Washington, 1855–61.

11. Gray, A. B. *Survey of a Route for the Southern Pacific Railroad on 32nd Parallel.* Cincinnati, 1856.

12. Kane, Paul. *Wanderings of an Artist Among the Indians of North America.* London, 1859.

13. Catlin, George. *Life Among the Indians.* London, 1861.

14. Ives, Joseph C. *Report Upon the Colorado River of the West.* Washington, 1861.

15. Mathews, Alfred E. *Pencil Sketches of Colorado.* New York, 1866.

16. Catlin, George. *O-Kee-Pa: A Religious Ceremony; and Other Customs of the Mandans.* London, 1867.

17. ———. *Last Rambles Among the Indians of the Rocky Mountains and the Andes.* London, 1867.

18. Mathews, Alfred E. *Pencil Sketches of Montana.* New York, 1868.

19. Hayden, F. V. *The Yellowstone National Park, and the Mountain Regions of Idaho, Nevada, Colorado and Montana.* Boston, 1876.

20. Dutton, Clarence E. *Tertiary History of the Grand Canyon District, with Atlas.* Washington, 1882.

THE GOLDEN AGE
1888–1938

21. Roosevelt, Theodore. *Ranch Life and the Hunting Trail.* New York, 1888.

22. Russell, Charles M. *Studies of Western Life.* New York, 1890.

23. Parkman, Francis. *The Oregon Trail.* Boston, 1892.

24. Remington, Frederic. *Pony Tracks.* New York, 1895.

25. ———. *Drawings.* New York, 1897.

26. ———. *Frontier Sketches.* Chicago, 1898.

27. Deming, Therese O. *Indian Child Life.* New York, 1899.

28. Russell, Charles M. *Pen Sketches.* Great Falls, Montana, 1899.

29. Eastman, Charles. *Indian Boyhood.* New York, 1902.

30. Remington, Frederic. *Done in the Open.* New York, 1902.

31. Wister, Owen. *The Virginian.* New York, 1902.

32. Austin, Mary. *The Land of Little Rain.* Boston, 1903.

33. Brady, Cyrus Townsend. *Indian Fights and Fighters.* New York, 1904.

34. Steedman, Charles J. *Bucking the Sage Brush.* New York, 1904.

35. White, Stewart Edward. *The Mountains.* New York, 1904.

36. Myrick, Herbert. *Cache la Poudre.* New York and Chicago, 1905.

37. Remington, Frederic. *The Way of an Indian.* New York, 1906.

38. Schreyvogel, Charles. *My Bunkie and Others.* New York, 1909.

39. Strahorn, Carrie Adele. *Fifteen Thousand Miles by Stage.* New York and London, 1911.

40. Wister, Owen. *The Virginian.* New York, 1911.

41. Linderman, Frank B. *Indian Why Stories.* New York, 1915.

42. Porter, Bruce *et al. Art in California.* San Francisco, 1916.

43. Grey, Zane. *Riders of the Purple Sage.* New York and London, 1921.

44. Dixon, Maynard. *Injun Babies.* New York, 1923.

45. Garland, Hamlin. *The Book of the American Indian.* New York, 1923.

46. Parkman, Francis. *The Oregon Trail.* Boston, 1925.

47. Santee, Ross. *Men and Horses.* New York, 1926.

48. James, Will. *Cow Country.* New York and London, 1927.

49. La Frentz, F. W. *Cowboy Stuff.* New York, 1927.

50. Russell, Charles M. *Trails Plowed Under.* New York, 1927.

51. Swan, Oliver G., ed. *Frontier Days.* Philadelphia, 1928.

52. Russell, Charles M. *Good Medicine.* Garden City, New York, 1929.

53. Leigh, William R. *The Western Pony.* New York, 1933.

54. Linderman, Frank B. *Blackfeet Indians.* Saint Paul, Minnesota, 1935.

55. Berger, John A. *Fernand Lundgren.* Santa Barbara, California, 1936.

56. Haley, J. Evetts. *Charles Goodnight.* Boston and New York, 1936.

57. Muller, Dan. *Chico of the Cross Up.* Chicago, 1938.

58. Pennoyer, A. Sheldon, ed. *This was California.* New York, 1938.

THE LAST QUARTER CENTURY

59. Dobie, J. Frank. *Apache Gold and Yaqui Silver.* Boston, 1939.

60. Cleaveland, Agnes Morley. *No Life for a Lady.* Boston, 1941.

61. Cushing, Frank Hamilton. *My Adventures in Zuni.* Santa Fe, New Mexico, 1941.

62. Dobie, J. Frank. *The Longhorns.* Boston, 1941.

63. Downey, Fairfax. *Indian-Fighting Army.* New York, 1941.

64. First Boy as told to James L. Long. *Land of Nakoda.* Helena, Montana, 1942.

65. Isaacson, Robert *Frederic Remington, a Painter of American Life.* Brooklyn, 1943.

66. Parkman, Francis. *The Oregon Trail.* New York, 1943.

67. Millier, Arthur. *Maynard Dixon, Painter of the West.* Tucson, Arizona, 1946.

68. Lea, Tom. *Calendar of Twelve Travelers Through the Pass of the North.* El Paso, 1946.

69. De Voto, Bernard. *Across the Wide Missouri*. Boston, 1947.

70. Luhan, Mabel Dodge. *Taos and Its Artists*. New York, 1947.

71. Santee, Ross. *Apache Land*. New York, 1947.

72. Conkling, Roscoe P. *et al. The Westerner's Brand Book*. Los Angeles, 1948 (actually issued in 1949).

73. Haley, J. Evetts, *et al. Some Southwestern Trails*. El Paso, 1948.

74. Wentworth, Edward M. *America's Sheep Trails*. Ames, Iowa, 1948.

75. Gann, Dan and Kitchen, Merrill A., eds. *The Westerners Brand Book*. Los Angeles, 1949 (actually issued in 1950).

76. Haley, J. Evetts. *The Heraldry of the Range*. Canyon, El Paso, Texas, 1949.

77. Spaulding, Edward S., ed. *Etchings of the West*. Santa Barbara, 1950.

78. Ross, Marvin C. *The West of Alfred Jacob Miller*. Norman, 1951.

79. Williams, J. R. *Cowboys Out Our Way*. New York, 1951.

80. McCracken, Harold. *Portrait of the Old West*. New York, Toronto, London, 1952.

81. Pach, Walter, *et al. New Mexico Artists*. Albuquerque, 1952.

82. Spaulding, Edward S., ed. *Borein's West*. Santa Barbara, 1952.

83. Taft, Robert. *Artists and Illustrators of the Old West, 1850–1900*. New York, 1953.

84. Widen, Albin. *Carl Oscar Borg*. Stockholm, Sweden, 1953.

85. Rathbone, Percy T. *Westward the Way*. Saint Louis, 1954.

86. (Eberstadt). *A Distinguished Collection of Western Painting, Catalogue 139*. New York, 1956.

87. Holden, Frances M., ed. *The Peter Hurd Mural*. Lubbock, 1957.

88. McCracken, Harold. *The Charles M. Russell Book*. Garden City, New York, 1957.

89. Spaulding, Edward Selden, ed. *Adobe Days Along the Channel*. Santa Barbara, 1957.

90. Matthews, Sallie Reynolds. *Interwoven*. El Paso, 1958.

91. Jackson, Helen Hunt. *Ramona*. Los Angeles, 1959.

92. McCracken, Harold. *George Catlin and the Old Frontier*. New York, 1959.

93. McDermott, John Francis. *George Caleb Bingham, River Portraitist*. Norman, 1959.

94. White, Leslie A., ed. *Lewis Henry Morgan; The Indian Journals, 1859–62*. Ann Arbor, 1959.

95. Ainsworth, Ed. *Painters of the Desert*. Palm Desert, California. 1960.

96. McCracken, Harold, ed. *Frederic Remington's Own West*. New York, 1960.

97. (Schiwetz). *Buck Schiwetz's Texas*. Austin, 1960.

98. Josephy, Alvin M., Jr. *The American Heritage Book of Indians*. New York, 1961.

99. Ward, Don. *Cowboys and Cattle Country*. New York, 1961.

100. Lockett, Clay. *A Navajo Sketch Book*. Flagstaff, Arizona, 1962.

101. Renner, Fred G. *Paper Talk*. Fort Worth, 1962.

PHOTOGRAPHY AND THE WESTERN SCENE

102. Townshend, S. Nugent. *Our Indian Summer in the Far West*. London, 1880.

103. *A Souvenir of Cattle Scenes on the Range*. Omaha, nd.

104. Ragsdale. *Views of San Angelo and Frontier Life in the Concho Country*. San Angelo, 1905.

105. Diller, J. S. *et al. Guidebook of the Western United States, Part D; The Shasta Route and Coast Line*. Washington, 1915.

106. Clark, Badger. *Grass Grown Trails*. Boston, 1917.

107. James, George Wharton. *New Mexico*. Boston, 1920.

108. Reeves, Frank. *The Story of the Highlands*. Marfa, Texas, 1936.

109. ———. *Hacienda de Atotonilco*. Yerbanis, Durango, Mexico, 1936.

110. Coolidge, Dane. *Old California Cowboys*. New York, 1939.

111. La Farge, Oliver. *As Long as the Grass Shall Grow*. New York and Toronto, 1940.

112. Weston, Charis W. and Edward. *California and the West*. New York, 1940.

113. Miller, Joseph, ed. *Arizona Pictorial*. Phoenix, 1944.

114. Wellman, Paul I. *The Callaghan*. Encinal, Texas, 1945.

115. Jackson, Clarence S. *Picture Maker of the Old West: William H. Jackson*. New York, 1947.

116. Fitzpatrick, George, ed. *Pictorial New Mexico*. Santa Fe, 1949.

117. Bryson, John. *The Cowboy*. Garden City, New York, 1951.

118. Hunter, J. Marvin and Rose, Noah H. *The Album of Gun-Fighters*.

119. Brown, Dee and Schmitt, Martin F. *Trail Driving Days*. New York, 1952.

120. Haley, J. Evetts. *Life on the Texas Range*. Austin, 1952.

121. Belden, Charles *et al. Cow Country, U.S.A.* Kansas City, Missouri, 1953.

122. Henderson, Paul C. *Landmarks on the Oregon Trail*. New York, 1953.

123. Horan, James D. and Sann, Paul. *Pictorial History of the Wild West*. New York, 1954.

124. Howes, Paul Griswold. *The Giant Cactus Forest and its World*. New York, 1954.

125. Robinson, Bert. *The Basket Weavers of Arizona*. Albuquerque, 1954.

126. Brown, Mark H. and Felton, W. R. *The Frontier Years*. New York, 1955.

127. Wilson, Neill C. *Rancheros Visitadores*. Santa Barbara, 1955.

128. Brown, Mark H. and Felton, W. R. *Before Barbed Wire*. New York, 1956.

129. La Farge, Oliver. *A Pictorial History of the American Indian*. New York, 1956.

130. Haley, J. Evetts. *Focus on the Frontier*. Amarillo (El Paso), 1957.

131. Kindig, R. H. *et al. Pictorial Supplement to Denver South Park and Pacific*. Denver, 1959.

132. Jennewein, J. Leonard and Boorman, Jane, eds. *Dakota Panorama*. Mitchell (Sioux Falls), South Dakota, 1961.

133. Burroughs, John Rolfe. *Where the Old West Stayed Young*. New York, 1962.

134. Slater, John. *El Morro: Inscription Rock, New Mexico*. Los Angeles, 1961 (but actually issued in Spring, 1963).

SINCE 1963
1964–1976

135. Babbitt, Bruce E. *Color and Light.* Flagstaff, 1973.

136. Hendricks, Gordon. *Albert Bierstadt, Painter of the American West.* New York and Fort Worth (but printed and bound in Japan), 1973.

137. Davidson, Harold G. *Edward Borein, Cowboy Artist: The Life and Works of John Edward Borein, 1872–1943.* Garden City, New York, 1974.

138. Krakel, Dean. *James Boren, a Study in Discipline.* Flagstaff, 1968.

139. Seeber, Louise Combes. *George Elbert Burr, 1859–1939.* (Catalogue Raisonne and Guide to the Etched Works with Biographical and Critical Notes). Flagstaff, 1971.

140. Lowman, Al *et al. José Cisneros at Paisano, an Exhibit: Riders of the Spanish Borderland, June 1969.* San Antonio, 1969.

141. Woloshuk, Nicholas, Jr. *E. Irving Couse.* Santa Fe, 1968.

142. Reed, William. *De Grazia the Irreverent Angel.* San Diego, 1971.

143. Burnside, Wesley M. *Maynard Dixon, Artist of the West.* Provo, Utah, 1974.

144. Perceval, Don. *Maynard Dixon Sketch Book.* Flagstaff, 1967.

145. Amaral, Anthony. *Will James, the Gilt Edged Cowboy.* Los Angeles, 1967.

146. Carroll, John M. *Eggenhofer: The Pulp Years.* Fort Collins, 1975.

147. Wearin, Otha D. *Clarence Arthur Ellsworth, Artist of the Old West.* Shenandoah, Iowa, 1967.

148. Balcomb, Mary N. *Nicolai Fechin.* Flagstaff, 1975.

149. Waters, Frank. *Leon Gaspard.* Flagstaff, 1964.

150. Harman, Fred. *The Great West in Paintings.* Chicago, 1969.

151. Getlein, Frank. *Harry Jackson.* New York, 1969.

152. McCracken, Harold. *The Frank Tenney Johnson Book.* Garden City, New York, 1974.

153. Harper, J. Russell. *Paul Kane's Frontier.* Fort Worth, 1971.

154. Laurence, Jeanne. *My Life with Sidney Laurence.* Seattle, 1974.

155. Ross, Marvin C. *The West of Alfred Jacob Miller.* Norman, 1968.

156. *Al Nestler's Southwest.* Flagstaff, 1970.

157. *The Sketches of Tom Phillips.* Kansas City, 1972.

158. Proctor, Alexander Phimister. *Sculptor in Buckskin.* Norman, 1971.

159. Ralston, J. K. *Rhymes of a Cowboy.* Billings, Montana, 1969.

160. Stenzel, Franz. *Cleveland Rockwell, Scientist and Artist.* Portland, 1972.

161. Krakel, Dean. *Tom Ryan, Painter in Four Sixes Country.* Flagstaff, 1971.

162. *Texas' Buck Schiwetz.* San Antonio, 1972.

163. Schiwetz, E. M. *The Schiwetz Legacy, an Artist's Tribute to Texas.* Austin and London, 1972.

164. Cole, Philip G. *Montana in Miniature.* Kalispell, 1966.

165. Horan, James D. *The Life and Art of Charles Schreyvogel.* New York, 1969.

166. *Gus Shafer's West.* Kansas City, 1973.

167. *Gordon Snidow, Chronicler of the Contemporary West.* Flagstaff, 1973.

168. Rosenfeld, Arnold, ed. *A Thomason Sketchbook: Drawings by John W. Thomason, Jr.* Austin and London, 1969.

169. Belknap, William, Jr. and Frances S. *Gunnar Widforss, Painter of the Grand Canyon.* Flagstaff, 1969.

170. *Tenth Annual Exhibition, Cowboy Artists of America.* Flagstaff, 1975.

171. Howard, James K. *Ten Years with the Cowboy Artists of America.* Flagstaff, 1976.

172. Beeler, Joe. *Cowboys and Indians.* Norman, 1967.

173. ———. *The Joe Beeler Sketch Book.* Flagstaff, 1974.

174. Green, Ben K. *The Last Trail Drive Through Downtown Dallas.* Flagstaff, 1971.

175. ———. *The Color of Horses.* Flagstaff, 1974.

176. Pirtle, Caleb. *XIT — American Cowboy.* Birmingham, 1975.

177. Ainsworth, Ed. *The Cowboy in Art.* New York and Cleveland, 1968.

178. Meigs, John, ed. *The Cowboy in American Prints.* Chicago, 1972.

179. Harding, Frank. *A Livestock Heritage.* Geneva, Illinois, 1971.

180. Galvin, John. *The Etchings of Edward Borein.* San Francisco, 1971.

181. McDowell, Bart. *The American Cowboy in Life and Legend.* Washington, D.C., 1972.

182. Forbis, William H. *The Cowboy.* New York, 1973.

183. McCracken, Harold. *The American Cowboy.* Garden City, New York, 1973.

184. Woloshuk, Nicholas. *Edward Borein, Volume II — The Cowboy.* Santa Fe, 1974.

185. Hassrick, Royal B. *Cowboys.* London (but printed in Hong Kong), 1974.

186. Ellis, George F. *Bell Ranch as I Knew It.* Kansas City, 1973.

187. (Wolfe). *The Sketchbook of Byron B. Wolfe.* Kansas City, 1972.

188. Pitz, Henry. *The Brandywine Tradition.* Boston, 1969.

189. Karolevitz, Robert F. *Where Your Heart Is . . .* Aberdeen, South Dakota, 1970.

190. Reed, Walt. *Harold Von Schmidt Draws and Paints the Old West.* Flagstaff, 1972.

191. Carroll, John M. *Von Schmidt — The Complete Illustrator.* Fort Collins, 1973.

192. Apgar, John F., Jr. *Frank Schoonover, Painter - Illustrator — A Bibliography.* Morristown, New Jersey, 1969.

193. Schoonover, Cortlandt. *The Edge of the Wilderness.* Secaucus, New Jersey, 1974.

194. ———. *Frank Schoonover.* New York, 1976.

195. Wyeth, Betsy James (Mrs. Andrew), ed. *The Wyeths.* Boston, 1971.

196. Allen, Douglas and Douglas, Jr. *N. C. Wyeth.* New York, 1972.

197. Horgan, Paul. *Peter Hurd: A Portrait Sketch from Life.* Fort Worth, 1965.

198. Meigs, John, ed. *Peter Hurd, the Lithographs.* Lubbock, 1968.

199. *W. H. D. Koerner, Illustrator of the West.* Los Angeles, 1968.

200. Dykes, Jeff. *Fifty Great Western Illustrators.* Flagstaff, 1975.

201. Reed, Walt. *The Illustrator in America, 1900–1960s.* New York, 1966.

202. Broder, Patricia Janis. *Bronzes of

the American West. New York, 1973.

203. Ewers, John C. *Artists of the Old West.* Garden City, New York, 1973.

204. Rossi, Paul A. and Hunt, David C. *The Art of the Old West.* New York, 1971.

205. Hedgpeth, Don *et al. The West of Buffalo Bill.* New York, 1974.

206. Renner, Frederic G. *Charles M. Russell, Paintings, Drawings and Sculpture in the Amon Carter Collection.* Fort Worth, 1966.

207. *Ibid.* New York, 1974.

208. Yost, Karl and Renner, Frederic G. *A Bibliography of the Published Works of Charles M. Russell.* Lincoln, 1971.

209. McCracken, Harold. *The Frederic Remington Book.* Garden City, New York, 1966.

210. Hedgpeth, Don. *The Art of Frederic Remington.* Cody, Wyoming, 1974.

211. Hassrick, Peter H. *Frederic Remington.* New York, 1973.

212. *The West and Walter Bimson.* Tucson, 1971.

213. Harmsen, Dorothy. *Harmsen's Western Americana.* Flagstaff, 1971.

214. *The McKee Collection of Paintings.* El Paso, 1968.

215. *Edward Borein: The Katherine H. Haley Collection.* Phoenix, 1974.

216. Carroll, John M. *The Black Military Experience in the American West.* New York, 1971.

217. ———. *Buffalo Soldiers West.* Fort Collins, 1971.

218. *Tom Lea, a Selection of Paintings and Drawings from the Nineteen-sixties.* San Antonio, 1969.

219. Lea, Tom. *A Picture Gallery.* Boston, 1968.

220. *Woolaroc Museum.* Bartlesville, Oklahoma, 1965.

221. Baird, Joseph A., Jr., ed. *The West Remembered.* San Francisco, 1973.

222. *Walking Westward: An American Journey.* New York, 1972.

223. *American Masters in the West.* Boise, Idaho, 1974.

224. Dary, David. *The Buffalo Book.* Chicago, 1974.

225. Chapman, Kenneth M. *The Pottery of San Ildefonso Pueblo.* Albuquerque, 1970.

226. Hedgpeth, Don. *Spurs Were a-Jinglin'.* Flagstaff, 1975.

227. Krakel, Dean II. *Season of the Elk.* Kansas City, 1976.

228. Scriver, Bob. *An Honest Try.* Kansas City, 1975.

229. Getlein, Frank *et al. The Lure of the Great West.* Waukesha, Wisconsin, 1973.

CHAPTER VI

A Range Man's Library

AS AN AMATEUR RANGE MAN I should not attempt to discuss the technical working tools of the profession. I would soon be out of my depth. On the other hand, I should not write as an established collector of the literature of the range. A collector has been defined as one who tries to accumulate all that has been written on a subject — the worthy and the unworthy. Certainly it would be out of place to urge that you buy the unworthy and become an all-out collector of range books. The late Charlie Everitt, beloved Americana dealer of New York City, tells this tale in his delightful book, *The Adventures of a Treasure Hunter* (Boston, 1951). A man walked into his shop one day and said, "I'll buy any damn thing that mentions a cowboy." Note the marks of the collector, "any damn thing." Later Charlie ran a total on his adding machine. The stranger tore off a piece of Charlie's wrapping paper and wrote a check for $1,243. The check was signed, "Philip Ashton Rollins." Rollins wrote *The Cowboy* (New York, 1922), one of the classics on the cowboy, his equipment and his work. He revised and enlarged it in 1936, and that is the best edition. Rollins was one of the great collectors of range life books, and the collection is still intact in the Princeton University Library.

My recommendations are restricted to the more recent books and pamphlets on the men and events of the range. They are also selective, mentioning mainly the worthy books that will help build a library rather than a collection. There are two primary reasons for sticking to the more recent books — cost and availability. While it does not hold for all kinds of books, most of the older range life books are both expensive and hard to find.

Balance Needed

There should be balance in a range man's library. There should be books about the range country, biographies and autobiographies of cowboys and cowmen, histories of their associations, accounts of the trails and trail drivers, ranch histories, studies of the range wars, books about cows, sheep and range horses, and the literature of the range including the novels, ballads, and art. These are the books that a range man should read and reread for pleasure and for an understanding and essential background of his profession.

It is perhaps happenstance that I am in a position to discuss recent range books. I am a collector of range books, but also I have two close associates, B. W. (Bill) Allred and F. G. (Fred) Renner, who collaborate on a monthly review column, "Western Book Roundup," carried by several magazines. In each of the past five years we have reviewed about 150 western books. Practically every new range book issued during that period has been reviewed by one of the three of us.

The Start

An indispensable first book in any range man's library is a good bibliography. Until December 31, 1959, when *The Rampaging Herd* (Norman, 1959) by Ramon F. Adams was issued such a book was not available. It lists a total of 2,651 books and pamphlets on men and events in the cattle industry. While it is by no means selective, it will provide much guidance to any range man building a library. As a collector, I have found J. Frank Dobie's *Guide to Life and Literature of the Southwest* (Austin and Dallas, 1942, and revised and enlarged, Dallas, 1952) very useful. In the chapters on "Range Life, Cowboys, Cattle, Sheep"; "Cowboy Songs and Other Ballads"; "Horses, Mustangs and Cow Ponies"; and "The Bad Man Tradition," Dobie comments on range books in his own particularly pithy and penetrating fashion. You will find this book highly entertaining as well as useful. Make no mistake — Frank Dobie is a range man with a deep love of the land, grass and animals that shines through everything he has written.

The greatest single book about a major segment of the range country is Dr. Walter Prescott Webb's *The Great Plains* (Boston, 1931). The first printing is now a collector's item. A much more recent book, *Grasslands of the Great*

Plains, Their Nature and Use (Lincoln, 1956) by J. E. Weaver and F. W. Albertson, with contributions by other experts including Bill Allred, brings together a tremendous amount of knowledge about the vegetation of the mid-continent prairie between the Saskatchewan and the Rio Grande. Carl Frederick Kraenzel's *The Great Plains in Transition* (Norman, 1955) is worthwhile.

Unfortunately, so far as I know there is no book about the intermountain ranges that is comparable in environmental coverage to these three. A book that will be harder to find but worth the search is *Western Grazing Grounds and Forest Ranges* (Chicago, 1913) by Will C. Barnes. Leon V. Almirall in *From College to Cow Country* (Caldwell, 1956) has some pertinent remarks to make on ranching at the nine-thousand-foot level. Two books which give considerable information on desert ranges are worth mentioning — Earl J. Larrison's *Owyhee, Life of a Northern Desert* (Caldwell, 1957) and Edmund C. Jaeger's *The North American Deserts* (Stanford, 1957). *This is the West* (New York, 1957) edited by Robert West Howard has much to say on the whole of the range country. It was issued first as a paperback at thirty-five cents and then in hard covers, with numerous fine illustrations, at six dollars — a bargain either way.

The Trail Driving Era

The days of the spread of cattle from Texas into the Northern Plains and of trail driving to railheads in Kansas is one of the most thrilling periods in the history of the West. This period has been very thoroughly documented in both fact and fiction. No book on trail driving will compare with Andy Adams's *The Log of a Cowboy* (Boston and New York, 1903). The first printing of this book is getting scarce but the publisher keeps it in print with colored illustrations (added in 1927) by another range man, R. Farrington Elwell — former manager of Buffalo Bill's Wyoming ranch and well-known western artist now living in Phoenix, Arizona. Frank Dobie's *Up the Trail from Texas* (New York, 1955), primarily for younger readers, is a dandy book about real trail drivers. Wayne Gard's *The Chisholm Trail* (Norman, 1954) is the best book in print on that drove road just as the late Walter S. Campbell's (Stanley Vestal) *Queen of Cow Towns, Dodge City* (New York, 1952) is the best book in print on Kansas cow towns. The late Floyd B. Streeter's *Prairie Trails and Cowtowns* (Boston, 1936) was issued in a small edition and is now very scarce and expensive but most of the text, revised and expanded, is available in his later book, *The Kaw* (New York, Toronto, 1941). *The Cattle Drives of David Shirk from Texas to the Idaho Mines, 1871 and 1873* (Portland, Oregon, 1956) was edited by Martin F. Schmitt and includes some later experiences of Shirk as a cattleman in eastern Oregon.

Cattle Kings

Some cowmen started as cowboys, many cowboys never became owners, and some owners were never cowboys. *Charles Goodnight* (New York and Boston, 1936) by J. Evetts Haley is the best biography ever written of a range man and may be the best biography ever written about a Westerner. The first printing of this great book is scarce and expensive but it has been kept in print by the University of Oklahoma Press since 1949. Edward F. Treadwell's *The Cattle King* (New York, 1931) is good on California's big cowman, Henry Miller. Like the Goodnight book the original publisher permitted Miller's biography to go out-of-print but another publisher recognized its value and reprinted it. Roscoe Sheller's *Ben Snipes, Northwest Cattle King* (Portland, Oregon, 1957) is a rags to riches story of a man whose cattle ranged over much of central Washington. He had competition from Pete French of Oregon. There is a book about French, too, and while it is classed as novel it is said to follow closely the life of this well-known cowman. It was written by Elizabeth (Lambert) Wood and is entitled *Pete French, Cattle King* (Portland, Oregon, 1951). Here is one more — *Pierre Wibaux, Cattle King* (Bismarck, 1953), a pamphlet reprinted by the State Historical Society of North Dakota. It is about a Frenchman who did well in cattle and became a well-know cow town banker. Frazier Hunt's *Cap Mossman* (New York, 1951) is a top biography. Mossman made his reputation as manager of the Hashknife in Arizona where his success in dealing with rustlers led to his appointment as Captain of the Arizona Rangers. Later Cap and his associates controlled a million acres of range, all under fence, in South Dakota. There are many books about cowmen but none better than these — and these have the added advantage of being readily available.

Associations

Historically, cowmen, beginning with the roundup, have worked together in solving their mutual problems. The books about their associations are a part of the history of the range. Maurice Frink's *Cow Country Cavalcade* (Denver, 1954) is on the eighty-year-old Wyoming association. Lewis Nordyke's *Great Roundup* (New York, 1955) is the saga of the Texas and Southwestern. Ray H. Mattison's *Roosevelt and the Stockmen's Association* (Bismarck, 1950) is of much interest. Teddy was quite an organizer.

Autobiography

The books about cowboys are many. The first was Charles A. Siringo's *A Texas Cowboy, or Fifteen Years on the Hurricane Deck of a Spanish Pony* (Chicago, 1885). The first printing is exceedingly rare, but it has been reprinted many times. Siringo claimed that a million copies of it were sold in his lifetime. This seems to be an exaggeration but it was justifiably popular — a rollicking account. Fortunately, it is again in print with an entertaining and informative introduction by J. Frank Dobie, illustrations by Tom Lea, typography by Carl Hertzog, and the Sloane imprint (New York, 1950). Rated just below the Siringo, and not much at that, is Ike Blasingame's *Dakota Cowboy* (New York, 1958). Ike was a Matador cowboy and bronc peeler and this is a tremendously entertaining book that is also down to earth on all cow country happenings. Fred Gipson's *Cowhand* (New York, 1953) is matter-of-fact on the day-to-day jobs of a working cowboy. Richmond P. Hobson, Jr., has written two very entertaining books about the discovery and development of the last great cattle frontier on this continent — *Grass Beyond the Mountains* (Philadelphia, New York, 1953) and *Nothing Too Good for a Cowboy* (Philadelphia, New York, 1955). Ranch life beyond the mountains in British Columbia was high adventure indeed. Walt Coburn's *Stirrup High* (New York, 1957) is his story of his first summer on the family ranch in Montana — it is completely charming.

Ranch Histories

Ranch histories include much on the owners and their hired help as well as operations, financing and stocking. *The King Ranch* (Boston, 1957) by Tom Lea, talented Texas writer and artist, is a handsome two-volume set, designed by the equally talented Texas typographer, Carl Hertzog. It belongs in any range man's library. *Life on the King Ranch* (New York, 1951) by Frank Goodwyn, is good on the life and legends of the Mexican vaqueros, who make up the working force on the ranch. Frank was raised on the Norias division where his father was the manager. J. Evetts Haley in *The XIT Ranch of Texas* (Chicago, 1929) spoke quite plainly about some folks who started their herds with XIT cows. A suit was filed and the unsold remainder of the first edition was impounded by the court. It is a very scarce and expensive book. However, with some changes, it is now again available with the imprint of the University of Oklahoma Press. The State of Texas traded the land which became the XIT to a Chicago syndicate for the Capitol building in Austin. *Flat Top Ranch* (Norman, 1957), edited by Bill Allred and the writer, is a different kind of a ranch history. It is the story of the creation of a ranch from a number of eroded, cropped-out farms and some depleted, brush-infested range. It also is the story, about the only one in book form as yet, of modern conservation ranching. Since neither Bill nor I receive a royalty from the sale of the book I am not too modest to say it also belongs in every range man's library. *Wyoming's Pioneer Ranches* (Laramie, 1955) is a big handsome encyclopedic volume on ranches of the Laramie Plain by three native sons, R. H. (Bob) Burns, A. S. (Bud) Gillespie and Willing G. Richardson. There are other ranch histories, of course, and nearly all of them are worth having.

The Women's Viewpoint

The viewpoint of the women on range life is entertaining and sometimes informative. Agnes Morley Cleaveland's *No Life for a Lady* (Boston, 1941) is generally conceded to be about the top account. It is certainly spritely enough without an overdose of sentiment but so is Sallie Reynolds Matthews's *Interwoven* (Houston, 1936 and El Paso, 1958). The beautiful reprint, designed by Carl Hertzog, is illustrated by E. W. (Buck) Schiwetz. Mary Kidder Rak's *A Cowman's Wife* (Boston and New York, 1934) and *Mountain Cattle* (Boston and New York, 1936) are sound matter-of-fact ranch history. Mary Taylor Bunton's *A Bride on the Old Chisholm Trail* (San Antonio, 1939) refutes the contention that women didn't go up

the trail. Emerson Hough's good historical novel *North of 36* (New York, 1923) really stirred up the critics because he has the young woman owner of the herd on the trail with it.

Range Wars

The range wars, the big owner versus small owners or nesters and cattle versus sheep, were often bloody. The moves and countermoves by the participants make interesting reading. The Johnson County Wyoming affair is perhaps the most widely publicized of all range wars. A. S. Mercer's *The Banditti of the Plains* (Cheyenne, 1894) was the first of several books on it and is now exceedingly rare. It has been reprinted several times. *The Longest Rope* (Caldwell, 1940) as told by Bill Walker to 'Mrs. D. F. Baber seems to be the only other account of the Johnson County troubles still in print. Will A. Keleher's *Violence in Lincoln County* (Albuquerque, 1957) is by far the most authoritative book on the so-called Lincoln County War. *Arizona's Dark and Bloody Ground* (Caldwell, 1936 and revised and enlarged, 1948) by Earle R. Forrest is an entertaining account of the Pleasant Valley War in Arizona.

County Histories

I want to call attention here to another type of book — the county history — which often contains biographies of early cowmen, accounts of the establishing of the first ranches, and something of the range troubles. I hope you will carefully scan the county histories available in your own state, for in them you will find range history not available else-

A Trail Herd *by R. Farrington Elwell*

where. Here are some of the recent examples of county histories of considerable range interest: George Francis Brimlow's *Harney County, Oregon and Its Range Land* (Portland, Oregon, 1951), Ira A. Freeman's *A History of Montezuma County, Colorado* (Boulder, 1958), Cornelia Adams Perkins's *Saga of San Juan* (Monticello, Utah, 1957), Harry N. Campbell's *The Early History of Motley County* (San Antonio, 1958). The latter is essentially the history of a great ranch, the Matador. Minnie Dubbs Millbrook's *Ness, Western County, Kansas* (Detroit, 1955) has a place of honor in my own collection because it was in Ness County that I learned some forty years ago that a cowboy is no longer "a hired man on horseback" much of the time.

Range Livestock

"No cows, no cowboys. No sheep, no shepherds. No livestock, not much American West." This quotation, I believe, should be credited to the late Colonel Eddie Wentworth, teacher, author, and longtime educational director for Armours. A range man's library will include books about the critters. The number one book is J. Frank Dobie's *The Longhorns* (Boston, 1941) based on a terrific amount of research and written as only "Mr. Southwest" could write it — a major contribution to the history of the West. The cattlemen took the lead in settling much of our West and it was the longhorns, walking to their new homes, that went with them. Paul C. Henlein's *Cattle Kingdom in the Ohio Valley* (University of Kentucky Press, 1959) adds some important links in the spread of the British breeds westward from the Atlantic. It was on the prairies and savannahs of the Ohio Valley that these breeds were first crossed with the longhorns of Spanish origin. Today the Hereford is the dominant beef breed in this country. The newest and best book about the whitefaces is Don Ornduff's *The Hereford in America* (Kansas City, Missouri, 1957). Robert J. Kleberg, Jr., of the King Ranch has written a pamphlet about the first beef breed to be developed in this country, *The Santa Gertrudis Breed of Beef Cattle* (Kingsville, n.d., and revised and improved in format by Carl Hertzog, El Paso, 1954). The Santa Gertrudis are becoming popular in the Gulf Coast country. Frank W. Harding's *Mostly About Shorthorns* (privately printed, 1947) is a little harder to find but real Shorthorn fans will do it. The books by Alvin H. Sanders on the Hereford, Shorthorn and Angus are now scarce but worthwhile. His *The Cattle of the World* (Washington, D.C., 1926) is profusely illustrated and somewhat easier to come by. The number one book about range horses is J. Frank Dobie's *The Mustangs* (Boston, 1952). This is one of the best, if not the very best of all of Dobie's books. In it his love of the wild and free sings on every page. Rufus Steele's *Mustangs of the Mesa* (Hollywood, 1941) is well written but no longer easy to find. Walker D. Wyman's *The Wild Horse of the West* (Caldwell, 1945) is based primarily on the written records and has a fine bibliography. Luis B. Ortega's *California Stock Horse* (Sacramento, 1949) is well illustrated with photographs and is informative. John A. Gorman's *The West-*

ern Horse (Danville, Illinois, 1939) is always in demand and therefore, in print. Wayne Gard's *Fabulous Quarter Horse: Steel Dust* (New York, 1958) is the story of one of the famous sires of this purely American breed so popular as cow horses.

Despite the importance of sheep in our range economy they have been practically ignored in range literature. A range man's library, to maintain balance, should include some books on sheep. Fortunately there are some very good ones. The best of all is the late Archer B. Gilfillan's *Sheep* (Boston, 1929), truly a western classic. It was reissued by the University of Minnesota Press in 1957 with an illuminating introduction by J. Frank Dobie. Hughie Call's *Golden Fleece* (Boston, 1942) is good social history as well as informative on sheepherders. Winifred (Thalmann) Kupper's two books *The Golden Hoof* (New York, 1945) and *Texas Sheepman* (Austin, 1951) are about sheep and sheep folks in the Hill Country of Texas where she grew up. Both are authentic and charming. Towne and Wentworth's *Shepherd's Empire* (Norman, 1945) is based on the writings of others but worthwhile. Colonel Wentworth's *America's Sheep Trails* (Ames, Iowa, 1948) brings together much information. It is not a book for reading but does have considerable reference value. Will C. Minor's *Footprints in the Trail* (Denver, 1959) is a delightful book of nature stories by a scribbling shepherd. Minor says sheepherding allows him more opportunity to study the whole of nature than any other manner of making a living he has yet discovered. Will Minor

may prove to be a worthy successor to Archie Gilfillan.

Literature Diverse

The literature of the range is certainly diverse. It encompasses the ballads and other verse, the legends and tall tales, the novels and short stories, the writings of certain range men, cartoons and art, and the heraldry of the range. I am also including here two additional books by Ramon F. Adams, *Cowboy Lingo* (Boston, 1936) and *Western Words* (Norman, 1944). Both were labors of love in which Ramon strives to preserve for posterity, in dictionary form, the idiom of early range days. With the possible exception of the Negro spirituals, cowboy songs and ballads are believed to be the major contribution of this country to folk songs. John A. Lomax spent thirty years collecting and preparing such ballads for publication. Any of the books of cowboy songs he has compiled and his *Adventures of a Ballad Hunter* (New York, 1947) are worthwhile. The late Badger Clark's *Sun and Saddle Leather* (Boston, 1915) received the approval of the severest critics of all, the oldtime range men. It is in print and enlarged to include the poems which appeared in a number of other small books of verse by Badger. "The Badger Hole," his log cabin bachelor home near Custer, South Dakota, is now a state shrine. Omar Barker's *Songs of the Saddle Men* (Denver, 1954) speaks to all those who love grass, blue skies, cattle and horses.

Novels

The novels of Andy Adams and of Eugene Manlove Rhodes are a part of the literature of the range but all are now believed out of print. Several of the Rhodes novels were reprinted in paperback series and can occasionally be found in the used book and magazine stores. Conrad Richter's *The Sea of Grass* (New York, 1937) is a beautifully written novel with a sound range conservation moral. Owen Wister's *The Virginian* (New York, 1902) was the beginning of the deluge of "westerns." It is still in print and while it does not smell strongly of cows, it has become an American range classic. The short stories and tall tales of Charles M. Russell, the great cowboy artist, are terrific. Many of them are included in *Trails Plowed Under*, first issued in 1927 but still in print. His *Good Medicine* contains a number of brilliantly illustrated letters. It was first issued in 1929 and is still available. Both the illustrations and Russell's words mirror the range. Russell illustrated many other range books but unfortunately nearly all of them are out of print. Mody C. Boatwright's *Tall Tales from Texas Cow Camps* (Dallas, 1934) is no longer easy to find but worth seeking. Dr. James Cloyd Bowman's *Pecos Bill* (Chicago, 1937) is the best of several books on this legendary cowboy.

Cartoons and Pictographs

The late J. R. Williams's *Cowboys Out Our Way* (New York, 1951) is a highly enjoyable true-to-life book of cartoons. J. Frank Dobie liked it and gave his reasons in the introduction he wrote for it. Ace Reid's *Cowpokes* (Kerrville, Texas, 1958) won't equal Jim Williams's expert work but Ace is a comer. The photographs by certain pioneer camera-men do much to document the flavor of the range. Brown and Felton's *Before Barbed Wire* (New York, 1956) reproduces many of the pictures of range life made by the pioneer Montana photographer, L. A. Huffman. *Life on the Texas Range* (Austin, 1952) is profusely illustrated with the very fine photographs made by the pioneer Texas camera artist, Erwin E. Smith. The text is by J. Evetts Haley. Ed Borein, like his friend Charlie Russell, was never a top cowhand because he was too interested in sketching the man, cow and horse action that is inevitable on the range. After Ed's death his friends published two handsome volumes — *Etchings of the West* (Santa Barbara, 1950) and *Borein's West* (Santa Barbara, 1952) — in which most of his great range sketches are saved for our future edification. Harold Bugbee illustrated several Haley books; Tom Lea several by Dobie; Ross Santee many of his own books, as well as range books by others. Will James stuck pretty much to illustrating his own works. These and such other great western artists as "Buck" Dunton, Maynard Dixon, R. Farrington Elwell, Nick Eggenhofer, Harvey T. Dunn, and Frederic Remington illustrated range books. Watch for books with drawings by these artists. They are marks of quality.

Life on the Range

A range library should also include books that cover the sweep of men, cattle, horses, and country in their relation to one another. Such a book, for example, is Ernest Staples Osgood's *The Day of the Cattleman* (Minneapolis, 1929 and reprinted 1954). Here, too, belongs

Granville Stuart's *Forty Years on the Frontier* (two volumes, Cleveland, 1925 and in one volume, Glendale, California, 1959). E. C. Abbott, better known as Teddy Blue, was Stuart's son-in-law. Teddy told his story to Helena Huntington Smith, and the book which resulted from their collaboration, *We Pointed Them North* (New York, 1939 and Norman, 1955, with Eggenhofer illustrations) is frank and highly entertaining. Walker D. Wyman's *Nothing But Prairie and Sky* (Norman, 1953), based on the notes of Bruce Siberts, is just as frank on the early days on the Dakota range. Both works deserve high literary ratings.

Three books have been compiled recently in which the records left by pioneer range men and those who reported their doings are made available to modern readers — Ramon F. Adams's *The Best of the American Cowboy* (Norman, 1957), *The Cowboy Reader* (New York, 1959) edited by Lon Tinkle and Allen Maxwell, and Clifford P. Westermeir's *Trailing the Cowboy* (Caldwell, 1955). Westermeir also wrote what is probably the most realistic book on the rodeo, *Man, Beast, Dust* (Denver, 1947). The classic book on brands is Oren Arnold and John P. Hale's *Hot Irons* (New York, 1940), but Duncan Emrich's *The Cowboy's Own Brand Book* (New York, 1954) is a minor classic for readers seven to seventy. It was only after reading Hortense Warner Ward's *Cattle Brands and Cowboys* (Dallas, 1953) that I learned why I couldn't read the Mexican brands I had encountered in the lower Rio Grande Valley thirty years ago. One or two of his own state or county brand books should be in each range man's library.

British Books

Some of the best writing ever done about the range is by educated men from the British Isles. The investment of foreign capital in livestock enterprises in the American West was a major financial phenomenon of the late seventies and early eighties. Younger sons, experienced breeders, and British visitors followed their capital to the West. Unfortunately, there isn't a book by one of these educated gentlemen in print today. Mostly, they are expensive and hard to find, yet a range man's library should include one or more of these volumes. Perhaps the best of all, and probably the most expensive, is John Clay's *My Life on the Range* (privately printed in Chicago, 1924). Clay, an educated Scot, was tenderfoot, ramrod, manager, owner and founder of a great commission firm. His book is tops in writing style and content. William French's *Some Recollections of a Western Ranchman* (London, 1927) and John Culley's *Cattle, Horses and Men* (Los Angeles, 1940) rate just below Clay's book. R. B. Townshend's *A Tenderfoot in Colorado* (London, 1923), *A Tenderfoot in New Mexico* (London, 1923), and *Last Memories of a Tenderfoot* (London, 1926) are all good. They were reissued in this country in the twenties and are somewhat less expensive than those mentioned above. The one range book by an English author you are most likely to find, *My Reminiscences as a Cowboy* (New York, 1930) by Frank Harris, is utterly worthless. It was issued in wraps in what must have been a huge printing and is still rather common. There are many others, fortunately, and most of them are good.

Western Frontier Library

There never was a time before when so many good books could be bought for so little. For example, Savoie Lotinville, the canny businessman and scholar, who heads the University of Oklahoma Press, is issuing a well-printed, hardboard-covered series, The Western Frontier Library at two dollars per volume. In this Library of classic western reprints of particular interest to range men are: Mercer's *The Banditti of the Plains* (1954) with a long introduction by William H. Kittrell; Pat F. Garrett's *The Authentic Life of Billy the Kid* (1954), a major Lincoln County War item with an introduction by this writer which shows it isn't so authentic; Charles L. Martin's *A Sketch of Sam Bass* (1956), a cowboy and trail driver who turned train robber, with an introduction by Ramon F. Adams; Nelson Lee's *Three Years Among the Comanches* (1957) with an introduction by Dr. Walter P. Webb (Lee was a horse and cow trader and trail driver to Louisiana before he was captured); Will Hale's *Twenty-four Years a Cowboy and Ranchman in Southern Texas and Old Mexico* (1959), one of the rarest and most sought-for range books; and General James I. Brisbin's *The Beef Bonanza or How to Get Rich on the Plains* (1959), one of the books credited with inducing eastern and foreign financiers to invest in the cattle business in the West. It was first issued in 1881 and was really an expansion of the first promotional piece of its type done for the Union Pacific Railroad — Dr. Hiram Latham's *Trans-Missouri Stock Raising* (Omaha, 1871), a very rare range book.

Other Reprints

The famous reprint house Grosset and Dunlap has included two great books in the Grosset Universal Library, issued in paper covers, to sell at $1.25 — Dobie's *The Longhorns* (1957) and Webb's *The Great Plains* (1957). Bantam Frontier Classics, issued in 1959 in paper covers to sell at four bits include Dobie's *The Mustangs,* Gipson's *Cowhand,* Santee's *Lost Pony Tracks* and Campbell's (Vestal) *Dodge City.* Pennant Books issued Dobie's *A Vaquero of the Brush Country* in wraps in 1954 to sell for two bits — this is a somewhat abridged edition of the 1929 *First* that is one of my favorites among all of Frank's fine books. Watch the racks of paperbacks in the book stores, newsstands and drug stores. More and more good range books are showing up on them. Also watch the remainder tables (sometimes labeled "Publisher's Overstocks") in the bookstores — occasionally a publisher overestimates the number of copies of a good range book the public will take at the original price and has to sell them cheaper.

Two other reprints in 1959, both by the Antiquarian Press of New York, rank in importance with the issuing of *The Rampaging Herd* as news in the field of range books. They are cheap only in comparison with the prices commanded by the originals when one or the other does infrequently appear on the market. James Cox's *Historical and Biographical Record of the Cattle Indus-*

try and the Cattlemen of Texas and Adjacent Territory (Saint Louis, 1895) and James W. Freeman's *Prose and Poetry of the Livestock Industry* (Denver and Kansas City, 1905) were the two reprinted in handsome numbered editions of 500. The Cox, in two volumes, has a new introduction by J. Frank Dobie — the Freeman one by Ramon Adams. The price of each is $100. This is the first reprint of each of these exceedingly rare books. A good copy of the first of either brings $500.

If you have the time, the patience, and the money, by all means get the first edition of all the books mentioned. The *firsts* will give you a feeling of pride of ownership as long as you live and will constitute a substantial addition to your estate. But, first editions are not mandatory in a range man's library. The reprints provide the same or an improved text at much less cost and can be had now. There is no valid reason for a range man to be without a library to supplement his working tools and to enrich his understanding of his calling.

CHAPTER VII

The Texas Ranch Today

THE YEAR WAS 1849, the place Grenada, Mississippi — my grandfather, William W. Dykes, received a letter from a cousin who had left Georgia a few months before he did to settle near Gonzales in southwest Texas. After a little family news, the letter dwelt on the rich deep prairie soils of Texas with their luxuriant cover of grass that could be bought for almost nothing, and it was enough to start my grandfather, tired of growing cotton on the eroding hills of northern Mississippi, on his way. Some days later, family legend has it, William stopped to spend the night with one of the numerous Cotham families at old Rough and Ready (now Monticello), Arkansas. Such were the charms of a daughter of the family, the dancing-eyed, poetry-writing Nancy, that William tarried and the lanky soft-speaking Georgian wooed and won her. Part of the bargain, however, was settling down in southern Arkansas.

Grandfather William is buried in an unmarked grave near the old Blue and Boggy Army Depot in what is now Oklahoma — the victim of the accuracy of Yankee gunnery. Grandmother Nancy, with her four sons, stuck it out for a while after the war was over, but history tells us that reconstruction days were pretty tough in Arkansas, and about

1870 she was on her way west after trading a section of land for a yoke of oxen and a covered wagon.

Grandmother Nancy took along the letter my grandfather got from his cousin in 1849 — who knows how much it had to do with her decision to move to Texas — and it is a treasured part of the cattle collection at the little house on Guilford Road.

The family of five settled first on Grapevine Prairie, lived a while in Bosque County, moved to Wilbarger County and then back to Dallas County. The particular significance of these moves is the constant proximity to the cattle trails — the Chisholm and the Western — of the family farming and ranching operations. My own father was never on a trail drive to Kansas but he knew many cowmen and cowhands. He was constantly on the Texas cattle frontier until he married at forty and settled down to run a feed store on the Courthouse Square in Dallas and later to breed some Jersey cattle. At our home in the Trinity bottom west of Dallas, when I was growing up, the number of places to be set for supper — the evening meal — was never known until dad drove in from the "store."

Such old brands as the XIT, Turkey Track, Hashknife, JA, Four Sixes, SMS, and 3D's; such old ranch names as the Matador, King, Spur, Pitchfork, Taft and League; such old range giants as John Chisum, Charles Goodnight, Thomas Bugbee, Oliver Loving, Shanghai Pierce, Barbecue Campbell, Buck Barry, Luke Brite and George Littlefield; and such Texas ranch families as the Swensons, Klebergs, Mitchells, Curetons, Slaughters, Kokernots, Reynolds, Matthews and the Waggoners, which produced not one, but several outstanding cowmen, call to mind a past era in the range history of Texas.

The talk at the table and before the fireplace in our living room was talk of the day of the open range, followed by huge fenced spreads; of the great trail drives of beef to rail's end in Kansas and Nebraska; of carousing cowboys in Dodge, Hays, or Abilene at the end of the trail; of drives of cows to stock the northern Plains just wrested from the hard-fighting Plains Indians; of Indian raids on isolated ranches; of the round-up; and of foreign capital invested in Texas lands and Texas cattle.

I could easily spend my allotted time in acknowledging our indebtedness to Mexico for the gifts of cattle and the *know-how* of handling them. For well over two centuries cattle have been of tremendous economic significance in Texas and even now two-thirds of the land area of the state is devoted to grazing. The trail drives, following the Civil War, hastened the economic recovery of the state by pouring an estimated two hundred million dollars into its business arteries. It would be easy to dwell, nostalgically, on this age of range romance about which I heard so much as a boy.

Some of the old brands and some of the old ranch names are still in use, and, while the range giants are all gone, many of the great ranch famiiles are still in the cattle business, having made — even taken the lead in — the adjustment to the modern way of ranching.

It is impossible in a paper of this length to trace properly the evolutionary changes from the old to the new — the influence of barbed wire, windmills, railroads, highways, new and improved grasses, new and improved breeds, rural electricity, and the application of soil and water conservation principles to range lands.

The Texan ranch of today is small by the old open range standards, although James C. Tanner, writing in the *Wall Street Journal,* recently stated that there are more than a hundred ranches of more than 100,000 acres in the state today. The modern Texan ranch is fenced and cross-fenced to permit rotation grazing. It has adequate water — at least, in non-drouth years — from living streams, stock ponds, and wells. There are electric lights in the ranch house and in the barns and electric pumps on some of the wells. The ranch is close by a paved road and a bus takes the ranch children to a modern school. There are some farming tools on hand and most of the supplemental feed needed to carry the cattle through the winter without loss of weight is produced on the ranch. The ranch family *eats its own beef,* carefully aged in its own deep freezer. The ranch owner is a cooperator with — and often a supervisor of — the locally organized and managed soil conservation district and is actively engaged in practicing soil and water conservation to assure the maximum production of a grass crop for harvest by his cattle.

"Are there cowboys on these modern Texan ranches?" you may well ask. Yes . . . some. But the cowboy is no longer the historic "Hired Man on Horseback," who was willing to do anything so long as it could be done from the topside of a horse. I learned this lesson the hard way forty years ago when I was a Kansas cowboy for a summer — I spent considerably more time on a Fordson tractor seat than I did in the saddle and about twenty times as many hours putting up hay as I did working cattle.

The cowboy of today is likely to be as expert in the handling of a Jeep as a horse. My good friend and fellow Texan in exile — in Maryland — Dr. Frank Goodwyn, in his book *Lone Star Land* (New York, 1955) shows a photo of a helicopter in use on a roundup on the Waggoner Ranch in Wilbarger County. I am not suggesting that a present-day cowboy must be a flyer, although a goodly number of Texas cowmen are members of the "Flying Ranchers" and pilot their own planes. Skill in operating and repairing machinery is as highly prized in present-day cowboys as skill in handling cattle.

Texas cattle, more than 8,000,000 in number, are still dominated by the Herefords. However, Texans are particularly proud of the Santa Gertrudis cattle, the only breed developed in America. They are a product of the great King Ranch. The use of Brahman bulls on grade cows has been a common practice in South Texas for many years and there are a good many ranches stocked with regis-

tered Brahmans — red or gray — to supply this bull demand. There are Angus and Shorthorn enthusiasts, but the white-face remains the favorite with the Texas cowman.

CONSERVATION RANCHERS

In describing the Texan ranch of today in general terms, I have pointed out the use of soil and water conservation practices on the range. The Texas ranchman of today is a "conservation rancher," a term applied to Charles Pettit, the owner of Flat Top Ranch at Walnut Springs, Texas, by the late Louis Bromfield, noted novelist and conservationist of Malabar Farm, Ohio. I will have much to say about Charlie Pettit and his ranch but for fear you will think he is unique, I want to mention several other outstanding Texas conservation ranchers.

Dolph Briscoe has root-plowed and re-seeded most of his Catarina Ranch in the Texas brush country. He systematically rests his pastures to maintain grass vigor and now has a Santa Gertrudis breeding herd. He has tripled his carrying capacity using the conservation system. There was a good story about Dolph and some of his neighbors in the January 3, 1959, issue of the *Saturday Evening Post*.

Horace K. Fawcett of Del Rio has been a staunch advocate of conservation since the beginning of the modern movement. He was a member of the first State Soil Conservation Board and has been following a conservation ranching system on his land for about twenty years. He says that despite seven years of drouth recently the grass is now better than it has been at any time since the ranch went under fence.

Clayton Puckett of Fort Stockton is a former soil conservation district supervisor and President of the Association of Texas Soil Conservation Districts. He also had his troubles with drouth during the early 1950s, but reduced stocking, resting pastures, pitting for moisture conservation, controlling mesquite and cedar, and reseeding have resulted in a materially improved ranch. He received some returns on his investment even during the worst of the drouth years.

Joe Boyd of San Angelo is a cooperator with the Upper Clear Fork Soil Conservation District. Water development, deferred grazing, and control of cedar plus some reseeding have paid off for Boyd. He is now extending the conservation program to other ranches that he owns.

W. B. Osborn of Rio Grande City started spraying mesquite in 1948 and has since reduced his stocking rate, chopped the smaller brush and done some reseeding. He produces 450-pound calves now and markets more beef from a smaller number of cows than he ran before starting his conservation program. He feels that the day of 350-pound calves on his ranch are gone forever — and for those interested, the deer are bigger and fatter now.

Joseph Vander Stucken of Sonora is a pioneer in the control of brush on his range. His system consists of chaining, then using goats to control the sprouts, followed by alternate grazing and resting. Livestock and deer come from neighboring ranges to this ranch because of the quality and quantity of the Vander Stucken grass.

The late Waters S. Davis of League City was a grandson of J. C. League, a sea captain, who like Captain King saw a future in Texas grass and cattle. Waters was a past president of the Texas Association and of the National Association of Soil Conservation Districts. In addition to improving the drainage and reseeding the home place at League City, he actively cooperated with the other districts in Texas and Louisiana wherever he owned farm and ranch lands.

And I mention with some pride that two of my very close friends and former associates in the Soil Conservation Service, Louis Merrill and W. H. (Bill) DuPuy are doing quite well, thank you, as conservation ranchers. Merrill's Running M brand, registered by his father in 1872 in Somervell County, is now used on the Ellis County ranch near Midlothian. DuPuy is taking advantage of the additional moisture, common to East Texas, to operate successfully in Anderson County.

No — Charlie Pettit is not the only conservation rancher in Texas — there are literally hundreds of them and the tribe increases daily as a result of the examples set by such pioneers in the movement as those I have mentioned. However, I want to use Flat Top as a specific example of what can be done to reclaim eroded, gullied and abused land with sound conservation practices and of how it can be made to pay with astute management. I offer no apologies for using Flat Top as my example — it happens to be the Texan ranch that I know the most about. There is also a certain amount of sentiment involved in my choice since my own father ran cows on a part of the present Flat Top range back in the eighties.

Pettit Buys a "Lemon"

Charlie Pettit grew up on a ranch in Archer County, and he never got over it. He taught school — one of his pupils was Dr. Walter Prescott Webb, one of the best-loved historians of this century — ran a country store, and finally made a considerable amount of money in the oil business. But the desire to own a ranch was ever with him and in 1936 he felt that he could spare some time for ranching and started looking for a suitable piece of land to buy. In 1938 he bought the 7,000 acres of brush-infested and overgrazed, nearly worn-out range known as Flat Top Ranch. Roy Bedichek, Texas naturalist and educator, who headed the Texas Interscholastic League when I was a young high school teacher and coach many years ago, called this piece of range "heartbreak land."

Frank Reeves, longtime ranch editor of the Fort Worth *Star Telegram,* saw the ranch shortly after Pettit bought it. His interest in the place had been whetted by a remark made by Bob Coody, an experienced West Texas rancher who had leased the place. Coody had asked Frank if he knew the man who had purchased Flat Top Ranch, and on being told that Frank did not, said, "I am sorry for that man Pettit. He certainly bought a lemon, and it will not take him long to find it out. I moved most of my cattle off before my lease was out to keep them from starving. Even if you had the feed, it would not be a good place to keep them."

Frank reported that the land looked "shabby, worn and depressing — the open parts were bare of grass and the ugly signs of erosion caught and held the eye — brush was so thick in many places there was very little room for grass to grow." It is most fortunate for all of us that Frank Reeves saw the ranch before the conservation practices were installed. He is one of the keenest observers of range and livestock operations in the Southwest.

Far from discouraged with his purchase, Charlie Pettit decided to buy more land to add to his original 7,000 acres. Over the years, he has bought many of the eroded, cropped-out farms adjoining the ranch, and Flat Top now consists of 17,000 acres. He was aware that this new land of his was in the native bluestem belt. The bluestem belt, the most productive native grassland of the primeval American continent, according to my associate B. W. (Bill) Allred, lay in the area extending from Lake Winnipeg, Canada, to the Gulf of Mexico. It was bounded on the east by the hardwood forest and on the west by the Great Plains — short grass country.

The important native grasses in this huge belt are big bluestem, little bluestem, Indian grass, switchgrass, sideoats grama, and the wild ryes. I am sure from many talks with him that Charlie Pettit could see, even in 1938, with his mind's eye, the bluestem belt restored in all its glory on his range. Why not? This was its own, its native land. Charlie Pettit recognized another asset that Bob Coody had failed to see — the East Bosque and its tributaries, Rough Creek and Flag Branch, and a tributary of the main Bosque, Tough Creek, and he was already seeing the acres of water that he would one day impound.

Charles Pettit's Flat Top Ranch at Walnut Springs, Texas. Credit: Charles J. Belden

The cowman's trinity — good grass, an abundance of clean water and well-bred cattle — were well known to the Flat Top owner. But he knew that he had to have the grass and water before he got the cattle and that grass was highly important in controlling run-off and in capturing and storing the water. While some water conservation measures were started almost immediately, the first real project on the new ranch was the improvement of the grass.

Grass

About a fourth of Pettit's land was covered with suffocating stands of trees and shrubs, and he immediately tackled the job of reducing this cover to give the grasses a chance. A good many different ways of ridding the ranch of the unwanted woody vegetation were tried over the years but the cheapest and most effective proved to be hand-cutting followed by spraying with 2,4,5-T. All brush under four inches in diameter was cut off and the stumps sprayed. Tree trunks were girdled and the cut space sprayed. Only about ten percent resprouted and required a second spraying.

There was a considerable acreage infested with cactus when the new owner took over. Hand grubbing, due care being taken to remove the "potato" — a tuber at the base of the plant usually several inches underground — was found to be the most satisfactory way of eradicating cactus at Flat Top. The grubbers assisted in reestablishing the grass by dropping and stepping on a few grass seed into the soil disturbed by the removal of each cactus plant. The native

grasses, given a chance by the elimination of competition, began to increase almost immediately.

There was another grave problem to be solved in restoring the bluestems — 3,400 acres had been cultivated by the various previous owners. About 2,400 of these acres should never have been plowed and had to be reseeded. This land was badly eroded, infertile and often caked as hard as flint. Native grass seed supplies were inadequate. Water conservation and control measures plus the use of heavy crust-breaking tools and nurse crops of small grain got the grass started, and a deferred grazing program of one to three years resulted in the restoration of the bluestem range.

On much of the rest of the ranch the bluestems needed only a chance to grow, and a program of deferred grazing gave them that chance.

The management of the restored range is a fetish at Flat Top — the policy is to leave almost half of the annual grass production on the ground for conservation and improvement. You may wonder how a cow can tell when she has eaten her fifty or sixty percent. She can't, of course, but managers can and there is where the real gift of management counts. This policy has paid off handsomely for Charlie Pettit. His "heartbreak land" was carrying 2,500 purebred Herefords before the drouth started in December, 1950. This was a cow to each seven acres — need I say more?

This management principle resulted in the progressive reduction of livestock numbers through the drought years of 1951–1956. In July 1956 the herd numbered only a thousand head. Charlie Pettit had practiced what he had preached — often a difficult thing to do — and disposed of fifteen hundred registered Herefords, but he had not overgrazed or destroyed his grass cover.

WATER

Along with the grass improvement program the water system was gradually developed. At the present time there are twenty-four wells and over sixty impounding dams of all sizes on the ranch. The ranch is divided into about one hundred enclosures, ranging from small traps to one pasture containing about one thousand acres. Nearly all the enclosures are grazed sometime during the year, and this means water must be available in each. For the most part the wells are located on high points on the ranch and water flows by gravity from substantial rock and cement or concrete storage tanks, located at each well, through pipes to concrete water troughs in the various pastures served by the particular well. There are windmills over eighteen of the wells and electric pumps on the other six.

While all the sixty dams that impound water are an important part of the ranch improvement program, those constructed on the East Bosque (five) and on its tributaries, Rough Creek (six) and Flag Branch (six), are making the greatest contributions. Water backs up in the stream channels along the gentle valleys from one dam to the downstream toe of the dam above it in the series. This has restored the water table in the valleys where formerly flash run-off from the denuded uplands had cut deep trenches in which the streams flowed. After the

flood run-off passed, the deeply entrenched channels had served as drains which lowered the water table. Approximately two hundred acres of land are now subirrigated by the restored water table in these valleys. As these fertile valleys have been cleared of scrub trees and brush, the tall native grasses have taken over. Now these valley meadows, if not cut, could hide a cow herd in summer.

Charlie Pettit has a real affection for his impounded water. He puts it this way, "An acre of water is worth much more to me than an acre of land." This is his way of saying than an acre of land will produce only its quota of grass, hay, or feed, while a surface acre of water — usually several acre-feet — can be used to irrigate or subirrigate several acres, with much greater production the result.

The reservoirs back of the dams will impound well over three thousand acre-feet of water in normal years. This will permit the irrigation of about eight hundred acres of bottom and benchland along the streams in addition to the two hundred acres which are subirrigated. The feed, hay, and grazing produced by this thousand acres, with the help of added water as needed, may approach the total of the forage produced on the rest of the ranch. The owner states, "I consider the thousand acres of irrigated and subirrigated land to be equal in value to the sixteen thousand acres of grazing land on the ranch."

Grass is the basic feed on the ranch the year round, but there are periods in Bosque County when most of the grasses are dry and low in feeding value. Supplemental feeds are used when the native grasses are dormant and the croplands are grazed for short periods during the growing season to rest the range. Sudan, alfalfa, oats, Madrid sweet clover, and button clover are the only cultivated crops raised on the ranch. While there is still some land dry-farmed, the supplemental feed program is tied closely to the one thousand acres that can be irrigated or subirrigated.

There are five stream miles of the East Bosque on the ranch and in July 1956, after five and one-half years of short rainfall, there was no water coming onto the ranch in its channel as it entered from the north. However, it became a living stream not long after crossing the boundary.

In July, 1956, one of Mr. Pettit's neighbors, living below Flat Top on the East Bosque, came to him to say, "I was pretty sore when you started building dams on the East Bosque, but, by God, you've made it into a flowing stream the year round. It always went dry during the summer when we had drouths before."

While there was no reason to doubt this good neighbor, this was something that had to be seen. On July 14, 1956, Mr. Pettit and this writer drove to the lower of the five dams on the East Bosque. We left the car, left the ranch by climbing through the fence, and some hundred yards or so below the dam, found a place where we could descend the rather steep bank to the bed of the stream. There was flowing water where we reached the stream bed, and as we followed it downstream the flow seemed to increase. Finally, it was too wet for us to walk and we turned back.

The changing of the East Bosque from a dry to a flowing stream as it crosses the ranch from the northwest to the southeast is not a miracle or even a mystery. Flat Top grass and Flat Top dams are responsible. They are also responsible for making Rough Creek and Flag Branch year-long flowing streams.

Flat Top grass is the most important factor in the changed water situation. Charles Pettit says, "Water is the thing that the ranching country runs short of too often. But there is one sure way to make the best use of the rain we get and that is get the ground coated with a heavy grass sod so that the water can quickly soak into the soil."

Together, run-off and evaporation used to get most of the water that fell on the ranch, but now rains soak into the ground to grow grass, and a considerable amount seeps slowly into underground channels, and part of it eventually reaches the natural drains — the stream beds — or breaks out as springs. Protective plant cover reduces evaporation losses to a minimum; growing vegetation gets the use of a large part of the total rain because it soaks deeply into the soil reservoir where it is recovered by plants as needed.

Flat Top grass and dams were ready when the excessive rains fell in the spring of 1957 and again in 1958. The forty-three ponds and lakes, created by the dams, were at low water level when the heavier rains started. Big Lake, a part of the East Bosque system, with a drainage area of nearly thirteen thousand acres and a hundred acres of water surface, filled slowly and it was not until April 29, 1957, after twenty and seven-tenths inches of rain in the year, that the water reached spillway height. It flowed over the spillway into the channel below for weeks as the springs and seeps continued to pour clear water into the lake. During the wet spring of 1957, and again in 1958, the East Bosque was never over about half bank full while neighboring streams flooded the bottoms, not once but several times.

Permit me to quote directly from *Flat Top Ranch* (Norman, Oklahoma, 1957) and the chapter I wrote on "Flat Top Water at Work" in the summer of 1956 after five and one-half years of drouth: "Perhaps the greatest unearned increment will accrue to those farmers and ranchers who live downstream on the East Bosque. For some distance they are going to have almost complete protection from floodwater damage to their bottomland fields and improvements. Until tributaries of sufficient size and number to put water over the banks enter the creek below the Flat Top boundary, there will be no floods." The statement I made with such finality in the dry year 1956 has been confirmed in the very wet years of 1957 and 1958 by the performance of Flat Top grass and dams.

CATTLE

Mr. Pettit is a Hereford enthusiast, not because the cherry red cattle with the white faces look good on his green grass — and that, they do — but because the sincerely believes in the superior beef-making qualities of the breed. This opinion is widely supported by his fellow cowmen — about eighty percent of the beef cattle today are Herefords.

Mr. Pettit started with polled Herefords but soon added some horned Herefords. He spent a lot of time in the pastures with his cattle and as soon as he had determined to his own satisfaction that the horned cattle outweighed and outgained the polled, he sold the muleys. He has been in the forefront in the American Hereford Association in fighting the trend to the smaller compact type which was in demand to compete with other breeds for honors at livestock shows. His early experiences with his father on the home ranch in Archer County convinced him that the roomier cows and bulls were the ones that paid the bills. So the big ones stayed to the delight of the ranch's commercial bull customers who stayed "old fashioned" almost to the man.

W. B. (Bill) Roberts, an excellent Hereford judge and cattle breeding expert, has been the resident manager of the ranch since 1941. Mr. Pettit and Bill Roberts are a real team — they agreed shortly after Bill came on the job that they were in the registered Hereford business to provide bulls which would improve the commercial herds of beef cattle of their customers. Bill puts it this way: "The goal is to produce a calf that will look good and weigh heavy at weaning time — the same calf to develop and look good and still weigh heavy at approximately eighteen months to two years."

The term "a Flat Top Bull" has come to have a special meaning in Hereford circles — big, ample bone, strong hindquarters, masculine head, and the inherent quality to do well on the range. This is because the motto of the ranch — "Dedicated to the Improvement of Herefords" — applies to the herd as a whole and not to just a few show cattle.

Some of the best Herefords in America are to be found at Flat Top and, despite the predominant attention to the business of providing bulls for commercial herds, it has had its share of show ring winners.

During the short time that the ranch had some commercial (grade) Herefords, two carloads of steers were fitted and shown at the Houston Fat Stock Show. Both won grand championships. Flat Top won the grand champion carload of bulls at the 1942 Fort Worth Fat Stock Show. *CP Tone,* the first great herd sire at Flat Top, was the grand champion at Fort Worth in 1942.

There have been other winners at the country's top shows but I believe that both Charlie Pettit and Bill Roberts get a bigger kick out of a telephone call from a Texas cowman ordering a half-dozen bulls — to be picked by Bill — than they do from winning a blue, or even a purple, at a show. Bill regards showing cattle as a necessary evil because it is one of the best forms of advertising. He likes better the repeat orders that follow his choice of bulls shipped to a customer unseen. This is the real pay-off — it shows the esteem in which Bill and his employer, Charlie Pettit, are held in Hereford circles.

RANCH IMPROVEMENTS

The first thing that Charlie Pettit did when he bought the ranch was to sell all the houses, barns, fences and other improvements to one of his neighbors for $500 with the proviso that they be removed in six weeks. The old shabby improvements were replaced by substantial, but by no means fancy, ones. Rock, plentiful on the ranch, was the main structural material used in the new improvements. Concrete, corrugated iron and iron pipe have been combined with the native stone to construct feed barns, hay barns, loading ramps, shelters and corrals that are, for all practical purposes, permanent and that blend into the landscape. These improvements were planned for efficient constant use, labor-saving the watchword.

The fences and cattle guards match the other improvements. After a considerable period in which various types of fences were tried, a staggered seven-wire fence, with four strands on one side of the post and three on the other, became the standard. This type of fence keeps the animals where they are supposed to stay and at the same time discourages young bulls from fighting through the fence. There are forty-five cattle guards on the fences dividing the various traps and pastures. The cattle guards, like all other improvements, are built to stay, using concrete, steel I-beams, and two-inch pipes on six-inch centers.

The one hundred different enclosures on the ranch are connected by about one hundred and fifty miles of graded, ditched, graveled and carefully maintained roads. Permanent bridges or concrete crossings are used over all streams of any appreciable size. Two cowboys using a two-horse trailer pulled by a car or pickup look after Flat Top cattle. The good roads and the cattle guards — they don't have to stop to open gates — make it possible for them to do the work that would ordinarily require ten or more cowboys, stationed at various places on the ranch. The roads and cattle guards save time and labor in the winter when it is necessary to put out feed to livestock in the pastures. The feed troughs are of concrete with heavy pipe dividers and are practically indestructible. Their weight minimizes the chances of their being tipped over and they are set on sloping ground — on south slopes or other protected spots — with a drain hole in the lower end for rain water to get out. I have already mentioned the water system which was planned and established with the same objectives in mind — permanence, minimum expenditure of time and material for maintenance, and the greatest efficiency of operations.

WILDLIFE

Soil and water conservation measures applied on farm and range lands are often of great incidental value to wildlife. Food, cover, and clean water are the fundamentals of a satisfactory wildlife habitat. The conservation treatment of the range has provided these essentials to an increasing wildlife population at Flat Top but there is nothing incidental about the wildlife program on the ranch. The original conservation plan developed for the ranch by Mr. Pettit, in cooperation with the Bosque County Soil Conservation District, provided for the improvement of 2,300 acres for wildlife. As other land was added, additional wildlife habitat improvements were included in their conservation treatment.

My Uncle Jack Bradley, a Confederate veteran, who was my fishing companion when I was a boy, and my own father both lived within sight of Flat Top Mountain in the eighties. Their tales of the abundance of game in Bosque County were enough to send me on a number of hunting trips along the East Bosque when I lived in neighboring Erath County in 1921–26. I sighted Flat Top Mountain more than once but very few doves or quail. When Mr. Pettit bought the ranch he estimated that there were no more than six coveys of quail on the seven thousand acres and no large game although a few predators were still around.

Today the white-tailed deer herd is estimated at between five hundred and a thousand animals. This herd has resulted from forty-nine animals released on the ranch in 1946 by the Texas Game, Fish and Oyster Commission although there is some indication that deer released on neighboring ranches, at about the same time, found Flat Top grass and water more to their liking and moved in. One of the real thrills on a visit to the ranch is a drive along the ranch roads in the East Bosque bottom at dusk to see numerous deer grazing the alfalfa and irrigated grasses.

The Commission released ten antelope does and six bucks on the ranch in 1941 and by 1945 there was a herd of eighty. But by 1953 there were only three does left — twenty-five does escaped through a water gap; the bucks fought among themselves, with many dying from infections of their wounds; and the herd refused feed offered to them. Two bucks were added in 1953 and by 1956 the herd had grown to fifteen animals. Antelope cannot jump the Flat Top fences — although deer can — and with their known migratory habits even the largest pasture — about a thousand acres — may not be a suitable habitat for them. Small antelope gaps are planned in some division fences and in the boundary fence between Flat Top and Rough Creek Ranch, which is owned by Mr. Pettit's daughter and son-in-law, to improve the antelope habitat.

It is estimated that the ranch population of wild turkeys has reached the one thousand mark. No turkeys may be shot on the ranch but Mr. Pettit feels that they earn their keep by eating huge quantities of grasshoppers.

Bobwhite quail are now found in abundance on the ranch and hunting is available for a fee, with a guaranteed limit of birds. This is made possible by the quail enterprise on the ranch — like all others, a paying proposition. About ten thousand quail are raised a year and the ranch sells fertile eggs, dressed birds, or live birds for release. The hunter who fails to reach the bag limit has the difference made up to him in dressed birds. One of the real disappointments to date has been the failure of the famed Texas prairie chicken to reestablish itself on the ranch. Two trials, 1951 and 1953, were made with the help of the Commission but both failed, for no known reason. They were there once in great numbers and with the almost complete recovery of the grassland there seems to be every reason to believe that they can and will find Flat Top a suitable habitat in the not too distant future. They belong there.

Mourning doves, although migratory, are at Flat Top the year round in great numbers. The "summer" doves fly south in the fall and are replaced by birds from the north and this process is reversed in the spring — the doves that wintered to the southward come home to the ranch to nest.

Prior to the construction of the Flat Top dams, migratory waterfowl passed the ranch up. Now three to five thousand ducks winter on the ranch each year. Duck hunting is permitted on part of the ranch but usually not over a hundred birds are killed a year. When the first ducks arrive in September, feed is put out on the shore of House Lake — the one close to the ranch house where no hunting is ever permitted. There is a great flight in to the lake each evening when the feed is scattered. The annual cost is about $500 for corn but Mr. Pettit says it is worth it to watch the evening flights.

Flat Top water, in addition to attracting migratory waterfowl, is stocked with fish — bluegills, redears, crappies, channel cats, and bass. The ranch staff and their families plus a few friends do most of the fishing at Flat Top although an area of about one thousand acres, with some fishing water, is leased for $2,500 a year to a group of businessmen who have formed a hunting club. The total cash take from hunting and fishing on the ranch probably averages $10,000 a year. And the value of game and fish used by ranch families is certainly considerable. However, the impact on the game population is negligible—one hundred ducks out of three to five thousand; seventy-five deer out of possibly a thousand; only half as many quail as are released annually from the breeding pens; and the doves are there in such abundance that those killed aren't missed. No antelope or turkey may be killed and the lakes and streams are really overstocked and need to be fished more than they are.

The story of Flat Top wildlife does not end with game — every kind of native or migratory bird or small animal common to Central Texas has found its way to the ranch. The scissor-tailed flycatchers and the roadrunners are among Mr. Pettit's favorites of the non-game birds. No attempt has been made to restore the so-called "balance of nature" on the ranch — some of the former wild creatures that were natives are frankly unwanted on a range now used primarily for the production of high value Herefords. In this unwanted group are bear, buffalo, panther, wolves, coyotes and bobcats. Their presence would simply not be in harmony with the grazing of fine Hereford cattle. The wildlife that is compatible with the main business of the ranch is wanted and provided for — food, cover, and clean water are there in abundance. Charlie Pettit says, "Whatever I do on the ranch, I would like for there to be a little profit in it." Flat Top wildlife pays in cash, in insects and rodents destroyed, and in the pure pleasure of the ranch owner, his friends and the Flat Top families.

RANCH ROMANCE

If I have given you the impression that the Texan ranch of today is just another place to make a living, it was unintentional. It is true that many of the ways of ranch life of yesteryear, considered to be of great romantic interest by the western fiction writers, are gone. The range war, the bucking horse, the brushpopper, the horse-breaker, the line rider, and the roundup rep are no more on most modern Texan ranches. The chuck wagon, if there is one at all, is used only when there are important visitors. Herd bulls no longer walk a thousand miles to their new home in Wyoming — they go by air, or if the distance is short, by truck. Few Texas cattle are herded today and most of the fence riding is done in a jeep. The line camps for the fence riders and the lone cowboys who guarded the outposts of the range are gone, too. The cowboys no longer ride to town in groups on Saturday for a night of wine, women and song. The fast gunman is for the movies and the shoot-outs are few and far between in these days.

Yes, it is another day in another age and these modern Texas conservation ranchers get their "kicks" in other ways — by changing spring floodways and summer dry streams into year-round living water; by restoring the native range to its former composition and vigor; by introducing new grasses and legumes; by turning back the invading cedar, mesquite and cactus; by producing more beef from fewer cows; and by community action through their soil conservation districts in preventing floods.

These modern conservation ranchers regard wildlife as an economic asset. They have time to hunt and fish — and do. They go on ranch tours and listen to a little bragging about a bull, a cow, the grass or all three and learn something they can take home and use on the home ranch. There are ranch libraries; radio is almost universal and TV is becoming common. Paved roads and automobiles put the pleasures of their city cousins only minutes away in most cases. The "kicks" are different but they are there, and who is to say, for sure, which ranch era offered the most?

As a professional conservationist, I am in a position to appraise the impact of this new breed of rancher on Texas land. They are good for it and are helping to preserve the bragging rights of future generations. The Charlie Pettits, the Dolph Briscoes and the hundreds of other modern conservation ranchers are showing the way by restoring the productive capacity of some of the best native grassland known to man which was overgrazed by another generation. With the grass competition removed, the mesquite, cedar and cactus moved in, gullies formed and the streams dried up in the summer when the need for water was the greatest. The damage that older generations permitted has made the job of the modern rancher a lot tougher, but he is meeting the challenge.

Frank Reeves in writing of Flat Top puts it this way, "I probably have seen as many ranches and as many beef animals in the past quarter century as any man in America. My job has made this not only possible, but necessary. One of the great rewards of my job as a range reporter and livestock editor is the regular opportunity to observe the continuing improvement of certain ranches. In no case that I can recall has the improvement of the range, the hay meadows, the water system, the houses, barns, fences, and the cattle been so constant as at Flat Top."

I am in agreement with Frank's statement but I know that there are others who are close on Charlie Pettit's heels. The closer they get, the better I like it, for then I know we have the leadership so essential to matching the safe and sound production of red meat to our ever-increasing population.

READING LIST
Texan Ranches

CALLAGHAN
Wellman, Paul. *The Callaghan.* Encinal, Texas, 1945.

FLAT TOP
Allred, B. W. and Dykes, J. C., eds. *Flat Top Ranch.* Norman, Oklahoma, 1957.

JA
Burton, Harley True. *A History of the JA Ranch.* Austin, 1928.

KING
Goodwyn, Frank. *Life on the King Ranch.* New York, 1951.

Lea, Tom. *The King Ranch* (2 volumes). Boston, 1957.

Rowe, James *et al. King Ranch, 100 Years of Ranching.* Corpus Christi, 1953.

MATADOR
Campbell, Harry H. *The Early History of Motley County.* San Antonio, 1958.

Pearce, William M. *The Establishment and Early Development of the Ranch, 1882–1890.* Abilene, Texas, 1951.

Warren, John and Colquet. *The Matadors.* Dickens, Texas, 1952.

SMS
Hastings, Frank S. *A Ranchman's Recollections.* Chicago, 1921.

Swenson, W. G. *SMS Ranches.* Stamford, Texas, 1956.

SPUR
Elliot, W. J. *The Spurs.* Spur, Texas, 1939.

Holden, William Curry. *The Spur Ranch.* Boston, 1934.

TAFT

Watson, May M. Green and Lillico, Alex. *Taft Ranch*. N.p., n.d.

North, Gene. *The Tafts Went to Texas*. Cincinnati, 1957.

XIT

Haley, J. Evetts. *The XIT Ranch of Texas*. Chicago, 1929.

Nordyke, Lewis. *Cattle Empire*. New York, 1949.

GENERAL

Evans, Will F. *Border Skylines*. Dallas, 1940.

Hamner, Laura V. *Short Grass and Longhorns*. Norman, Oklahoma, 1942.

Harper, Minnie Timms and George Dewey. *Old Ranches*. Dallas, 1936.

Williams, J. W. *The Big Ranch Country*. Wichita Falls, Texas, 1954.

Willis, W. S. *A Story of the Big Western Ranches*. Comanche, Texas, 1955.

Texas Ranchmen

Anderson, August. *Hyphenated*. N.p., 1916. (Swenson)

Dobie, J. Frank. *A Vaquero of the Brush Country*. Dallas, 1929. (John Young)

Douglass, C. L. *Cattle Kings of Texas*. Dallas, 1939. (King, Kenedy, Chisum, Slaughter, Loving, etc.)

Emmett, Chris. *Shanghai Pierce*. Norman, Oklahoma, 1953.

Haley, J. Evetts. *Charles Goodnight, Cowman and Plainsman*. Boston, New York, 1936.

———. *George W. Littlefield, Texan*. Norman, Oklahoma, 1943.

Hamner, Laura V. *The No Gun Man of Texas*. Amarillo, 1935. (Goodnight)

Holden, William Curry. *Rollie Burns*. Dallas, 1932.

Keith, Noel L. *The Brites of Capote*. Fort Worth, 1950.

Kupper, Winifred, ed. *The Golden Hoof*. New York, 1945.

———. *Texas Sheepman*. Austin, 1951.

Jones, J. O. *A Cowman's Memoirs*. Fort Worth, 1953.

Matthews, Sallie Reynolds. *Interwoven*. Houston, 1936 and El Paso, 1958. (Matthews, Reynolds)

Siringo, Charles A. *A Texas Cowboy*. Chicago, 1885 and New York, 1950.

Sonnichsen, C. L. *Cowboys and Cattle Kings*. Norman, Oklahoma, 1950. (Swensons, Evans, Kokernots, etc.)

Wallis, George A. *The Cattle Kings of the Staked Plains*. Dallas, 1957. (Slaughters, Chisum, Goodnight, Littlefield, etc.)

Texas Cattle and Range Life

Adams, Andy. *The Log of a Cowboy*. Boston, 1903.

Adams, Ramon F. *Cowboy Lingo*. Boston, 1936.

Cox, James. *The Cattle Industry of Texas and Adjacent Territory*. Saint Louis, 1895.

Dobie, J. Frank. *The Longhorns*. Boston, 1941.

———. *The Mustangs*. Boston, 1952.

———. *On the Open Range*. Dallas, 1931.

Haley, J. Evetts. *Life on the Texas Range*. Austin, 1952.

Kleberg, Robert J., Jr. *The Santa Gertrudis Breed of Beef Cattle*. Kingsville and El Paso, 1954.

Ridings, Sam P. *The Chisholm Trail*. Guthrie, Oklahoma, 1936.

Webb, Walter Prescott. *The Great Plains*. Boston, 1931.

CHAPTER VIII

Billy the Kid Was My Friend

IT SEEMS THAT MOST of the old-timers who told or wrote of their experiences in the Pecos Valley of New Mexico, or the Texas Panhandle, in the late 1870s knew William H. Bonney, better known as Billy the Kid. Of well over sixty personal narratives of these old-timers included in my Kid bibliographical check list, only three come to mind that do not include a claim that the narrator was personally acquainted with the little outlaw. Teddy Blue, Ike Fridge and J. L. Hill told of the Kid but admitted their tales were hearsay only. Of course, not all the narrators introduced the subject of the boy desperado with the statement, "Billy the Kid was my friend." There were variations — "The Kid was my buddy"; "The Kid was drinking at the bar when I rode up"; "Billy was a Chisum hand when I went to work for Uncle John"; and many others including, "I saved Billy the Kid's life."

Most personal narratives defy classification — that is, particularly when told or set down half a century after the events described, it is difficult to say they are either fact or fiction. More often they are a combination of both — fact limited by time-dimmed memory, and tempered with camp-fire and barroom tales, folk legends and hearsay. A clear majority, I believe, can be described as "tall tales"

and as such, belong to the field of folklore rather than history.

Perhaps you have accepted the flat statement made by practically every historian that Billy was born in New York City (some say Brooklyn) in 1859. There is at least one dissenter — Deadwood Dick, in his book *The Life and Adventures of Nat Love,* claims that he met the Kid at Holbrook, Arizona, in the fall of 1880 and that they rode to Silver City together. Near Silver City the Kid pointed out the log cabin where he was born. Dick also states that he arrived at Fort Sumner the very night that the Kid was killed — Billy "was laying dead at Pete Maxwell's ranch." Nice timing!

The Kid's First Victim

Or perhaps you have long accepted Pat Garrett's version of the killing of the burly ruffian who had insulted Billy's mother as his first act of violence. Perhaps it would be more accurate to call it Ash Upson's version, since William A. Keleher offers strong evidence in his excellent book, *The Fabulous Frontier,* that the entire volume was written by the pioneer newspaper man. You remember the story — the insult, the saving of the boy from a bad beating at the hands of the ruffian by Ed Moulton, and the knifing of the ruffian as he was about to strike Moulton with a heavy chair during a barroom fight. "Once, twice, thrice his arm rose and fell. Then rushing through the crowd, his right hand above his head grasping a pocketknife, blade dripping with blood, he went out into the night, an outcast and a wanderer, a murderer self-baptized in blood." Billy was "about twelve" at the time.

Pat's, or Ash's, version has been widely accepted and much copied. Certainly, it is a romantic enough beginning of a killer's career but a good many of the old-timers tell it differently.

For example, Mrs. Edith M. Bowyer in *Observations of a Ranchwoman in New Mexico* (London, 1898), repeats the story as she heard it in the Mesilla Valley in the early 1890s. A young dishwasher is ill-used by a big burly man cook in one of the towns of the territory. The dishwasher wounds the bully with a pistol shot and flees the town. He turns up some days later, half-starved, at Morton's (Tunstall's) ranch. The dishwasher is the Kid and he repays the kind Englishman for his care and protection with a passionate devotion.

John Lord has a different version of a cook being the Kid's first victim. In *Frontier Dust* he states that the Kid was working for John Chisholm (Chisum) and got in an argument with the camp cook. The enraged cook threw some hot grease on Billy and, of course, Billy jerked out his gun and killed the cook. He rode away an outlaw.

As Ike Fridge told the story to Jodie D. Smith (*History of the Chisum War, or, Life of Ike Fridge*), Billy visited a Mexican sheep herder's camp. He prepared a meal, and when the Mexican returned and objected, the Kid killed him. Reason? "Self-defense" — the Mexican ran at him with a knife.

Fred E. Sutton in his reminiscences in *The Trail Drivers of Texas* uses the old dime novel story of the Kid knifing a boy companion to death in New York City. This version of the beginning of the Kid's career also appeared (perhaps first appeared), in a brief article in *The National Police Gazette,* August 13, 1881.

As John Young told the story to J. Frank Dobie (*A Vaquero of the Brush Country*), the Antrims (Billy's mother and step-father) had a restaurant at Fort Union, and Billy helped as a waiter. The cowboys nicknamed the boy "Billy the Kid." He liked the name but not the corruptions of it such as "Billy the Goat," used by the negro soldiers stationed at Fort Union. They also "bleated" at him as he passed, and on one occasion the proud boy threw a rock at one of his tormentors. The soldier went for a gun and so did Billy — result? One less soldier for the government to support.

In George Griggs's *History of Mesilla Valley,* the Kid is credited with killing twenty-seven men — his first was a miner who ran off with the Kid's fifteen-year-old sister. The Kid follows the couple, and he tells the miner to marry the girl, but the miner couldn't do it as he was already married. Billy buys a six-shooter and kills the miner.

Colonel Maurice G. Fulton discovered four chapters of a personal narrative in the incomplete files of the Las Vegas *Optic* for 1882. On a visit to Billy's camp the narrator learned from the outlaw that his first victim was a Chinaman whose throat he cut from "ear to ear" for revealing that he had bought a keg of butter from him. Billy had sold his employer's butter and pocketed the money. The four stray chapters are available in *Folk-Say: A Regional Miscellany,* edited by B. A. Botkin, and issued by the University of New Mexico Press in 1930. This account gives Billy's birthplace as the county Limerick, Ireland.

Fighting and Fun

With the Kid's career safely launched with whichever version you prefer, we turn to some of his early experiences. J. E. Sligh, a partner of Judge Ira A. Leonard in an assay office in White Oaks in 1880, in an article in the *Overland Monthly,* July, 1908, tells a very thrilling story of one of the Kid's encounters with the Apaches. A rancher named Irvington leaves his wife and four children at home (near Fort Bayard) to go to the mountains, some five miles away, for a load of timber. Four renegade Apaches watch his departure and then surprise Mrs. Irvington and the children. One Apache guards the door; one the window; one seizes Mrs. Irvington; and one the oldest child, a "well-grown" girl of ten. Mrs. Irvington puts up a valiant fight but is knocked senseless. The three younger children hide under the bed. Just as Mrs. Irvington's captor is about to place her on the bed, the Kid makes a dramatic appearance, kills three of the Apaches and drives the other off. The author states "probably no other man on earth would have acted just as he did and accomplished what he did."

Kyle Crichton reports, in *Law and Order, Ltd.,* a visit to Albuquerque made by Elfego Baca and the Kid. Elfego and Billy ride from Socorro to Isleta, stable their horses with the Indians at the pueblo, and walk the thirteen miles into Albuquerque. Horses are not safe in Albuquerque, and rather than take a chance with the thieves the boys (Billy, seventeen and Elfego, sixteen) make the long walk in their high-heeled cowboy boots. On arriving in the "metropolis" they rest near a telegraph pole on First Street and almost immediately learn about "justice."

A policeman and a friend are talking as a man approaches. The man gets about ten steps past the policeman when the policeman hails him. As the man turns, the policeman shoots him down as the policeman's friend fires in the air. The friend places his smoking gun in the dead man's hand and takes the dead man's gun and places it in his own holster. Of course, the policeman is in the clear — self defense, and as he modestly admits, "I got the draw on him."

Elfego and the Kid visit the Martinez Bar in Old Town. (The Kid could have endeared himself to all at that famous old bar by playing the piano — "it was marvelous playing that Billy the Kid did" — but he was not in the mood.) The Kid has a short stubby revolver, and to the consternation of the customers he suddenly fires three shots into the rafters. The tough bouncer decides the Kid fired the shots since he is the calmest person in the bar; he searches Billy, but does not find the gun. A little later the Kid repeats the three shots into the rafters; he is searched again, and again the bouncer fails to locate the gun. The bouncer de-

A shifty-eyed characterization of Billy the Kid done by H. O. Rawson in 1930

cides to throw the boys out, anyway, but the customers interfere. They finally leave and Billy reveals the location of the gun to Elfego — it is on top of his head adequately protected by his big "John B."

I want to point out that while the Kid was once seventeen and Elfego was once sixteen, it was not at the same time. According to author Crichton, Elfego was one year old in 1865, and that places the year of his birth as 1864. According to Garrett, the Kid was born in November, 1859, so Elfego was about five years younger than Billy.

"Billy the Kid's Lost Years" is the title of an article written for *The Texas Monthly,* September, 1929, by my friend Ramon Adams of Dallas. It is based on an interview with "Cyclone" Denton, old-time cowhand and frontiersman and later a two-gun man with Buffalo Bill's Wild West Show. "Cyclone" told Ramon that he worked with the Kid on the Gila Ranch in Arizona — the Kid was about sixteen at the time and Cyclone was nineteen. Cyclone said that the Kid was a good roper, a good rider, and a top hand. Billy was already a two-gun man, and he taught Cyclone how to use two guns — a skill that Cyclone utilized later in his act for Buffalo Bill's Show.

The Kid had an eye for a horse, and so did Cyclone, who owned a fine horse named Topsy. The Kid tried to trade Cyclone out of Topsy and, being unsuccessful, asked permission to ride him. Cyclone finally agreed, but on the condition that the Kid not use spurs, a quirt, or stiff bits. Topsy gave the Kid quite a ride — the Kid got a bloody nose, lost his hat, and finally pulled leather. Neither the Kid nor any other member of the crew ever asked to ride Topsy after that.

Cyclone remembered the Kid as smiling when he wasn't pleased and said that "a man who smiles that-a-way is dangerous." The Kid made a lot of friends on the Ranch, and Cyclone was his "buddy." Cyclone stated that even if the Kid did graze in the wrong pasture he liked him.

The Kid and Jesse James

Dr. Hoyt, the first practicing physician in the Texas Panhandle, in his fine book, *A Frontier Doctor,* tells about beating the Kid in a footrace at Tascosa. In the chapter "I Become a Bartender and Eat with Jesse James," he tells about the meeting between the Kid and James, who was traveling under his alias of "Mr. Howard." The two outlaws consider a merger, but Billy backs down. Homer Croy, in *Jesse James Was My Neighbor,* says it was the other way around — Jesse would have no part of the Kid.

John J. Collison in *Bill Jones of Paradise Valley,* Oklahoma, has a greatly different story to relate. Bill Jones goes to work for Dave Pool at his ranch in Colorado. Pool is a Missouri native and an old Quantrill raider. A rather good-looking young man, "more like a tenderfoot than a cowboy," rides up to the ranch looking for work. Though it is toward spring, Pool tells the young stranger that it is too early to put him to work but that there might be a job for him in two or three weeks. The young stranger sticks around taking many long rides to learn the range (or so he reports). One morning the stranger disappears and so does a considerable bunch of horses and some cattle. The same day, six well-armed riders arrive, and Jones learns that they are the real owners of the ranch. One of the men introduces the group to Jones — Frank James, Jesse James, Cole Younger, Bill Gregg, Ike and George Berry. Reinforced with some cowboys, the gang takes the trail of the young stranger (and the cattle and horses). They meet some cowboys and learn that the rustler is no other than Billy the Kid. Under the leadership of Frank James, they press the pursuit and finally catch up with the Kid and his gang of nine. They kill eight of the Kid's men — only the Kid and one other escape under cover of night. The Kid does not last long after this fight as he is shot down by Pat Garrett. The Kid is twenty-three at the time he is killed and has twenty-three killings to his credit.

Captain Tom and the Kid

The Young Pioneer — When Captain Tom Was a Boy quotes in full a letter from the Chief of Chaplains, War Department and includes a publisher's preface — both lending an air of authenticity that is undeserved. Captain Thomas Marion Hamilton's story about his life on the frontier is worthless as history but is a good example of the kind of "tall tale" spun for the grandchildren of a "participant." Almost half of the book is devoted to stories about Billy the Kid.

Captain Tom, at fourteen, is a cowboy on the McDermott ranch in New Mexico. The sheriff's posse traps the Kid in the Salinas cave. The Kid makes a deal with the deputy in charge of the posse when it comes under his guns in an open place near the mouth of the cave. The Kid orders Captain Tom to come to him, and he places his horse, Black Bess, in Captain Tom's charge since he has no horse feed in the cave. The posse begins the agreed withdrawal, but Sheriff Pat Garrett arrives and vetoes the arrangement. The posse settles down to starve the Kid out. A few days later Captain Tom wounds a mountain lion and trails it to another entrance to the cave. This entrance to the cave is unknown to the posse, and the Kid escapes through it just in the nick of time as the posse closes in on him. The grateful Billy presents his horse, Black Bess, to Captain Tom; the Kid's sweetheart, Maria Monette, is rescued from a gang of drunken Apaches by Captain Tom. She recognizes Black Bess and thereby Captain Tom. She is carrying the payroll from the bank in Santa Fe to the ranch when attacked by the Apaches.

The Kid is living in Arizona, under the name of Williams, and is going straight when he is arrested by mistake for killing a yearling that does not belong to him. It is a case of mistaken identity, but just as the Kid is cleared, Pat Garrett walks into the Tombstone courtroom. Pat sticks a gun into the Kid's back, but the Kid sidesteps and ducks and Pat's shot misses him. The Kid knocks Pat down with a blow to the jaw, but in the fight that follows the Kid is finally overpowered and captured. Maria Monette comes to Tombstone and helps the Kid escape to Mexico.

Later, the Kid warns Judge Fountain not to take his "last buckboard ride." The Judge ignores the warning, and both he and his young son are shot down by the Tate gang of cow thieves. Their bodies are buried in the White Sands. The foul deed is witnessed by the Kid and he becomes "The Mounted Ghost of Crawling White Sands" until the last member of the Tate gang is wiped out by his flaming guns. The Kid rides a white horse (with enormous rag boots tied to his feet), wears a white robe and lives at an Indian oasis in the White Sands until the last Tate is killed. (Note: Colonel Fountain and his son disappeared in 1896.)

Captain Tom becomes a mine owner in Mexico and the Kid visits him on several occasions when it gets too hot for him north of the border. During one of these visits the Kid helps Captain Tom clean up the Poe gang. This gang is trying to drive Captain Tom out of Mexico to gain possession of his mine.

Pat Garrett knows that the Kid visits Maria Monette occasionally. Pat goes to Maria and leads her to believe that if the Kid will surrender that he can persuade the judge and prosecuting attorney to let the Kid off with a light sentence of two or three years. Maria believes that Pat is sincere and arranges for the Kid to meet Pat at her ranch. The Kid arrives and is shot down by Pat who had concealed himself in Maria's garden. The furious girl tries to kill Pat but he disarms her. Captain Tom doesn't think much of Pat.

The Killing of Carlyle

Fred Sutton, peace officer as a young man, and Oklahoma oil man and banker in later years (and already mentioned), claims that Carlyle did not dive out of a window at the Greathouse ranch. Carlyle walked out the door, and Sutton knew, because he walked out with him. Sutton states that he accompanied Jimmy Carlyle on the fatal visit to the Greathouse ranch house and that the two of them were three-fourths the way back to the posse when the Kid's gang sent an avalanche of lead at them killing Carlyle, Sheriff William Bradley (Brady?) and George Hindman. Somehow, Sutton is not named as a posse member in any other account. In *The Trail Drivers of Texas*, Sutton offers no explanation for his own miraculous escape, but perhaps his story in the *Saturday Evening Post*, April, 10, 1926, provides a clue. In the *Post* article, Mr. Sutton tells how he saved Billy the Kid's life at a dance in Hays City. A greedy man is about to shoot the Kid in the back when Mr. Sutton knocks his gun up and shouts to warn the Kid. A few days later the Kid sends word that he will not forget that Sutton saved his life. In his book, *Hands Up!*, the dance and the saving of the Kid's life seem to have occurred at Tascosa. Take your choice.

The Journal of a Sister of Charity

The dates in the journal of a Sister of Charity, *At the End of the Santa Fe Trail* (Columbus, Ohio, 1932), must be considered to be editorial, since they do not check with established facts. According to the journal, Sister Blandina nurses a member of the Kid's gang and saves the lives of Trinidad's doctors by "getting the grateful Kid to grant her a favor." The favor is, of course, the sparing of the lives of the doctors. This incident occurs in September, 1876, and despite the care given the wounded bandit, he dies December 2, 1876.

Sister Blandina encounters the Kid again on June 9, 1878. She is en route by stage from Trinidad to Santa Fe when the Kid stops the stage, probably to rob it. He recognizes Sister Blandina and rides away.

In January, 1881, her journal entry states that the Kid is using his gun freely, and that Governor Wallace's interviews with him have had no effect.

The entry for July 23, 1881, reveals that the Kid is "playing high pranks" and that there are big rewards offered for his capture.

On May 16, 1882, Sister Blandina goes to see the Kid in jail — he is chained hand and foot. He asks nothing for himself but entreats the good Sister to do what she can for Kelly, a fellow prisoner and first offender.

The entry for September 8, 1882, records the killing of "poor, poor Billy the Kid" by Sheriff Pat Garrett.

Later Harry C. Gibbs wrote a one-act play, *Chico,* around the first Billy the Kid incident recorded in Sister Blandina's journal.

Mob Scene at Las Vegas

"I was there" seems to be a favorite term in many personal narratives, particularly as concerning major events. At least three "eye-witness" accounts of the mob scene at Las Vegas are available in addition to Pat Garrett's matter-of-fact statement in his *The Authentic Life of Billy the Kid*. In fact, the last part of Pat's book can easily be classed as a personal narrative as it is a rather matter-of-fact account of a manhunt and is set down in Pat's plain language. If Ash Upson "wrote" the entire book, it seems certain that the description of events, after Pat personally became a participant, is by Pat and that he allowed Ash few liberties in changing his words in the process of writing down the story as he related it.

Albert Hyde's account was printed in the *Century Magazine,* March, 1902. Hyde, a young Tennesseean, was in Las Vegas when Pat Garrett arrived there with his prisoners after the surrender at Stinking Springs. His article, though written sometime later, is an eyewitness account of Pat's coolness in the face of danger when the mob demanded his prisoners. The Mexican population at Las Vegas was bitter towards Dave Rudabaugh, who had killed the jailer there in making good his escape from the jail a few months before. The mob seemed much more intent on getting its hands on Rudabaugh than it was in taking the Kid. From a vantage point, on top a nearby box car, Hyde observes the action of the officers and the prisoners. He states that Rudabaugh smoked a cigar and seemed uninterested while the Kid became very excited and asked Pat to return his guns should the mob attack. Garrett gives a very different version of the reactions of the prisoners and states that he promised the prisoners he would arm them should there be a fight with the mob.

Hyde is high in his praise of Pat's conduct on this occasion.

Jim McIntire, in *Early Days in Texas: A Trip to Hell and Heaven* (Kansas City, 1902), states that he was City Marshal at Las Vegas when Sheriff Pat Garrett, Jim East, and two other deputies brought in the Kid, Dave Rudabaugh,

Tom Pickett, Bill Wilson and Tom Fowler. McIntire noted the gathering of the mob and fearing that it would try to take Rudabaugh by force, he went into town and gathered up a few guns with which to arm the prisoner in the case of violence. However, Sheriff Pat Garrett stood firm and as the train started with a jerk, the Kid opened a window and let out a war whoop which scattered the Mexicans in all directions. The Kid is called the "notorious Mexican outlaw" by McIntire.

Former Governor Miguel Antonio Otero in his first book, *My Life on the Frontier — 1864–1882,* tells the story of the mob's attempt to prevent Pat taking Rudabaugh on to Santa Fe. The Governor "quotes" Pat's speech to the mob, made from the car of the train that was to take the prisoners to Santa Fe. The Governor's father, one of the town's most substantial citizens, then climbs to the car platform and, after shaking hands with Pat, urges the mob to disband. He assures the people of Las Vegas that Pat is a man of his word and that the prisoners will be delivered to the proper authorities at Santa Fe. The mob disbands.

The Governor and his brother ride the train from Las Vegas to Santa Fe with Pat and his prisoners. They talk with the Kid and Rudabaugh, an old acquaintance. They visit the Kid many times at the jail at Santa Fe. The Governor likes the Kid and his appraisal of the Kid's character is supported by Mrs. Jaramillo (of Fort Sumner) and Don Martin Chaves. The Governor concludes that the Kid was "a man more sinned against than sinning."

1881 — The Final Scenes

Tex Moore "was there" when the Kid escaped at Lincoln. In his book, *The West,* this is the story: "Tex," his "pard" Steve, and Billy Kind are eating dinner at the Wortley Hotel in Lincoln, hear the shot that kills Bell, and see the Kid kill Bob Ollinger. The Kid waves goodbye and shouts, "So long boys," to them as he rides out of Lincoln.

Frederick William Grey wrote the story of his American experiences some years after returning to England. His book, *Seeking Fortune in America* (London, 1912), gives Kip McKinney's version of the killing of the Kid. Grey works with Kipp Kinney (Kip McKinney) on a mining venture in the Southwest, and from him hears the story of the killing of the Kid told in this book. Grey compares the Kid with Ben Thompson and gives Ben all the best of it. He states that the Kid never fought fair, being a half-breed Indian. As he recalls the story told him by Kipp, Pat Garrett learns that the Kid will visit his Mexican sweetheart. Pat and Kipp arrive at her home before the Kid, and they tie up and gag the girl. Pat hides behind a sofa while Kipp stands guard outside. As the Kid enters his girl's house he shows clearly in the open door for a moment, and Pat shoots him down. Grey comments, "This was not showing much sporting spirit."

John Lord, mentioned earlier, tells it this way: The Kid is in love with a Mexican girl, whose father works for Pete Maxwell at Fort Sumner. Maxwell's foreman, fine young Mexican, loves the same girl. The girl and her mother favor

Pat Garrett kills Billy the Kid. Illustration by R. Farrington Elwell.

the Kid but the girl's father prefers the ranch foreman. The father knows when the Kid is due to call because the women do an especially good job of cleaning the house. Through the foreman, the father gets word to the Sheriff.

Lord arrives at Maxwell's to buy some cattle and Maxwell assigns his own bedroom to Lord. Deputy Pat Garrett, having received word that the Kid is due, arrives disguised as a Mexican. Lord and Pat go to bed in Maxwell's bed — Pat is fully clad and occupies the back half of the bed which is quite aways from the wall. They hear the Kid coming and Pat slides off the bed and squats between the bed and the wall, with cocked gun in hand. Billy steps in the room and Pat raises up and shoots right over Lord. Billy falls dead with a bullet through his heart. Billy is twenty-four and had killed twenty-four men at the time of his death.

I want to recommend that you read Tom Blevins's tale in the late Lloyd Lewis's *It Takes All Kinds* (New York, 1947). This is probably the wildest of all the old-timer tales of the Kid.

I have purposely omitted the personal narratives of Charley Siringo (*A Texas Cowboy*), George Coe (*Frontier Fighter*), John W. Poe (*The True Story of the Death of Billy the Kid*) as being entirely too factual and too well known to fit into the theme of this presentation. I hope the material chosen was partially new, at least to most of you, and that you are tantalized enough by this sample to take the trail of the Kid in many other personal narratives. And perhaps you can then help me understand why good men and true vie for the honor of "having known" such killers as Billy the Kid.

CHAPTER IX

Ranger Reading

FORTY YEARS AGO last month, I read my first Texas Ranger book. My mother gave me *The Boy Captive of the Texas Mier Expedition* (San Antonio, 1909), by Fanny Chambers Gooch-Iglehart, on my twelfth birthday. It is still a treasured part of my collection although somewhat battered and worn from frequent readings. Big Foot Wallace was a fellow prisoner of the young hero and he spun many a tale of his frontier experiences to help the boy through the dreary days of captivity. Big Foot was one of the most famous of the early Texas Rangers and, so far as I can remember, I have turned down only one Wallace item offered to me in the last forty years — recently I successfully resisted the opportunity of buying a copy of the first edition of A. J. Sowell's *Life of Big Foot Wallace* (San Antonio, 1899) for $500. I didn't have the $500 and I did have a good reprint, issued at Bandera, Texas, by J. Marvin Hunter in 1927.

Of course, I am not claiming that I have been a Ranger collector for forty years. Actually, even after being introduced to the Texas Rangers by *The Boy Captive,* I accumulated the usual miscellaneous juveniles of the period, including many by Alger, Henty, Burt L. Standish (Gil Patten), etc. It was nearly a quarter of a century later — on April 21,

1937, to be exact — after many years of "accumulating" books, that I decided to seriously try to build a Texas Ranger collection. I know the exact date because beginning that day I kept a diary of my experiences with books, dealers and writers, for six years.

In my entry that day, the 101st anniversary of the battle of San Jacinto, I credited the stories told me by Captain Jim Gillett for the decision to collect Ranger books. Thinking back over what actually happened, I know now that my friend and collecting associate of many years, Louis P. Merrill of Fort Worth, Texas, was really responsible for my change from "accumulator" to "collector." Merrill had already begun the building of his now-famous collection on the range livestock industry and in addition to talking up the pleasures of collecting, he provided some literature on the subject. After reading Winterich's *A Primer of Book Collecting* and Herbert Faulkner West's *Modern Book Collecting for the Impecunious Amateur,* I decided to limit my collection to Texas Ranger items.

My purpose is to tell you about the Ranger books I have found the most entertaining to read. The books I will mention will not be the rarest items in this field, though some can be properly classed as rare; nor will they necessarily be the best books from a literary viewpoint, though some have achieved some reknown as American literature. I have restricted those to be named here to the most readable books in my own collection and this selection, while strictly one man's opinion, is guaranteed to provide entertaining reading as well as much information on the many Rangers in our history.

I have already mentioned the thrilling tales I've heard Captain Gillett tell — some to large audiences and some in his own book-lined den at his home in Marfa. Fortunately, he also wrote many of them down and they are available to you in *Six Years with the Texas Rangers* (Austin, Texas, 1921). This entertaining personal narrative, in case you are not the possessor of the scarce first edition, has been reprinted three times — by the Yale University Press in 1925; by the World Book Company in 1927 (with the title *The Texas Rangers*); and at Christmas, 1943, it became a Lakeside Press Classic.

Much has been written about Big Foot Wallace but to me John C. Duval's *The Adventures of Big-Foot Wallace* (Philadelphia, 1871) is by far the most entertaining. I know that many collectors (and quite a few dealers) are still hoping to secure a copy of the Macon (Georgia), 1870 edition but my own advice is to "quit struggling." There is an edition so dated but it is far from the "first." The mystery of the "Macon, 1870" edition was cleared up in J. Frank Dobie's fine tribute to *John C. Duval, First Texas Man of Letters* (Dallas, 1939). This is also a fine Ranger book as Duval served

with Wallace in Captain Jack Hays's company in 1845. "Texas John" or Jack Duval's book on Wallace is usually available in one of the numerous later issues but the "Philadelphia, 1871," or first edition, is definitely rare.

Numerous dime novels were written about Big Foot. I like best *Big Foot Wallace, the King of the Lariat; or Wild Wolf, the Waco* by Buckskin Sam (Samuel Stone Hall) issued as Beadle's New York Dime Library No. 204 on September 20, 1882. Hall served in the Texas Rangers prior to the War Between the States and his own "biography," with particular emphasis on his Ranger experiences, appeared as *Plaza and Plain; or, Wild Adventures of "Buckskin Sam," (Major Sam S. Hall), the Noted Texas Ranger, Scout, Guide, Ranchero, and Indian Fighter of the South-west Border* on April 4, 1882, as Beadle's Boy Library No. 17. It was written by Colonel Prentiss Ingraham. Hall appeared in many other dime novels written by Ingraham and Hall did almost as well in keeping Wallace's "adventures" before the boys of the 1880s in his fifty-odd novels published by Beadle.

Dime novels about the Texas Rangers had been appearing regularly for some years when the two mentioned above were issued. I believe the first of these by a highly respected teacher and newspaperman, C. Dunning Clark, who used the pen name "William J. Hamilton" for his subliterary fiction. It appeared as Beadle's Dime Novels 232 with the title, *The Prairie Queen; or, Tom Western, the Texas Ranger* (New York, 1871). This "thriller" about the troubles the Rangers had with horse thieves and marauding Comanches was "in print" for at least fifteen years in the various Beadle series, sometimes with a somewhat changed title.

So far as I know, the first book about the Texas Rangers was Samuel C. Reid's *The Scouting Expeditions of McCulloch's Texas Rangers* (Philadelphia, 1847). It was primarily concerned with the events of the Mexican War but it also contains short biographies of McCulloch, Hays, and Walker, three of the famous Rangers leaders of that period.

Many years ago, an entertaining biography of McCulloch appeared. It was written by another old Ranger, Victor M. Rose, with the title, *The Life and Services of General Ben McCulloch* (Philadelphia, 1888).

It is interesting to note that we have had to wait until this year for a full-length biography of Colonel Jack Hays, close associate and friend of McCulloch. It was written by the well-known Texas historian, James K. Greer, and is simply titled — *Colonel Jack Hays* (New York, 1952). After serving together in the Texas Rangers, Hays and McCulloch both went to California, and to me, it is quite interesting to note that at the same time that Hays served San Francisco as its first sheriff McCulloch served Sacramento in the same capacity.

Additional material on Samuel Walker was hard for me to find. I finally heard of a pamphlet issued by the Wyoming Historical Society about Walker. Suffice to say that after much correspondence with Cheyenne and Laramie, and with many dealers all over the country, I discovered that the correct "Wyoming" was the Wyoming Valley in Pennsyl-

vania. Publication No. 3, *Proceedings of the Wyoming Historical and Geological Society* (Wilkes Barre, 1883), contains Edmund L. Dana's *Incidents in the Life of Capt. Samuel H. Walker, Texas Ranger.* There is also much on Walker in the books about the Colt revolvers since he helped the inventor design the "Walker" (or "Texas") Colt for the hard usage it was to have on the frontier. Of these, I think you will enjoy the excellently printed *Sam Colt's Own Record* (Hartford, 1949), compiled by John E. Parsons and issued by The Connecticut Historical Society in an edition of 1,000 copies.

Another interesting little item that it took me months to secure was George E. Hyde's *Rangers and Regulars* (Denver, 1933). Our fellow *Westerner,* the late John Van Male, was the publisher and did all he could to help me find a copy. Finally he sent me a list of all the purchasers and I began the tedious task of contacting each of them. I received courteous replies from nearly all of them saying, "Sorry, I'm not interested in selling my copy." I did not receive a reply from one purchaser in Omaha, Nebraska, and I decided to follow up on that copy. My fellow collector, G. E. Connely of Omaha, finally found the owner of the missing copy in a hospital there. He was old and nearly blind and willing to part with his copy for a "consideration." Through Mr. Connely I bought the copy, and was mighty happy I did as John wrote me that the printer actually delivered only forty-three copies of the book to him. This little book was reprinted, with additions, by Long's College Book Store, Columbus, Ohio, 1952.

A goodly number of the old Rangers, in addition to Captain Gillett, wrote their own stories. The personal narratives that I found highly readable include N. A. Jennings's *A Texas Ranger* (New York, 1899), an issue with an introduction by J. Frank Dobie, (Dallas, 1930); Sergeant W. J. L. Sullivan's *Twelve Years in the Saddle* (Austin, 1909); J. B. (Red) Dunn's *Perilous Trails of Texas* (Dallas, 1932); Captain Dan W. Roberts's *Rangers and Sovereignty* (San Antonio, 1914); and Ira Aten's *Six and One-Half Years in the Ranger Service* (Bandera, Texas, 1945).

Worthwhile Texas Ranger biographies are quite numerous. J. Evetts Haley's *Charles Goodnight* (Boston, 1936) is the greatest biography of a cowman produced to date and it is properly classed as a Ranger item because Goodnight served as scout and guide for the Texas Rangers during the War Between the States. James K. Greer's *"Bucky Barry," Texas Ranger* (Dallas, 1932) is fine reading as is Haley's *Jeff Milton, a Good Man with a Gun* (Norman, 1948). Dora Neill Raymond's *Captain Lee Hall of Texas* (Norman, 1940) and Albert Bigelow Paine's *Captain Bill McDonald, Texas Ranger* (New York, 1909) rank high. Incidentally, Paine's book was sold by subscription in three bindings — plain blue cloth; red cloth with a photo of Captain Bill mounted on the front cover; and full leather. The text does not differ in the three issues and it is almost certain that each is the true first edition but differently bound to suit the pocketbooks of the various subscribers.

Many entertaining histories have been issued about Texas counties and many of them contain Ranger material not otherwise available. I have selected two examples of local history that I can recommend for their readability: Cliff D. Cates's *Pioneer History of Wise County* (Decatur, Texas, 1907) and O. Clark Fisher's *It Occurred in Kimble* (Houston, 1937).

There has been no single outstanding novel about the Texas Rangers. Two old-timers, Honorable Jeremiah Clemens's *Mustang Gray* (Philadelphia, 1858), and Charles W. Webber's *Old Hicks the Guide; or, Adventures in the Comanche Country in Search of a Gold Mine* (New York, 1848) are probably the best of the long list. A good many collectors have refused to class *Old Hicks* as fiction, and there seems to be little doubt that it describes some incidents in the adventurous career of the author, who served as a Texas Ranger on the frontier. But it is fiction and right entertaining. Clemens fought in the Mexican War and later served his state, Alabama, in the United States Congress. His hero "Mabry Gray" was probably Mabery B. Gray, a fellow soldier and noted frontiersman. Clemens collected the material for his novel during the Mexican War and he used some of the "Mustang" Gray's experiences in the book, but it is still fiction. Fellow Westerner, William MacLeod Raine, is the author of *A Texas Ranger* (New York, 1911), but nearly ten years ago he told me that he could not recommend it as it was just two short stories rather loosely tied together. Of course, my copy, which he so kindly inscribed for me, has an honored place in my collection, but for my money his *The Damyank* (Boston, 1942), in which Captain

Lee Hall is an important character, is a much better Texas Ranger novel.

The short stories about the Texas Rangers are legend and many are very good indeed. William S. Porter's (O. Henry) *Heart of the West* (New York, 1907) contains several "corkers." H. S. Canfield's *A Maid of the Frontier* (Chicago and New York, 1898) is well worth reading. There is a dandy Ranger yarn in William S. Hart's *The Law on Horseback* (Los Angeles, 1935) and Stewart Edward White, in *Arizona Nights* (New York, 1908), tells how a few old Texas Rangers founded the city of Yuma.

Some years ago I talked to a group in Philadelphia on the services of our numerous Ranger companies to our country. After I completed my remarks, a gentleman from New Hampshire approached me and said, "You left out the most important Ranger of all." After listening to my feeble excuses, he identified this important omission as The Lone Ranger and stated, "My brother-in-law writes him." In case you are a relative of his creator, of The Lone Ranger, or of Tonto, I'll mention the book that "reveals all." Fran Striker's *The Lone Ranger Rides* (New York, 1941) is a good western and from it we learn that The Lone Ranger is really a Texas Ranger — the last of a company wiped out by the Indians He was wounded nearly "unto death" but nursed back to health by Tonto. So far as I know, he never did report back to Ranger headquarters but carries on his good work to this day while AWOL.

So far as I know, we still lack a collection of verse about the Texas Rangers. However, many books of western ballads include one or more about them. Francis D. Allan's *Lone Star Ballads* (Galveston, 1874) includes several about the Ranger leaders and companies from Texas in the War Between the States. B. Metchim's *Wild West Poems* (London, 1871) also includes two or three in a somewhat more humorous vein. John Lomax has included several Ranger ballads in his various collections.

I am sure that many of you know that Pat Garrett, after killing Billy the Kid, was a Captain in the Texas Rangers. I hope you appreciate the restraint I have exercised in not including a number of Billy the Kid books in my recommendations. Actually, the Lincoln County War was one of the most violent of our numerous western range wars and some real good writers have had their say about it. The Fulton-Garrett version, *The Authentic Life of Billy the Kid* (New York, 1927), is the best single book about that war and the killing of the Kid. Colonel Maurice G. Fulton's serious research and historical footnotes added to Pat's (and Ash Upson's) original version makes this book the foundation on which to start your reading or collecting on this subject.

And, speaking of choosing a single book, if I had to limit my Texas Ranger reading to just one book, I'd take Dr. Walter Prescott Webb's *The Texas Rangers — A Century of Frontier Defense* (Boston and New York, 1935). Here is history, backed by intelligent research and by an understanding of the genius of the force (they could ride like Mexicans; trail like Indians; shoot like Tennesseans; and fight like the devil!), and the psychology of the men by actual contact with them, presented with vigor and clarity that makes it better reading than most fiction.

In my diary entry for May 12, 1937, I find the following entry: "I finished reading Dr. Webb's *The Texas Rangers* tonight. More entertaining than fiction." I have read all of it more than once since and parts of it many times and the 1937 decision stands. Incidentally, according to my diary entry for August 5, 1937, the limited edition (205 signed copies) of Dr. Webb's book was my first catalogue order. My copy, no. 184, came from Wright Howes's Catalogue No. 49, and I still stick with my diary statement on receipt of the book — "I think I am going to agree with Herbert Faulkner West that catalogue shopping is one of the finer experiences of collecting," although there is nothing that can really replace the close personal relationship between the collector and certain of his dealer friends.

California Rangers

Perhaps another diary entry serves to explain how so many other Rangers invaded my Texas Ranger collection: "October 28, 1937 — At Home: Received from the Eastern Book Co., of New York City, Major Horace Bell's *Reminiscences of a Ranger* (Santa Barbara, 1927). I am quite disappointed as Major Bell was a California Ranger instead of a Texas Ranger, a fact not disclosed in the catalogue description. However, it is quite entertaining, and I shall keep it." Yes, the California Rangers moved in just that easily, and I had a new reading interest. The first edition of this ranger item was the first cloth-bound book to be entirely produced in Los Angeles. It was published in 1881 by the firm of Yarnell, Caystile and Mathes.

The California Rangers were created by the California Legislature for the specific purpose of ending the career of Joaquin Murieta, the outlaw scourge of the miners. Harry Love, late of Texas, was the Captain with several old Texas Rangers as members and they did the job assigned. The most entertaining item it has been my privilege to read is the Grabhorn Press's American Reprint No. 1, *Joaquin Murieta* (San Francisco, 1932). This is a reprint from the old "California Police Gazette" version of 1859 that seems to have been "pirated" from John R. Ridge, the original "biographer" of the outlaw. That "Yellow Bird's" (Ridge's) biography was mostly fiction is clearly set forth in Joseph Henry Jackson's *Bad Company* (New York, 1949) and well worth reading. *Roy Bean, Law West of the Pecos* (New York, 1943) by C. L. Sonnichsen is the best of a number of biographies about the "Judge," onetime member of the California Rangers. General Patrick Edward Connor was another California Ranger who made history in the West and Major Fred B. Rogers's *Soldiers of the Overland* (San Francisco, 1938) tells his story very well indeed.

One of the interesting by-products of the Rangers-versus-Murieta contest involved a young poet, Cincinnatus Hiner Miller. So intrigued was young Miller, a visitor to California shortly after the killing of Murieta, with the growing legend, that his second book, *Joaquin Et Al* (Portland, 1868 or 1869), was devoted to the outlaw. In a footnote to the poem "Joaquin Murietta" in *The Complete Poetical Works of Joaquin Miller* (San Francisco, 1897), the poet states that this is a much "revised and cut down" version of the original poem from the book and that it was from the book and the poem that he was, in derision, called "Joaquin." The name stuck and few today recall that the name of the "Poet of the Sierras" was really Cincinnatus Hiner.

George W. Perrie wrote his own story (edited by C. G. Rosenberg), *Buckskin Mose* (New York, 1873), and in doing so presented a highly colorful account of the Buckskin or Susanville (California) Rangers, organized to fight the Indians in 1859–60. It has been said that Perrie could have written a very interesting book by sticking to the simple truth but that "he stretched the blanket to the splitting point."

Arizona Rangers

The Arizona Rangers had a short but worthwhile life in the early years of this century. The best general history of this state police force appears in *Our Sheriff and Police Journal,* volume 31, number 6, June, 1936. It is by Winsor Mulford with the title "The Arizona Rangers." Since the definitive history of the Arizona Rangers is still to be written (I've urged friend Raine to do it), it is fortunate that their story has been told by some of their famous leaders. *Gun Notches* (New York, 1931) is the autobiography of Captain Thomas H. Rynning as told to Al Cohn and Joe Chisholm. *Cap Mossman* (New York, 1951) told his story to Frazier Hunt. Both are

thrilling accounts. *Cap's* biography was one of the best ten western books of 1951 as selected by the Chicago Westerners. I also recommend fellow Westerner Raine's *Bucky O'Connor* (New York, 1910), a fine tale of the Arizona Rangers. Some years ago our friend told me that while he was not a member of the Arizona Rangers, he had the permission of the Governor "to ride" with them and that, on occasion, he did so. He has told some of his experiences while riding with them in fictional form, but I still think he is the logical man to write their history.

Colorado Rangers

About the only information that I have been able to find about the short-lived Colorado Rangers is in Bruce Smith's *The State Police* (New York, 1925). It is not a thrilling book, but as it is the only one mentioning the Colorado Rangers, it is a "must."

Rogers Rangers

Frederic Remington's *Crooked Trails* (New York and London, 1898) includes a fine chapter on the Texas Rangers, "How the Law Got into the Chaparral," and I bought it many years ago for that reason. It also includes "Joshua Goodenough's Old Letter" that introduced me to Rogers Rangers. It also introduced me to the spirited art of the author-artist and led me into additional collecting fields. About the time that I bought *Crooked Trails* there appeared a great novel, *Northwest Passage* (Garden City, New York, 1937), about Rogers Rangers by Kenneth Roberts. These two books did a very thorough job of convincing me that there was thrilling "Ranger Reading" to be had about the companies that operated east of the 100th meridian: *i.e.,* the "Smith and Weston" line, and finally the decision was made to encompass all the Rangers in my collection.

Major Robert Rogers, organizer and commander of the Rangers, who fought for the English in the French and Indian War, was an intriguing rascal but a great fighter and leader. He wrote his story, *Journals of Major Robert Rogers* (London, 1865), and it is, so far as I know, the first Ranger book as well as prime source material for the novelist or historian. Generals Israel Putnam and John Stark of Revolutionary War fame served their apprenticeships with Rogers Rangers. The first attempt at biography in America was Colonel David Humphrey's *Essay on the Life of the Honorable Major-General Israel Putnam* (Hartford, 1788). It is not a great biography by present-day standards, but it is our first and mighty good on "Old Put." A number of biographers of General John Stark are available, but I like best the brief account, by Edward Everett, in *The Library of American Biography — Vol. I* (Boston and London, 1834).

One of my most prized items is Remington's *A Rogers Ranger in the French and Indian War* (reprinted from *Harper's Magazine,* November, 1897). When I examined it shortly after buying it, the text seemed familiar and, sure enough, it was "Joshua Goodenough's Old Letter" as I had read it in *Crooked Trails*. I recognized that it was the first "separate" of a fine story and that it preceded the appearance in *Crooked Trails* by some months. But the statement that

assured it of a place of honor on my shelves appeared under the description of the item in the catalogue of Rains Galleries' Auction Sale No. 553 and is from a note found among Merle Johnson's papers. The note reads, "This pamphlet is probably the rarest of all Remington books." While I do not agree with Johnson on this point, I do agree that it is rare enough to husband.

The best buy in the Rogers Rangers field is Kenneth Robert's *Northwest Passage* as issued in two volumes in a limited printing of 1,050 numbered and signed sets. Volume I is the novel — one of our best of the historical type and based on much research. Volume II reprints the primary source material on which the essentials of the novel are based.

Rangers in the Revolution

Rogers remained true to the Crown in the Revolutionary War and helped organize the Queen's Rangers to aid the British in putting down the rebellion. The real leader of the Queen's Rangers, and later Governor-General of Canada, was *John Graves Simcoe* (Toronto, 1910) whose biography was written by Duncan Campbell Scott.

Another company that fought for the British in those days, notorious in fiction and in some historical writings for its cruelty during the raids on the Wyoming and Cherry Valleys, was known as Butler's or The Tory Rangers. Howard Swiggett in his excellently done historical book *War Out of Niagara — Walter Butler and the Tory Rangers* (New York, 1933) has done much to correct the false legends that have been handed down about Butler and his company.

The colonists also had some Rangers on their side in that war. One company is almost forgotten yet one of its members is known to every schoolboy. Colonel Thomas Knowlton organized a company of rangers to be the eyes and ears of Washington's army before New York. This company was known as Knowlton's or the Connecticut Rangers. Ashbel Woodward's *Memoir of Colonel Thomas Knowlton* (Boston, 1861) is good on this old ranger, who in addition to his services in the Revolution is credited with saving the life of "Old Put" in the French and Indian War.

It was Colonel Knowlton, later killed in the battle of Harlem Heights, who sent one of his rangers (he volunteered) into New York City to seek information for Washington. The young school teacher, turned soldier and ranger in the best tradition of our citizen-soldiers, was captured and executed as a spy. By now I am sure that you have guessed that the young ranger was the immortal Nathan Hale. Of the very great number of books about the young martyr, I have selected a fairly recent book, Henry Phelps Johnston's *Nathan Hale* (New York, 1901) because, in addition to providing all the essential facts about Hale's career, it includes much new material — Hale's army diary, ten Hale letters, descriptions of the Hale memorials, and much of interest not in the older Hale biographies.

United States Rangers

Rangers in the Army of the United States seemed to have been especially recruited in time of war, rather than forming a permanent part of it. Ranger companies were active on the western frontier during the War of 1812, but the only written records I have of their services are the bills (and the reports on them), some of them introduced in Congress as late as 1820, praying for the pay promised them. So far as I know, they were never paid.

Nathan Boone, son of Daniel Boone, commanded a company in Missouri but since they were not mentioned in the bills, it is likely arrangements for the pay of the several ranger companies varied by location.

The mounted rangers authorized by Congress during the Black Hawk War in 1832 were much more fortunate. Probably no other rangers did so little, and were written about so much. One of the really rare items in my collection is the *Rules and Regulations for the Government of the Mounted Rangers* (Washington, D.C., 1832) issued by Major General Alex Macomb, Commanding the Army. From it I learned that the U.S. Ranger of 1832 received one dollar a day for services, and for use of his arms, horse, and equipment. The uniform was "The Hunting Dress of the West" and furnished by the ranger. The government agreed to furnish each ranger "a pair of pistols and a sword" but he had to furnish his own rifle. My great-great-great-uncle, Jesse Bean, organized a company in Arkansas and since the situation in Illinois was under control by the time the company was mustered into service, it was ordered to Fort Gibson, Indian Territory. Washington Irving, in *A Tour of the Prairies* (Philadelphia, 1835), and Charles Joseph Latrobe, in *The Rambler in North America* (New York, 1835), told the story of the tour they made with the rangers in the winter of 1832. Many others have followed suit and of these I will mention only that most worthwhile book by Grant Foreman, *Pioneer Days in the Early Southwest* (Cleveland, 1926).

The Mounted Rangers of 1832 were in service for less than a year. They were reorganized into the First Dragoons as a part of the regular army in March, 1833, and quickly made up for their rather indolent life at Fort Gibson by fighting Indians throughout the West. Captain Nathan Boone, already mentioned, was one of the United States Rangers of 1832 to serve long and well with the dragoons. His journal was printed the first time in Louis Pelzer's *Marches of the Dragoons in the Mississippi Valley* (Iowa City, 1917), which also covers the transition of the Rangers to Dragoons in fine fashion.

Rangers in the War Between the States

I have already mentioned the services of the Texas Rangers to the United States Army in the Mexican War. And there were ranger companies on both sides in the War Between the States. Fighting for the South was that spectacular, hard-riding and almost legendary force organized by the great cavalry leader, Colonel John S. Mosby. Much has been written about the sensational rides and raids of Mosby's Rangers. J. Marshall Crawford's *Mosby and His Men* (New York, 1867) was the first, and Virgil C. Jones's *Ranger Mosby* (Chapel Hill, 1944) was the last book written about these famous Virginians. They are among the best, but I recommend any or all of the books about Mosby and his rangers.

Not all Virginians favored dissolution of the Union and among the number were many neighbors and relatives of Mosby's men. The story of these men, reinforced by a number of recruits from Maryland, is told by Briscoe Goodhart in the *History of the Independent Loudoun Virginia Raiders* (Washington, D.C., 1896). The Loudoun Rangers were in frequent conflict with Mosby's Rangers and it was often truly brother against brother. While their overall value to the North was not as great as that of Mosby's men to the South, they seemed to have held their own in the skirmishes between the two—honors were about even when Ranger met Ranger.

It is interesting to note that George W. Arrington, the Captain of the Texas Rangers responsible for driving the thieves and outlaws out of the Texas Panhandle, served with Mosby. Dr. Webb in *The Texas Rangers* credits Mosby with developing Arrington into a strict disciplinarian and with teaching him the tactics that enabled him to deal with the outlaw bands in Texas while earning him the honorary title of the "Iron-Handed Man of the Panhandle." It seems that Arrington was not the name used by the Ranger Captain when he served with Mosby, but in those days it was not considered polite to inquire closely into such a private matter.

Since we are again on the subject of Texas Rangers, I want to mention a recently issued separate from the *Papers* of the Bibliographical Society of America with the enchanting title, *Texans in Leopard Skin Pants* (n.p., 1950). It is by

Robert B. Brown and is primarily the story of a rare book on the services of a company of Texas Rangers in the War Between the States . . . W. W. Heartsill's *Fourteen Hundred and Ninety-One Days in the Confederate Army, or Camp Life; Day by Day of the W. P. Lane Rangers* (Marshall, Texas, 1876?). Despite the fact that I am the good friend and college classmate of Heartsill's grandson, I have, so far, failed to secure a copy of his diary. Brown locates nine copies and I think I can match his nine — but I'm not telling where until one copy rests in the library of the little house on Guilford Road.

Our Newest Rangers

In World War II the United States Army again found use for the special talents of groups of tough fighting men. Volunteers from among the troops were given special training — reputed to have been the toughest course of "sprouts" ever given soldiers. Those who passed were formed into ranger companies and served hard and well. The books about these rangers are now beginning to appear and I recommend one, Lieutenant James J. Altieri's *Darby's Rangers* (Durham, North Carolina, 1945).

Border Rangers

So far the rangers mentioned have been members of military, semi-military, or state police companies. The term was appropriately used, however, for another group of fighting men. In the early days of Western Pennsylvania, Kentucky, West Virginia, and Ohio the settlements employed individual rangers "to range the frontier to prevent surprise attacks by Indians." Among the best known of these border Rangers were Simon Kenton, Lewis Wetzel and Samuel Brady. I have selected one interesting book about each of these famous old frontier scouts: John McDonald's *Biographical Sketches of General Nathaniel Massie, General Duncan McArthur, Capt. William Wells and General Simon Kenton* (Cincinnati, 1838); Cecil B. Hartley's *Life and Adventures of Lewis Wetzel, the Virginia Ranger* (Philadelphia, 1859); and *Sketches of the Life and Indian Adventures of Capt. Samuel Brady* (Lancaster, 1891). I also recommended one book that contains material about all three — John Frost's *Border Wars of the West* (Sandusky City, Ohio, 1853).

Bushrangers

My boyhood readings introduced me to another type of ranger. One of my favorite heroes in those days was Jack Harkaway, the English schoolboy who "adventured" over just about the entire globe. In Australia, Jack was involved with the "Bushrangers," the name applied to the escaped convicts of that continent. When I decided to expand my collection to include all the rangers, I naturally sought out some of the books about the bushrangers. I found most of them vastly entertaining as well as informative about the early history of Australia. Strangely enough, I nominate a novel as the book to read about the bushrangers — Henry Kingsley's *The Recollections of Geoffry Hamlyn* (Cambridge, 1859), one of the famous old "three-deckers" of England which has been described as the "Bible of Australian Faith." Marcus Clarke, according to

George Mackaness in an article in *The Amateur Book Collector,* April, 1952, described *Geoffry Hamlyn* as "The best Australian novel that has been and probably will be written."

Forest and Park Rangers

Books about the Forest Rangers of the United States Forest Service and the Park Rangers of the United States Park Service form an important part of my ranger collection. Major John D. Guthrie, author of *The Forest Ranger* (Boston, 1919), now retired from the Forest Service, helped me greatly in developing a Forest Ranger want list and in securing many of the scarce early items. One of the best of these is a book ordinarily rated as a novel but the old-timers in the Forest Service tell me that it is only too true — Hunter Stephen Moles's *Ranger District Number Five* (Boston, 1923). Another novel, based on facts, that I'm sure you would enjoy is Stewart Edward White's *The Rules of the Game* (New York, 1910).

Space does not permit me to mention readable books about numerous other ranger outfits, including the New Hampshire, Albany, Pennsylvania, Virginia, South Carolina, Georgia, Alabama, DeKalb (Saint Louis), Little Fork, Backwoods, Partisan, Connaught, Sherwood and York Rangers. Many of them are highly entertaining and of great historical value. Ranger material has supplied most of my reading for the past sixteen years and a considerable part of it for forty. For thrilling true stories of little-known and all-but-forgotten incidents in the history of our country, for truth stranger than fiction, and for much above average historical fiction, I recommend that you get your book dealer, or your library, to supply you some Ranger Reading!

CHAPTER X

Buckskin Sam

FEW OF US REALIZE our boyhood ambitions. Sam Hall did. Sam wanted to go west to fight the Indians! Sam went west — before he returned to his New England home he had been a Texas Ranger and a Confederate soldier on the Texas frontier — and his primary job had been Indian fighting!

Samuel Stone Hall was of sound New England stock. His father, Oliver, a native of Leominster, Massachusetts, was born on April 28, 1810 and died there on January 3, 1893. His mother, Clarissa D. (Stone) Hall, was born in Dorchester, Massachusetts, in 1815 and died in Leominster, December 22, 1899. Sam was born on July 23, 1838, during the fifteen years (1835–1850) his parents lived in Worcester, Massachusetts. The family moved back to Leominster when Sam was twelve. Oliver Hall was a leader in the fruit-growing industry and had a sizeable orchard near West Street where Leominster High School stood in 1948. The Halls had two other children — a son, Oliver, and a daughter, who married a man named Cleveland. Both settled down near their parents in Leominster. But not Sam — he was through with school at fifteen, reputed to be incorrigible. Accompanied by another Leominster boy, Joe Booth, Sam worked his way west. In 1858, Sam and Joe

reached San Antonio, Texas and enlisted in Captain Edward Burleson's company of Mounted (Texas) Rangers. The roll of Burleson's company for the campaigns of the "bloody years" of 1858–59 is missing from the Archives in the Texas Capitol at Austin but the roll for 1860 is on file and both Sam and Joe are listed as members of the company.

An unpublished paper by Roy Harris, Sam's grand-nephew, is on file in the Leominster Public Library and provides considerable information about the Hall family and Sam's boyhood ambitions. In 1948, Florence E. Wheeler, Librarian, Leominster Public Library, provided this writer much valuable information (based on the Harris paper and other records) on Sam and the Hall family.

The Burleson company of Texas Rangers was inducted into the Confederate Army at the beginning of the Civil War. Sam and Joe served the Confederacy on the Texas frontier during the opening years of the war. Sam's sympathies were primarily with the Union but as long as he did not actually have to fire at the Boys in Blue he was content to fight the Comanches and other hostile Indians who tried to take advantage of a frontier weakened by the large number of Texans serving in the Confederate Army. Sam joined Baird's Regiment in the spring of 1863 and accompanied Lieutenant Colonel Daniel Showalter on his expedition after the marauding Indians in the winter of 1863–64. The Indians raided several times that winter, concentrating in Cooke County, Texas, where they murdered men, women and children. These were sudden forays with the Indians retreating rapidly. The State troops failed to catch up with them. Sam was in North Texas with Showalter at the time of General Nathaniel P. Banks's drive up the Texas coast from Brownsville to Lavaca. However, when it became apparent that Banks, after evacuating the Texas coast, would attack from the east, Sam felt that he could no longer postpone his plan to desert rather than to fight the Union troops. According to the War Department Records, Washington, D.C., Sargeant Samuel S. Hall, Company F, deserted from Baird's Regiment, Colonel Spruce M. Baird, Commanding, Texas Cavalry, Texas Confederate States Army, on April 22, 1864, at Camp Ford, Texas. This Regiment was also known as Showalter's Regiment, after its Lieutenant-Colonel, and as the Fourth Regiment, Arizona Brigade. The regiment was authorized in a Texas Headquarters general order of February 2, 1863 and was slated to be formed in Arizona and New Mexico but was actually enrolled in Texas.

After his desertion, Sam made his way to the Union forces in Louisiana and finally home, traveling by water from New Orleans to New York. He rested a short time and on July 15, 1864, he enlisted in the Union Army at Somerville, Massachusetts. He was mustered in at Readville, Massachusetts, on July 25,

1864, and served as a private in Company Six, Fifth Regiment, Massachusetts Militia Infantry. He was in poor health when honorably discharged on November 16, 1864, and went home to rest up. He paid his first long visit to the members of his family in nearly ten years. However, Sam was full of wild tales of the frontier and fond of drink and it was not long before he was in bad in Leominster. He didn't suit Leominster and Leominster didn't suit him. He drifted west again and rumor has it, back to New York where he became a hotel clerk.

Despite the repeated newspaper statements that Sam was a clerk in a hotel in New York City in the early seventies, the New York City directories of the period do not list Samuel Stone Hall, a Samuel S. Hall or a S. S. Hall. The 1874 Directory lists the name Samuel Hall twice — one a "driver" of 1126 Second Avenue and one "laborer" of 531 West Forty-third Street. The 1875 Directory lists a Samuel Hall, a "watchman" of 59 Orchard Street. The 1876 Directory lists a Samuel Hall, "driver" of 1125 Second Avenue. The Worcester City Directory for 1871 lists a S. S. Hall, "ornamental painter, boards Richard." There is nothing to definitely identify any of these listed Halls as "Buckskin Sam."

The dime novel war between Beadle, Tousey, Munro, and Street and Smith was on in full force in the seventies and the tales were getting wilder by the issue. Sam, while serving as a hotel clerk, had time to read the works of Colonel Prentiss Ingraham, Ned Buntline, Edward S. Ellis, Gerald Carlton, and others who were picturing the life on the western frontier. He had the opportunity to compare the experiences of their fictional and real heroes with his own experiences as a Texas Ranger and with the camp-fire tales he had heard as a Ranger and while serving in the Confederate Army. While visiting his relatives in Leominster in 1876, Sam came under the influence of the temperance advocate, George M. Dutcher.

Dutcher lived in Leominster, Massachusetts, Sam's old home town, from 1872–77. The Leominster Directory for 1876–77 lists Dutcher as a "Temperance Lecturer" and as residing at a house on Willow Street. At the Leominster City Hall the birth on December 4, 1872, of Dutcher's daughter, Marietta, is recorded. The birth record showed Dutcher's place of birth as Cairo, New York and that Mrs. Dutcher was born in Worcester, Massachusetts. Sam met Dutcher on his last trip home in 1876 and perhaps members of Sam's family, who knew Dutcher in Leominster, urged Sam to follow Dutcher to Wilmington in hopes of Sam's final reformation under Dutcher's influence.

Dutcher arrived in Wilmington on Monday, April 16, 1877 and so successful were his efforts in fighting demon rum that the grateful citizens of Wilmington presented him a home on Thanksgiving Day that same year. Dutcher was one of the ablest temperance advocates of the day — he lectured 4,000 times in the United States and Canada, talking to over 2,000,000 people and leading 250,-000 to take the pledge. At the height of his campaign in Wilmington fifty saloons were closed and the sale of liquor fell off $800 a week. Dutcher was the author of *Disinthralled: A Story of My Life,* published by the Columbian Book Co. of Hartford, Connecticut, in 1874. His reform as described in the book was pure fiction, but he was able to cover up his misconduct until 1879 when his frequent absences from Wilmington aroused the suspicion of a newspaper reporter. He was exposed and when tried by the citizens who had been his strongest supporters, was convicted of drunkenness, hypocrisy, and improper and unjudicious conduct. He left Wilmington accompanied by Wilful Widow Watson who had followed him there.

When Dutcher moved to Wilmington, Delaware, in 1877, Sam followed him there. Sam, encouraged and assisted by Dutcher, completed his first dime novel for Beadle in 1877. In this novel, *Kit Carson, Jr.,* Sam turned temperance advocate (or perhaps Dutcher supplied the words) — "Oh, you who legislate in favor of a license for the sale of, and you who vend this vile poison, which brings more misery, suffering, crime and woe into this favored land than all other evils combined, think you that you will be held guiltless of its work in the great day when all profit from its sale will be as naught to you?" Despite this statement, Sam had been a drinking man for some years and from time to time until his death he was to fall-from-grace and shoot-up his adopted home town, Wilmington.

When Dutcher was driven from town in 1879, his family was left without means. At the time, Sam Hall was living in a tent in the yard of the home the citizens of Wilmington gave to Dutcher, and he did his best to support the

Dutcher family. Sam stepped up his dime novel output and in the few years before he died, he delivered an additional fifty novels to Beadle and found time to write a few for Beadle's competitors. Sam's earnings, while not great, were enough to keep the wolf from the door of the Dutcher family. When Sam went on one of his periodic sprees, the good people of Wilmington, knowing his role of provider for the family of his friend, were ever ready to forgive him. Sam lived his last years in unselfish service of the Dutcher family. So far as is known, Sam never married. He died of pneumonia in Wilmington on February 1, 1886. The two Wilmington papers, *Morning News* and *Every Evening,* for February 4, 1886, state that Sam was buried in the Riverview Cemetery, Thirtieth and Market Streets, Wilmington. *The Leominster Enterprise* for June 6, 1901, states that Sam's grave is in Leominster's Evergreen Cemetery in the Cleveland (Sam's sister married a Clevelander) lot. It seems probable that the family eventually had the body moved from Wilmington to Leominster.

Sam Hall lived less than a half century. In the seven years, 1858–65, he was a Texas Ranger; he wore the grey; he deserted; and he wore the blue. In the seven years, 1879–86, he was a quiet hero and a prolific dime novelist. Buckskin Sam wrote out of his experiences and background in the West. He was one of the few dime novelists who could.

BUCKSKIN SAM, RANGER

If, as has often been said, one's first novel is likely to be autobiographical, we can assume that Hall really was, at least, an acquaintance of Big Foot Wallace, Rip Ford, Ben and Billy Thompson and other historical characters who make up much of the personnel of *Kit Carson, Jr., The Crack Shot of the West (A Romance of the Lone Star State)*. Sam is one of the Rangers, though not an important character, and Cortina and his raiding Mexicans provide most of the opposition.

The Texas Archives reveal that Sam was a member of Captain Edward Burleson's company of Mounted Rangers in 1860. Joseph Carson, age twenty-six, was the Second Lieutenant of Burleson's company and while Sam makes "Kit Carson, Jr." somewhat younger in the novel, it seems likely that Lieutenant Carson was the model for Sam's hero. According to Dr. Walter Prescott Webb's *The Texas Rangers* (Boston, 1935), Burleson's company was authorized by Governor Sam Houston on January 4, 1860. On January 20–21 Governor Houston issued his "Orders to Ranging Companies" — Burleson was to locate his quarters on the Nueces to the south. The company was to be divided into detachments and was to patrol the frontier at least five miles beyond the settlements. The officers were to permit no horse racing, gambling, or drinking among the men. Colonel Rip Ford was at this time vigorously prosecuting the Cortina War and there is no record to indicate that Burleson's Company left its post on the Nueces to participate in the doings on the Rio Grande.

Joseph E. Booth, age twenty, the "Reckless Joe" of Sam's novels, is also listed as a member of the company. The roll of the company reveals that most of

BUCKSKIN SAM

A sketch of Samuel Stone Hall, or "Buckskin Sam," by William Loechel

the members were in their twenties but there was a scattering of eighteen- and nineteen-year-olds including Third Corporal William E. Barton, age eighteen. Edward Quinn at forty-three was the "old" man of the company. Trail driver George N. Steen, then twenty-two, who spent his latter days at Bryan, Texas, was a member of the company. In *The Trail Drivers of Texas* (San Antonio, 1920), Steen tells about Captain Bill George of Seguin joining him in crossing the Indian Territory while on a drive to Abilene, Kansas, in 1868. Perhaps this was the William A. George who was a member of the company. There was a James W. King in the company and this may have been the Jim King who sold a 7,000-acre ranch in Karnes County to Captain Tom Dennis in 1874. Toby A. Long was a member of the company and perhaps he liked the Nueces County where the company was stationed and settled down there. Jim and "Tobe" Long are recorded at putting up a trail herd on the Nueces for Smith Brothers of Prairie Lea in 1871 (J. M. Hankins in *The Trail Drivers of Texas*). The size of the company, sixty-nine officers and men, was rather large for a Ranger company of that period and the fact that Houston authorized companies of that size at that time reinforces the idea that they were to be used in furthering his Grand Plan — the conquering of Mexico.

Burleson had commanded a company when Ford as Senior Captain led the Rangers on the expedition against the Comanches on the Northern frontier early in 1858. The roster of Burleson's Company in that campaign is not available. Sam states in one of his novels that he was a member of the Company in 1858 and both his dime novel biographers make the same claim. There seems to be little reason to doubt it. Even if Sam didn't take part in the campaigns of '58 and '59, doubtlessly some of Burleson's old Rangers in the campaigns of the Bloody Years re-enlisted in his company in 1860, and from them the twenty-one-year-old Hall heard many a campfire tale that became his own adventure or otherwise appeared in one of his novels some time later. Much later N. A. Jennings in his fine narrative, *A Texas Ranger* (New York, 1899), used the same techniques — he placed himself as a McNelly Ranger some months before he actually joined up in order to use the first person in telling a part of the McNelly saga in which he had not participated. He heard the stories from the other Rangers who had been there.

William M. Walton in his *Life and Adventures of Ben Thompson, the Famous Texan* (Austin, 1884), quotes Thompson as picking Buckskin Sam to accompany him on a scout for Burleson in the campaign of 1858–59 against the Comanches. Sam and Ben are caught in a stampede of buffalo driven by 80 to 100 Comanches. They run before the herd but Ben's horse is injured and finally goes down. Sam refuses to leave Ben and they fight from behind Ben's horse. They kill the leaders of the pursuing Comanches but there seems to be little hope in the face of the odds against them. Burleson and the Rangers rescue them at the last possible moment. Sam is wounded in the arm and leg by Comanche arrows in this fight.

Two dime novel biographies of Buckskin Sam, the Ranger, were written by two of the most prolific of all dime novelists, Colonel Prentiss Ingraham and Colonel E. Z. C. Judson (Ned Buntline). Both Ingraham and Judson lived dime novel lives and were able to draw on their own experiences for many of their exciting tales. Ingraham's life of Hall was titled *Plaza and Plain; or, Wild Adventures of Buckskin Sam (Major Sam S. Hall), the Noted Texas Ranger, Scout, Guide, Ranchero and Indian-Fighter of the Southwest Border*. It was issued by Beadle and Adams on April 5, 1882, as No. 17 in Beadle's Boy's Library of Sport, Story, and Adventure. Later it was reissued as No. 27 in Beadle's Boy's Library.

Judson's contribution *Buckskin Sam, the Scalp-Taker* was issued by Street and Smith on June 25, 1891, as No. 119 in the Log Cabin Library. This was five years after the death of both Hall and Judson — Judson having outlived Sam only from February to July. The first appearance of *The Scalp-Taker* in print has not been determined but Ralph F. Cummings of Fisherville, Massachusetts, dean of the dime novel buffs, knows that it appeared in *Wildwood's Magazine* and believes it appeared in the famous old boy's paper, *New York Weekly*.

Ingraham and Judson agree on but few of the details of Hall's career. So diverse are their accounts that one wonders if there were two Buckskin Sams. Neither can be considered accurate enough to add anything of importance to our knowledge of Sam's life. Ingraham also used Buckskin Sam as a character in several of his novels about Buffalo Bill and Buck Taylor. Beadle and Adams encouraged their writers to use other Beadle and Adams authors in their stories whenever possible to build their popularity and to give authenticity to their novels. The Buffalo Bill stories were reprinted many times in this country and in England and kept Buckskin Sam's name before the public well into this century.

Sam Hall's duties when he became a Confederate soldier on the Texas Frontier did not change. The companies charged with protecting the frontier fought Indians, pushed the raiding Mexican bandits back across the Rio Grande and did their part in controlling the outlaws and cow thieves on the border. The terms of enlistment were short in these ranging companies but Sam seems to have been continuously in the Confederate service until his desertion in April, 1864. Baird's Regiment was ordered to East Texas to protect the Confederate ordnance plant at Camp Ford near Tyler in Smith County. Banks's Union army was threatening to invade Texas from the east and this made a clash with the Texas troops seem almost a certainty. Sam carried out his plan to desert rather than to fight the Union soldiers and successfully made his way to the Union lines in Louisiana. Sam was fortunate in getting river transportation to New Orleans almost immediately. The Confederates under General Dick Taylor, son of Zachary Taylor, defeated the Union forces at Mansfield, Louisiana, near the Texas border in a bloody battle. The boys in blue were driven back in disorderly retreat to Alexandria and the threat of Union invasion of Texas from the east ended. So far as is known Sam's old regiment (Baird's) remained on guard duty at Camp Ford and did not take part in the Battle of Mansfield.

Buckskin Sam, Writer

Samuel Stone Hall was one of the few major dime novelists having a background of experience in, and knowledge of, the West to write on western subjects. In the short period of nine years, 1877 to 1886, while writing for Beadle, he produced fifty-one dime novels for that firm. The total circulation of the first issues of these novels ran into the millions, Beadle kept them in print for some years and reprinted many of them in his other series, sometimes with changed titles.

Despite the fact that Sam was only a sergeant in the Confederate army when he deserted and that he served only a few months in the Union army, he became *Major* Sam S. Hall as a dime novelist. It seems likely Editor Orville J. Victor of Beadle and Adams suggested that the title was in order. A large number of other Beadle writers used honorary military titles or pseudonyms. So widespread was the practice among Beadle writers it seems that it was company policy. The explanation of the nickname "Buckskin Sam" seems much simpler — any frontier character fond of wearing buckskins was likely to have the adjective prefix added to his name. In 1949 Colonel Charles D. (Buckskin Bill) Randolph of Iowa furnished this writer with a list of other frontier scouts who used the "Buckskin" prefix. The list included "Buckskin Johnny" (John Thomas Spaulding); "Buckskin Jack"

(John W. Russell); "Buckskin Frank," also known as "Antelope Frank" (Frank Leslie) and "Buckskin Mose" (J. W. Perrie).

In addition to the dime novels he wrote, Sam was a major contributor to *Beadle's Weekly*. This was in the publisher's words "a weekly magazine in newspaper form devoted to stories, narratives, personal experiences, biographies, recitals of pioneer work and other kindred material relating to American history, manners, customs, and conditions." Among Sam's contributions was an important book in installments, *Heroes and Outlaws of Texas,* dealing with Jack Hays, Nelson Lee, Cortina, the Knights of the Golden Circle and other famous figures and events in Texas. He also wrote a series titled *Texas Life Sketches,* many shorter articles and stories including "Sam Houston's Expedition of 1859," and several poems. *Beadle's Weekly* was issued weekly for more than twenty-seven years under various titles. In each of the three years, 1882, 1883 and 1884, Sam had thirteen novels published. All of these except two were published by Beadle. In 1885, Beadle published eight of Sam's novels and two others were published by other firms. So these last four complete years of Sam's life account for about ninety percent of his total output of novels. If he had lived and continued his pace of 1882–1885, he might well have rivaled his biographers, Ingraham and Judson.

Sam's work must be classed as Western Americana despite the fact that he was a native of Massachusetts and actually did no writing for publication until he became a resident of Wilmington,

Delaware. At least, it is a part of the "Sub-Literature of the West" since he used that setting for practically all of his novels and claimed, with reason, that their contents were based on his own and his associates' experiences in Texas and the Southwest.

Sam believed in the direct approach, and his novels are full of action. While he didn't bother much with description in his novels, he could do a neat job on occasion. For example, he opens *The Black Bravo* with a description of the setting of his tale — "Our first scene opens on the Rio Frio, a tributary of the Rio Nueces. Both of these streams wind through vast stock-raising districts of Southern Texas. It is on the bank of the first-named, and directly south from the Bandera Hills . . . winding snake-like from the hills just mentioned, its waters lovingly shielded from the sun by towering pecan trees and oaks — the moss-draped branches of which formed a verdant archway — was a small stream or creek."

Edward Pearson in his book, *Dime Novels* (Boston, 1929), reports that Orville J. Victor, for many years Beadle's editor, had to give particular attention to Sam's English, which isn't surprising since Sam left home at an early age and that ended his formal schooling.

Competition from DeWitt, George P. Munro and later Norman Munro, Tousey, and Street and Smith finally forced Beadle to abandon his policy of issuing only works meeting the exceptionally moral standards under which his business developed in the sixties. Beadle's policy is clearly stated in "Gilbert Patten and His Frank Merriwell Saga" by John

Levi Cutler (*The Maine Bulletin,* University of Maine, May, 1934). In the seventies, when Hall started his sub-literary labors, many of the early traditions had vanished. The hero no longer had to be the perfect example for young America — he could smoke, chew, drink, and instead of using good English was permitted to lapse into the rich dialect of the border. A high standard of sexual morality was maintained to the end, however.

Hall's stories are often semi-historical and with Beadle's assistance he introduced numerous historical border characters to young Americans.

Big Foot Wallace appears as a major character in a number of the stories and has a part in at least nine of the Beadle novels. In addition, Sam wrote a lengthy poem, "Big Foot Wallace and His Panther," which appeared in *Beadle's Weekly,* May 5, 1883. In the October 27, 1883, issue of the same story paper Sam added to the Big Foot legend with another poem "Big Foot Wallace on the Trail." Rip Ford appears in four Beadle tales and in one Nickle Library story. Cortina and his invaders are the villains of at least five Beadle novels. Cochise, the Apache, is the villain of a West-of-the-Pecos tale. Ben and Billy Thompson appear in three Beadle tales.

The character that appears most frequently in Hall's tales, however, is "Old Rocky" Young, a Texas Ranger, who may be a historical character but is more likely a fictional creation of Buckskin Sam based on one or more of his Ranger "pards." "Old Rocky" appears in twelve Beadle novels and in two issued in the Nickel Library. In addition, he is an important character in the two dime novel biographies of Hall. Sam also paid tribute to Young in verse. His poem "Old Rocky" appeared in *Beadle's Weekly,* March 17, 1883. "Reckless Joe" Booth, Sam's chum from Massachusetts, appears in both the biographies and in four of Hall's novels published by Beadle and in two published in the Nickel Library. "Single Eye," a pal of "Old Rocky," appears in six novels and a friendly Indian, "Turtle, the Tonkaway," in six, "Big Foot, the Comanche," "Creeping Cat, the Caddo" and several others appear more than once in the pages of Hall's novels.

Hall was an addict of the alliterative title — in fact, along with Ingraham, he was one of the real developers of the *Diamond Dick, the Dandy from Denver* style. The alliterative title habit was so strong that Sam used it in naming several of his poems for *Beadle's Weekly.* Perhaps the most striking example appeared December 1, 1883 — "The Howling Hyena from Houston." (See the bibliographical check list of Hall's writings.)

Hall was also one of the true exponents of the Victorian ending which was extremely popular among dime novel authors. J. Donald Adams, in his column, "Speaking of Books" (*The New York Times Book Review,* September 5, 1943), says: "That was a comfortable amiable practice indulged in by many of the Victorian novelists and some of the predecessors, of rounding off a tale by reassuring their readers as to what turn of fortune was the ultimate fate of the book's characters. They took it for granted that if they succeeded in the

course of several hundred pages in engaging your interest in what befell their people, it was only fair that you should know how everything worked out for everybody in the end." Sam's prize Victorian ending was that of his first novel for Beadle — *Kit Carson, Jr., the Crack Shot of the West.* Sam never quite equaled that one and perhaps with reason. Perhaps he doubted the wisdom of permanently disposing of all his characters after marrying off his pard, "Reckless Joe" Booth, in *Kit Carson, Jr.* Joe, of course, figures in a number of Sam's other Ranger novels — furnishing with the Indian heroine, the Rose of the Tonkaways, the romantic interest in *Bow & Bowie; or, Ranging for Reds* (Nickel Library No. 295) and its sequel No. 296. Incidentally, *Bow & Bowie* is one of the very few Hall novels that missed the Victorian ending — a simple tie forward to the next issue sufficed.

Sam appeared as a character in his Ranger novels though he did not often assign himself a prominent role. *Bow & Bowie* and its sequel, *Old Rocky's Ruse; or, The Underground Camp,* provide an exception in this respect. Joe is captured by the Comanches and Sam helps "Old Rocky" rescue Joe and his heroine. Sam uses the terms "Little Pard" and "Little Yank" for himself in several of the novels, perhaps confirming the reports that he was below average size.

Another tale told by men who were boys when Hall lived in Wilmington has to do with Sam's testing of his novels. He is described as having long brown hair, imperially trimmed scout whiskers and as being a spare man of middle age, a trifle below average height.

A cartoon depiction of the mother of Buckskin Sam as literary critic

He wore a flannel shirt flowing loosely from the neck, a sombrero, wide and spreading enough to serve as an umbrella, and buck trousers flaring at the ankle with lacing to the knee. He wore much gaudy jewelry. The boys of Wilmington followed him up and down Market Street and often as not ended up at his tent in the yard of the Dutcher home to listen to his "latest" (dime novel). Sam would watch his auditors, noting every expression, as he read his manuscript to them. The merit of his plot and the thrill of his story were reflected on the faces of his listeners and as long as he accepted their verdict his stories were "surefire." It was said that only when he relied on his own judgment did his thrillers "flatten."

His young critics perhaps were short on the appreciation of literature but they knew good stories. Nearly all of his novels were reprinted several times in their original series and then reissued in another series indicating that the Beadle management also recognized the fact that Sam could spin a good yarn. Despite the popularity which Sam's novels enjoyed with the general public, they were regarded as "trash" by his mother. The way the folks around Leominster tell it is that Sam mailed a copy of each new novel home but that his mother just as regularly burned it unread. Sam's writings are now widely sought — both by the dime novel collectors and by the collectors of Western Americana. In the O'Brien sale (*American Pioneer Life* — a remarkable collection of dime novels assembled during twenty years by Dr. Frank P. O'Brien of New York City, Auction Catalogue—Sale Number 1500,

The Anderson Galleries, New York, May 10, 1920), *Kit Carson, Jr.* sold for $17. *Wild Wolf, the Waco; or, Big-Foot Wallace to the Front* brought $19 at the same sale. However, Ingraham's biography of Sam, *Plaza and Plain,* sold for a higher price than either of Sam's own, bringing $21. It only happens occasionally that a "Buckskin Sam" novel can be secured at any price today. The Texas stories, particularly those in which Big Foot Wallace appear, are scarce to very rare.

To the extent that they can be found, the first printings of Hall's novels are, of course, the most desirable. After a quarter of a century of earnest seeking, however, this writer has had to be content with any printing available. Others, including the New York Public Library (*Bulletin,* vol. 26, no. 7, July, 1922), have had the same experience. Any printing of a "Buckskin Sam" novel is *a collector's find*.

A BIBLIOGRAPHICAL CHECKLIST
OF THE WRITING OF
SAMUEL STONE HALL

Burke, John M. *Buffalo Bill's Wild West*. Hartford. The Calhoun Printing Co., 1885. Colored pictorial wraps., (32) pp. Salutatory, illustrated. Includes "Cody's Corral; or, The Scouts and the Sioux," a poem by "Buckskin Sam," reprinted from *Beadle's Weekly,* April 21, 1883.

Sutton, H. J. (Happy Jack). *Great Wild West and Mirror of the Plains*. New York. Popular Publishing Co., 1888. Colored pictorial wraps., (16) pp., illustrated. Includes "'Old Rocky' as Prisoner, Judge and Jury," a poem by

"Buckskin Sam," reprinted from *Beadle's Weekly,* March 17, 1883.

Beadle's New York Dime Library

Issued by Beadle and Adams, New York, wraps., 8½″ x 12½″, black and white front cover illustration. Part or all of the back wrap. used to list other Beadle publications.

This series started as Frank Starr's New York Library. The first printing of *Kit Carson, Jr.* bears the imprint of Frank Starr & Co., Platt & William Sts., New York. Starr was the foreman of Beadle's printing staff and his address was that of Beadle's plant. All the "novels" bearing the Starr imprint are really Beadle publications. By issue No. 26 of this particular series, the name had been changed to The New York Library and by the time No. 30 appeared, the name had been adjusted to its final form, Beadle's New York Dime Library. So far as is known the reprints of *Kit Carson, Jr.* were all issued in the Beadle's New York Dime Library as were the other early numbers originally issued in Frank Starr's New York Library and The New York Library.

So far as is known Edward Morrill & Son, Boston, was the first book dealer to use the advertisements on the back wraps of Beadle's publications to identify the first issues (Catalogue 7, *American Fiction*). As many as possible of the first printings of Hall's Dime Novels have been identified by examination of the novel lists on the back wraps. The issues in the writer's collection have been checked against the copyright deposit copies in the Library of Congress. Unfortunately the Library of Congress file is incomplete and the writer's collection contains many Hall items that are not first printings.

No. 3. *Kit Carson, Jr., the Crack Shot of the West. (A Romance of the Lone Star State.)* New York: Frank Starr & Co. 27 pp. and (5) pp. of advs., issued June 7, 1877. (Big Foot Wallace, Rip Ford, Reckless Joe Booth, Cortina, Ben Thompson, Billy Thompson.) First printing lists No. 4 as "Ready June 20th" on back wrap.

No. 90. *Wild Will, the Mad Ranchero; or, The Terrible Texans. (A Romance of Kit Carson, Jr., and Big Foot Wallace's Long Trail.)* 22 pp. and (2) pp. of advs., issued March 24, 1880. (Big Foot Wallace, Reckless Joe, Kit Carson, Jr.) First printing lists No. 93 as "Ready May 5" on back wrap.

No. 178. *Dark Dashwood the Desperate; or, The Child of the Sun. (A Tale of the Apache Land.)* 22 pp. and (2) pp. of advs., issued March 22, 1882. (Big Foot Wallace, Ben Thompson, Billy Thompson, Reckless Joe, Old Rocky Young.) First printing lists No. 180 as "Ready April 5" on back wrap.

No. 186. *The Black Bravo; or, The Tonkaways Triumph.* 30 pp. and (2) pp. of advs., issued May 17, 1882. (Cortina, Turtle, Big Foot Wallace, Ben Thompson, Reckless Joe.) First printing lists No. 188 as "Ready May 31st" on back wrap.

No. 191. *The Terrible Tonkaway; or, Old Rocky and His Pards.* 23 pp. and (1) p. of advs., issued June 21, 1882. (Old Rocky.) First printing lists No. 192 as "Ready June 28th" on back wrap.

No. 195. *The Lone Star Gambler; or, The Maid of the Magnolias. (A Ro-*

mance of Texan Mystery.) 26 pp. and (6) pp. of advs., issued July 19, 1882. First printing lists No. 198 as last novel on back wrap.

No. 199. *Diamond Dick, the Dandy from Denver. (A True Story of the Mines of New Mexico.)* 23 pp. and (1) p. of advs., issued August 16, 1882. First printing lists No. 201 as "Ready Aug. 30th" on back wrap.

No. 204. *Big Foot Wallace, the King of the Lariat; or, Wild Wolf, the Waco.* 30 pp. and (2) pp. of advs., issued September 20, 1882. (Big Foot Wallace.) First printing lists No. 208 as last novel on back wrap.

No. 212. *The Brazos Tigers; or, The Minute-Men of Fort Belknap. (A Tale of Sport and Peril in Texas.)* 28 pp. and (4) pp. of advs., issued November 15, 1882. (Big Foot Wallace, Single Eye.) First printing lists No. 213 as last novel in Beadle's New York Dime Library inside the back wrap.

No. 217. *The Serpent of El Paso; or, Frontier Frank, the Scout of the Rio Grande.* 22 pp. and (2) pp. of advs., issued December 20, 1882. (Cochise.) First printing lists No. 219 as last novel on back wrap.

No. 221. *Desperate Duke, the Guadaloupe "Galoot"; or, The Angel of the Alamo City.* 24 pp., issued January 17, 1883. (Old Rocky, Jack Hodge, Cortina.) First printing lists No. 224 as last novel on back wrap.

No. 225. *Rocky Mountain Al; or, Nugget Nell, the Waif of the Range. (A Story of New Mexico.)* 23 pp. and (1) p. of advs., issued February 14, 1883. First printing lists No. 226 as last novel on back wrap.

No. 239. *The Terrible Trip; or, The Angel of the Army. (A Romance of the Lone Star State.)* 30 pp. and (2) pp. of advs., issued May 23, 1883. (Single Eye.) First printing lists No. 243 as last novel on back wrap.

No. 224. *Merciless Mart, the Man-Tiger of Missouri; or, The Waif of the Flood.* 24 pp., issued June 27, 1883. (Single Eye, Old Rocky, Turtle.) First printing lists No. 247 as last novel on back wrap.

No. 250. *The Rough Riders; or, Sharp Eye, the Seminole Scourge. (A Tale of the Chaparral.)* 29 pp. and (3) pp. of advs., issued August 8, 1883. (Rip Ford, Old Rocky, Cortina.) First printing lists No. 254 as last novel on back wrap.

No. 256. *Double Dan, the Dastard; or, The Pirate of the Pecos.* 29 pp. and (3) pp. of advs., issued September 19, 1883. First printing lists No. 259 as last novel on back wrap.

No. 264. *The Crooked Three; or, The Black Hearts of the Guadaloupe.* 29 pp. and (3) pp. of advs., issued November 14, 1883. First printing lists No. 267 as last novel on back wrap.

No. 269. *The Bayou Bravo; or, The Terrible Trail.* 27 pp. and (5) pp. of advs., issued December 19, 1883. (Old Rocky, Single Eye.) First printing lists No. 273 as last novel on back wrap.

No. 273. *Mountain Mose, the Gorge Outlaw; or, Light Horse Leon's Five Fights for Life.* 24 pp., issued January 16, 1884. First printing lists No. 276 as last novel on back wrap.

No. 282. *The Merciless Marauders; or, Chaparral Carl's Revenge.* 23 pp. and (1) p. of advs., issued March 19, 1884. (Cortina.) First printing lists No. 287

as the last novel on back wrap.

No. 287. *Dandy Dave, and His Horse, White Stocking; or, Ducats or Death.* 27 pp. and (5) pp. of advs., issued April 23, 1884. First printing lists No. 290 as last novel on back wrap.

No. 293. *Stampede Steve; or, The Doom of the Double Face.* 28 pp. and (4) pp. of advs., issued June 4, 1884. First printing lists No. 297 as last novel on back wrap.

No. 301. *Bowlder Bill, the Man from Taos. (A Tale of the New Mexico Mines.)* 27 pp. and (5) pp. of advs., issued July 30, 1884. First printing lists No. 303 as last novel on back wrap.

No. 309. *Raybold, the Rattling Ranger; or, Old Rocky's Tough Campaign.* 28 pp. and (4) pp. of advs., issued September 24, 1884. (Old Rocky, Big Foot the Comanche, Turtle the Tonkaway.) First printing lists No. 313 as last novel on back wrap.

No. 322. *The Crimson Coyotes; or, Nita, the Nemesis.* 27 pp. and (5) pp. of advs., issued December 24, 1884. First printing lists No. 328 as last novel on back wrap.

No. 328. *King Kent; or, The Bandits of the Bason.* 23 pp. and (1) p. of advs., issued February 4, 1885. (Turtle, Old Rocky, Single Eye.) First printing lists No. 331 as last novel on back wrap.

No. 342. *Blanco Bill, the Mustang Monarch.* 29 pp. and (3) pp. of advs., issued May 13, 1885. First printing lists No. 351 as last novel on back wrap.

No. 358. *The Prince of Pan Out; or, The Beautiful Navajo's Mission.* 22 pp. and (2) pp. of advs., issued September 2, 1885. First printing lists No. 362 as last novel on back wrap.

No. 371. *Gold Buttons; or, The Up-Range Pards.* 27 pp. and (5) pp. of advs., issued December 2, 1885. First printing lists No. 374 as "Ready December 23" on back wrap.

No. 511. *Paint Pete, the Prairie Patrol; or, The Rival Rancheros.* 30 pp. and (2) pp. of advs., issued August 8, 1888. First printing lists No. 517 as "Ready September 19" on back wrap.

No. 1035. *Kit Carson, Jr., the Crack Shot of the West.* A reissue of No. 3 by M. J. Ivers & Co., April, 1900. (Beadle completed his run of 1,009 issues in 1898 but Ivers took over to extend the run to 1,103, reprinting earlier issues or numbers from the Camp Fire Library.)

No. 1070. *The Lone Star Gambler; or, The Maid of the Magnolias. A Romance of Texan Mystery.* A reissue of No. 195 by M. J. Ivers & Co., March, 1903.

Beadle's Half Dime Library

Issued by Beadle and Adams, New York, wraps. 8¼" x 12", black and white front cover illustrations. Part or all of back wrap. used to list other Beadle publications.

No. 234. *Old Rocky's "Boyees"; or, Benito, the Young Horse-Breaker.* 16 pp., issued January 17, 1882. (Old Rocky, Single Eye.) First printing lists No. 236 as last novel on back wrap.

(Half-Dime No. 234 is not in the Library of Congress files or in the writer's collection. In 1948, George French, Bloomfield, New Jersey, kindly loaned his treasured copy of this issue to the writer to help complete the check list.)

No. 246. *Giant George, the Ang'l of the Range. (A Tale of Sardine-Box, Ari-*

zona.) 14 pp. and (2) pp. of advs., issued April 11, 1882. First printing lists No. 249 as "Ready May 2d" on back wrap.

No. 275. *Arizona Jack; or, Giant George's Tender-Foot Pard.* 16 pp., issued October 31, 1882. First printing lists No. 278 as last novel on back wrap.

No. 297. *The Tarantula of Taos; or, Giant George's Revenge.* 14 pp. and (2) pp. of advs., issued April 3, 1883. First printing lists No. 302 as last novel on back wrap.

No. 307. *The Strange Pard; or, Little Ben's Death Hunt.* 15 pp. and (1) p. of advs., issued June 12, 1883. (Old Rocky, Turtle.) First printing lists No. 309 as last novel on back wrap.

No. 318. *Ker-Whoop, Ker-Whoo; or, The Tarantula of Taos on the War-Path.* 16 pp., issued August 28, 1883. First printing lists No. 320 as last novel on back wrap.

No. 327. *Creeping Cat, the Caddo; or, The Red and White Pards.* 14 pp. and (2) pp. of advs., issued October 30, 1883. First printing lists No. 329 as last novel on back wrap.

No. 332. *Frio Fred; or, The Tonkaway's Trust. (A Tale of the Lone Star State.)* 14 pp. and (2) pp. of advs., issued December 3, 1883. (Old Rocky, Turtle.) First printing lists No. 336 as last novel on back wrap.

No. 344. *The Fighting Trio; or, Rattlesnake, the Tonkaway. (A Tale of Texas.)* 15 pp. and (1) p. of advs., issued February 26, 1884. (Single Eye.) First printing lists No. 350 as last novel on back wrap.

No. 349. *Wild Wolf, the Waco; or, Big-Foot Wallace to the Front. (A True Tale of Texas.)* 16 pp., issued April 1, 1884. (Big Foot Wallace.) First printing lists No. 350 as last novel on back wrap.

No. 357. *The Ranch Raiders; or, the Seige of Fort Purgatory.* 15 pp. and (1) p. of advs., issued May 27, 1884. First printing lists No. 361 as last novel on back wrap.

No. 364. *Snap-Shot, the Boy Ranger; or, The Snake and the Dove.* 16 pp., issued July 15, 1884. First printing lists No. 366 as last novel on back wrap.

No. 375. *Chiota, the Creek; or, The Three Thunder Bolts. (A Tale of the Bandera Hills.)* 14 pp. and (2) pp. of advs., issued September 30, 1884. First printing lists No. 378 as last novel on back wrap.

No. 381. *Bandera Bill; or, Frio Frank to the Front. (A Companion to "Chiota, the Creek.")* 14 pp. and (2) pp. of advs., issued November 11, 1884. (A sequel to No. 375.) First printing lists No. 384 as last novel on back wrap.

No. 392. *Romeo and the Reds; or, The Beleaguered Ranch.* 14 pp. and (2) pp. of advs., issued January 27, 1885. (A sequel to Nos. 375 and 381.) First printing lists No. 396 as the last novel on back wrap.

No. 404. *Little Lariat; or, Pecan Pete's Big Rampage.* 15 pp. and (1) p. of advs., issued April 21, 1885. (Cortina, Rip Ford.) First printing lists No. 408 as last novel on back wrap.

No. 414. *The Daisy from Denver; or, The Renegade Red.* 15 pp. and (1) p. of advs., issued June 30, 1885. First printing lists No. 419 as last novel on back wrap.

No. 427. *The Three Trailers; or, Old Rocky on the Rampage. (A Tale of the Rio Concho.)* 13 pp. and (3) pp. of advs., issued September 29, 1885. (Old Rocky,

Creeping Cat the Caddo.) First printing lists No. 430 as last novel on back wrap.

No. 442. *Bluff Bill; or, The Lynx of the Leona.* 15 pp. and (1) p. of advs., issued January 12, 1886. (Big Foot Wallace, Cortina.) First printing lists No. 444 as last novel on the back wrap.

No. 455. *Little Lone Star; or, The Belle of the Cibolo.* 14 pp. and (2) pp. of advs., issued April 13, 1886. First printing lists No. 460 as "Ready May 18" on the back wrap.

No. 634. *Cache Carl, the Chico Giant; or, The True Hearts of Red-Eye Roost.* 14 pp. and (2) pp. of advs., issued September 17, 1889. First printing lists No. 640 as "Ready October 29" on back wrap.

Beadle's Pocket Library

Issued by Beadle and Adams, New York, wraps., 6″ x 8″, black and white front cover illustrations. Charles Bragin in *Dime Novels: Bibliography 1860–1928* (Brooklyn, New York, 1938, pictorial wraps., 29 pp.) reveals that it is really a pocket edition of the Half Dime Library, reprinting tales from this series, and somewhat rarer as a smaller edition was published.

No. 189. *Old Rocky's Boys; or, Benito, the Young Mustang-Breaker.* (A reissue of Half-Dime No. 234), August 24, 1887.

No. 217. *Bald Head of the Rockies; or, The Ang'l of the Range.* (A reissue of Half-Dime No. 246), March 7, 1888.

No. 248. *Giant George's Pard; or, Arizona Jack, the Tenderfoot.* (A reissue of Half-Dime No. 275), October 10, 1888.

No. 267. *Giant George's Revenge; or, The Boys of "Slip-Up Mine."* (A reissue of Half-Dime No. 297), February 20, 1889.

No. 285. *Old Rocky's Pard; or, Little Ben's Chase.* (A reissue of Half-Dime No. 307), June 26, 1889.

No. 297. *Arizona Giant George; or, The Boyees of Sardine-Box City.* (A reissue of Half-Dime No. 318), September 18, 1889.

No. 304. *Bald Head's Pards; or, Creeping Cat's Cunning.* (A reissue of Half-Dime No. 327), November 6, 1889.

No. 311. *Frio Fred in Texas; or, Old Rocky to the Front.* (A reissue of Half-Dime No. 332), December 25, 1889.

No. 317. *Buckskin Ben of Texas; or, Single Eye's Plucky Pards.* (A reissue of Half-Dime No. 344), February 5, 1890.

No. 342. *Snap-Shot Sam; or, Ned Norris's Nettle.* (A reissue of Half-Dime No. 364), July 30, 1890.

No. 348. *Sharp-Shoot Frank.* (A reissue of Half-Dime No. 375), September 10, 1890.

No. 355. *Texas Frank's Crony; or, The Girl Mustang Rider.* (A reissue of Half-Dime No. 381), October 29, 1890.

The War Library

Issued by the Novelist Publishing Co., New York, wraps., 8″ x 12″, black and white front cover illustrations. This was probably a Street and Smith publication. Part or all of back wrap. used to list issues of The War Library.

No. 140. *Wild Bill, the Union Scout of Missouri. (A True and Thrilling Story of the Famous Borderman.)* 23 pp. and (1) p. of advs., issued May 16, 1885. First printing lists No. 149 as "Ready July 16" on back wrap.

No. 282. *Wild Bill, the Union Scout of Missouri.* (A reissue of No. 140), February 4, 1888.

The Nickel Library

Issued by the Nickel Library Co., New York, wraps., 5¾" x 8½", black and white front cover illustrations. Part or all of back wrap. used to list other issues in The Nickel Library.

No. 145. *Honest Rube; or, Rangers of the Great Northern Divide,* by Weldon J. Cobb, Jr. 31 pp. and (1) p. of advs., issued June 12, 1880. Also contains "Chased by Bloodhounds — A Story of the War," pp. 27–31, by "Buckskin Sam." (Sam.)

No. 209. *Thorny Trails; or, Meanderings in Mexico.* 31 pp. and (1) p. of advs., issued (August 20) 1881. (Sam, Cortina, Ben Thompson, Rip Ford.) First printing lists No. 214 as "Ready Sept. 24" on back wrap. Reissued as No. 561.

No. 295. *Bow and Bowie; or, Ranging for Reds.* 30 pp. and (2) pp. of advs., issued October 28, 1882. (Sam, Reckless Joe, Old Rocky, Rip Ford.) First printing lists No. 297 as "Ready Nov. 11" on back wrap. Reissued twice — as No. 636 and as No. 877.

No. 296. *Old Rocky's Ruse; or, The Underground Camp.* (A sequel to No. 295.) 30 pp. and (2) pp. of advs., issued November 4, 1882. (Sam, Reckless Joe, Old Rocky.) First printing lists No. 297 as "Ready Nov. 11" on back wrap. Reissued twice — as No. 637 and as No. 878.

The American Library

Issued by American Library Co., New York, wraps., 8¼" x 12", black and white front cover illustration. Part or all of back wrap. used to list other issues of The American Library.

No. 8. *Prince of the Platte; or, Buffalo Bill's Long Trail.* 24 pp., issued December 5, 1885. (Major Frank North.) First printing lists No. 9 as last novel on back wrap.

Saturday Library

Issued by Saturday Library Co., New York, wraps., 8¼" x 11½", black and white front cover illustration. Part or all of the back wrap. used to list other issues of Saturday Library.

No. 35. *Prince of the Platte; or, Buffalo Bill's Long Trail.* 24 pp., issued August 21, 1886. First printing in this library lists No. 36 as last novel on back wrap. (A reissue of The American Library, No. 8.)

Beadle's Weekly

An eight-page weekly magazine in newspaper form, 14⅛" x 21¼", and illustrated, was issued by Beadle and Adams, New York, under various titles. It started on March 19, 1870, as the *Saturday Star Journal,* Vol. I, No. 1. With No. 97, in 1872, it became the *New York Saturday Star Journal.* In 1874, beginning with No. 243, it became the *New York Saturday Journal.* With Vol. X, No. 460, the name was changed to the *Star Journal* but with Vol. XI, No. 521, the name was changed back to *New York Saturday Journal.* This was shortened to *Saturday Journal* with issue No. 625 early in 1882 but before the year was out another change was made and the last issue to have the title *Saturday Journal,* No. 661, appeared November 11, 1882. The old volume and issue numbers were dropped and Vol. I, No .1 of *Beadle's Weekly* appeared November 18, 1882. The last change, to *Banner Weekly,* was made with Vol. III, No. 157, in 1885, and under this name the story paper appeared through Vol. XV, No. 758, issued May 22, 1897, with which number publication ceased. Whole number of issues, 1,419; pages, over 11,000; columns per page, 5, with about 1,800 words per column or about 100,000,000 words.

Vol. IX — *New York Saturday Journal*

No. 436, July 20, 1878–No. 448, October 12, 1878. "Wild Will, the Mad Ranchero; or, The Terrible Texans." (A serial which was reprinted as No. 90, Beadle's New York Dime Library, in 1880.)

Vol. X — *Star Journal*

No. 475, April 19, 1879. "Old Rocky's Opine of Buffalo Bill" (poem).

No. 477, May 3, 1879. "Lasso-Bound" (short story).

No. 493, August 23, 1879. "Claude Duval of America" (short story).

No. 494, August 30, 1879–No. 498, September 27, 1879. "Texas Life Sketches" (a "fact" serial).

No. 500, October 11, 1879. "The Perfidy of the Washita Reserve; or, Sam Houston's Expedition of 1859" (article).

No. 502, October 25, 1879. "Down de Brazos" (poem), [and] "After the Doctor" (letter to the editor).

No. 504, November 8, 1879. "Viva Cortina" (short story).

No. 506, November 22, 1879. "The 'Carmago Tap' " (short story).

No. 511, December 27, 1879. "Mavericks" (article).

Vol. XII — *New York Saturday Journal*

No. 594, July 30, 1881–No. 618, January 14, 1882. "Prairie Pards; Tales of Border Trails, Told by a Plainsman." (A campfire tales serial that includes "Buckskin Sam's Triple Duel," "Ben Thompson's Vendetta," etc.)

Vol. I — *Beadle's Weekly*

No. 15, February 24, 1883. "Our Cibolo Stampede" (short story).

No. 18, March 17, 1883. "Old Rocky" (poem).

No. 19, March 24, 1883. "Missouri's Leap to Death" (short story).

No. 21, April 7, 1883. "Bully Bill Finds a New Pard" (poem).

No. 23, April 21, 1883. "Cody's Corral" (poem).

No. 25, May 5, 1883. "Big Foot Wallace and His Panther" (poem).

No. 27, May 19, 1883. "The Bandits of Alazan" (story story).

No. 34, July 7, 1883. "Death in the Chaparrals!" (poem).

No. 43, Septemeber 8, 1883. "Little Ben" (poem).

No. 50, October 27, 1883. "Big Foot Wallace on the Trail" (poem).

Vol. II — *Beadle's Weekly*

No. 55, December 1, 1883. "The Howling Hyena of Houston" (poem).

No. 69, March 8, 1884. "Capt. Jack Hayes; or, The First Six-Shooter Charge Ever Made" (article).

No. 72, March 29, 1884. "General Woll's Invasion of Texas" (article).

No. 87, July 12, 1884. "Diablos Texanos" (short story).

No. 91, August 9, 1884. "The Church War" (article).

No. 92, August 16, 1884. "The Comanches" (article).

No. 93, August 23, 1884. "Sam Houston's Last Speech" (article).

No. 94, August 30, 1884. "The True Story of Old Maverick" (letter to the editor).

No. 98, September 28, 1884. "Phil Coe" (short story).

No. 101, October 18, 1884. "Little Jim" (short story).

Vol. III — *Beadle's Weekly*

No. 112, January 3, 1885–No. 121, March 1885. "Heroes and Outlaws of Texas." (A "fact" serial including chapters on Jack Hays, Nelson Lee, Cortina, etc.)

CHAPTER XI

Dime Novel Texas

THE RIFLE CAME STEADILY to Jack's brawny shoulder and poured out its fierce jet of flame, the "painter" gave one convulsive bound and fell heavily among the crashing underbrush, *dead*.

There needed no second bullet, and when, with a ringing whoop of triumph, the hunter came striding up to finish his work, his only anxiety seemed to be to ascertain if his bullet had gone just to suit him, and it undoubtedly had.

Why did it suit him?

Because a single glance assured him that the panther had been *shot in the eye* — plumb and true, without the deviation of a line.

This brief Dime Novel Texas scene is from Chapter I, *Jack Long; or, The Shot in the Eye,* issued by Robert M. DeWitt, New York, in 1868 as No. 20 of the series "DeWitt's Ten Cent Romances."

Dime Novel Texas was the creation of a handful of skillful blenders of fact and fiction who wrote for Beadle, Munro, DeWitt, Tousey, and the other owners of nickel and dime fiction "mills" during the period 1860 to 1900. During that forty-year stretch they kept their creation, *their Texas,* before the public with something over two hundred novels that sold for five and ten cents. Hundreds of thousands — yes, millions — of American boys read the history of that fictional state, Dime Novel Texas. One of several distributors, the American News Company, had a standing order for 60,000 copies of each new Beadle publication as it appeared. Dime Novels were passed from hand to hand and were literally read to "pieces," a fact that is reflected in their present rarity.

Probably ninety-five per cent of the impressions of Texas during the period came from reading, and probably ninety-five per cent of the impressions from reading came from the little booklets that sold for ten cents each — thus Dime Novel Texas was *the Texas* of most of America's youth. The Dime Novels were readily available; they were priced within the reach of all; they were readable; and in so far as literature about Texas is concerned, they were practically without competition. The writer recalls only two Texas items issued during the period with sufficient reader appeal to challenge the popularity of the Dime Novels — Charley Siringo's *A Texas Cowboy; or, Fifteen Years on the Hurricane Deck of a Spanish Pony,* first issued in 1885 and destined to sell a million copies during the lifetime of its author, and John C. Duval's *The Adventures of Big-Foot Wallace, the Texas Ranger and Hunter,* first issued in 1871, with the second edition in 1872, a third printing in

1873, a fourth printing and third edition in 1885, and steady popularity to this day resulting in a total of seven printings.

Recent re-readings of these two favorites do not indicate that the stories were in violent disagreement with the legendary Texas of 1860 to 1900.

Dime Novel Texas was populated with villainous Mexicans, cunning Apaches, treacherous Comanches and Kiowas, friendly Tonkawas, thieving Navajos, an infrequent renegade white, beautiful and virtuous maidens, poor but proud "Colonels" from the old South, brave Texas Rangers, daring Indian fighters, faithful soldiers, rough trappers and hide-hunters with hearts of gold, hard-riding cowboys, enterprising mustangers, sharpshooting hunters; an occasional lisping Englishman, stuttering Dutchman, or scary negro for comedy relief; herds of longhorns, wily mustangs, and buffalo; a profusion of other wild game; and, of course, handsome young heroes to dominate each dramatic situation.

The situations were standard, too — a wagon train (an isolated fort or a lone ranch house) attacked by Comanches (Kiowas, Apaches or Navajos) and the Texas Rangers (soldiers or cowboys) to the rescue — Mexicans (Lipans, Comanches, or Navajos) raiding a settlement (a hunter's camp or a ranch) to steal the horses (or cattle), the pursuit and the inevitable "lesson" taught the redskins ("greasers" or "hoss-thieves") — a beautiful maiden held captive for ransom (revenge or spurned love), the long search, the daring recovery, and marriage to the hero — family feuds transferred from Kentucky (Tennessee or

Virginia), the wrongs righted and the families united — thrilling hunts for mustangs (buffalo or bears), fancy shooting and hand-to-hand encounters with wild beasts — war with the Mexicans (Comanches or Apaches), reverses, final victory and its sweet reward — and always plenty of redskins (Mexicans or outlaws) biting the dust!

These were the people and these were the most frequent happenings in Dime Novel Texas.

Were the impressions all wrong? Indeed not. Most Dime Novels are short historical novels — many are semi-biographical or based on actual incidents. While in most instances they are properly classified as "lurid sub-literature," they did much to teach the young American his history lesson and to encourage him to read other and better historical fiction and narratives. After all, it is but a short step from Buckskin Sam's *Wild Wolf, the Waco; or, Big-Foot Wallace to the Front* to Duval's *The Adventures of Big-Foot Wallace, the Texas Ranger and Hunter.* The bound volume by Duval doubtlessly looked rather formidable to many a young reader — but then why should he hold back? Was it not about his frontier hero, "Ole Big-Foot," and bound to be exciting — and true? Many a boy first risked a dime for Rathborne's *The Hunter Hercules; or, the Champion Rider of the Plains* before making the greater expenditure of twenty-five cents for a paper-covered or $1.00 for a cloth-bound Siringo's *A Texas Cowboy.* Charles J. Finger, in his fine book, *After the Great Companions,* lauded the exciting "derring-do" Dime Novels for leading their readers to seek enlarged experiences in the field of action literature — Irving, Cooper, Scott, and Dana.

THE CREATORS

Gerald Carlton (Munro), Major Samuel S. Hall, and Colonel Prentiss Ingraham (both Beadle authors) were the leaders, but there were several other faithful workers in the sub-literature of Dime Novel Texas including Oll Coomes, Captain Mayne Reid, Edward S. Ellis, Joseph E. Badger, Jr., Frederick Whittaker, Edward Willett, and C. Dunning Clark, all Beadle laborers.

Little is known about the private life of Gerald Carlton, but the other two members of the Big Three were rather well known — in a kind of blend of fact and fiction, dime-novelish sort of way. Major Sam S. Hall, "Buckskin Sam," was a New York boy who went to Texas at the age of fifteen. He is reported to have joined the Texas Rangers and participated in many border battles with Indians and Mexicans. One particularly romantic episode was his first meeting with Buffalo Bill. Sam was in the Confederate Army — Bill wore the blue — and their meeting was under a flag of truce to bury a mutual comrade of border days. In 1882, Ingraham wrote the story of Sam's early experiences for "Beadle's Boy's Library," large series (121 issues, 1881–1884), under the title *Plaza and Plain; or, Wild Adventures of Buckskin Sam — Major Sam S. Hall — The Noted Texas Ranger, Scout, Guide, Ranchero, and Indian-Fighter of the Southwest Border*. It was reissued at least twice — as No. 27 in "Beadle's Boy's Library," small series (319 issues, 1884–1890), with the original title and as No.

418 in "Beadle's Pocket Library" in 1892 under the title *Buckskin Sam's Wild Ride; or, Plaza and Plain*. Buckskin Sam wrote at least thirty novels for "Beadle's Dime Library" and twenty for "Beadle's Half Dime Library." During his latter years he lived at Wilmington, Delaware, where it is said he occasionally "shot up the town." He was a small, wiry man. His grammar was faulty and required the careful supervision of Orville J. Victor, Beadle's editor for nearly fifty years.

Colonel Prentiss Ingraham was a real soldier of fortune. He fought for the Confederacy, refused to take "the oath," and went to Mexico to fight for Juarez. He fought for Austria against Prussia in 1866 and later fought against the Turks on Crete. He was in the Cuban "ten years' war" for independence, was captured and sentenced to death by the Spaniards. He escaped and returned to American to embark on a literary career that was to result in more than six hundred novels, of which a few less than fifty were about Dime Novel Texas. He wrote the story of the life of Texas Jack Omohundro for "Beadle's Boy's Library," large series, with the title *Texas Jack, the Mustang King; Thrilling Adventures in the Life of J. B. Omohundro, "Texas Jack," the Noted Scout, Indian Fighter, Guide, Ranchero, Mustang Breaker and Hunter of the Lone Star State*. It is quite likely that he was the real author of the Dime Novels credited to Omohundro and to Buffalo Bill. He used, as did many of the Dime Novel writers, a number of pen names including Major Dangerfield Burr, Captain Albert Taylor, Colonel Leon La Fitte, Colonel Jo Yards, Lieutenant L. Lounsberry, Dr. Frank Powell, and Dr. Noel Dunbar. As he was a real military man and somehow during his crowded career had found time to study medicine, his pen names were considered quite appropriate.

Both Badger and Coomes were frontier boys and knew much of the West. Badger used one of his pen names, A. H. Post, to write his own life's story with the title *Roving Joe: The History of a Young "Border Ruffian,"* for "Beadle's Boy's Library," large series. He killed his first Indian before he was eleven years old. Coomes outlived the Dime Novel Texas he helped create and was killed in an auto accident in Iowa in 1920.

Captain Mayne Reid had a colorful career before becoming a writer. His biographer (his widow) fails to mention his close association with Beadle. It was to Reid that Beadle paid the record price of $700 for *The White Squaw*, No. 12 in "Beadle and Adams 20¢ Novels." Most of his stories were reissued in cloth when Dime Novel days were done and were favorites of boys in both England and the United States for many years.

The records say but little of Willett or Captain Frederick Whittaker. Edmund Pearson, in his fine book *Dime Novels,* records the Captain as rising to the defense of the morality of the Dime Novels after an editorial attack by the New York *Tribune* in 1884. Both Willett and Whittaker wrote some thrilling Dime Novel Texas tales.

The author of the first Texas Dime Novel, Edward S. Ellis, dedicated his life to literature on the occasion of his selling *Seth Jones,* "Beadle's Dime Novels" No. 8, to Beadle for $75. *Seth Jones*

sales totaled over 600,000 and had much to do with the soundness of the financial foundation of Beadle's Dime Novel factory. Ellis was nineteen at the time. He wrote many Dime Novels, many juveniles, and much biography and history, finally achieving recognition by *Who's Who* through his literary efforts. His contributions to Dime Novel Texas, while written without the firsthand knowledge of a Hall, a Badger, or a Reid, were sound.

C. Dunning Clark was a well-known historian and produced his dime novels under the pen name of W. J. Hamilton.

In fact, Dime Novel Texas was particularly fortunate in having, as its main creators, writers with a broad general knowledge of pioneer life and times as well as much intimate and personal contact with the characters who populated that fabulous Texas.

THE LITERATURE

Beadle, and rightly so as the leader in the field for nearly forty years, published the first Dime Novel about Texas. The author was Ellis, then twenty, and the year was 1861. It appeared as one of the famous yellowbacks, No. 32, in the original series "Beadle's Dime Novels" with the title *Irona; or, Life on the Southwest Border.* It was (and is) an interesting tale of a flatboat trip up the Rio Colorado to a point beyond Austin, an overland journey to the mountains, encounters with Comanches, and, as an added attraction, the White Steed of the Prairies appears for the first, but by no means last, time in a Dime Novel. Thus began the legend that resulted in Dime Novel Texas.

Apparently the next Dime Novel having a Texas setting was Gerald Carlton's *Scar-Cheek, the Wild Half-Breed; or, A Chase After the Savages of the Frontier,* issued by George Munro and Company, New York, in 1864, as No. 28 in "Munro's Ten Cent Novels." It was written under his favorite military pseudonym of "Captain Latham C. Carlton." Carlton was a heavy contributor to the creation of Dime Novel Texas.

Erastus P. Beadle and associates had issued *Malaeska* by Mrs. Ann Stephens, the first complete book of fiction to sell for ten cents, in June, 1860, as No. 1 in the famous yellowback series "Beadle's Dime Novels." After *Irona* by Ellis in 1861, it was 1869, however, before the Beadle authors began to contribute heavily to the Texas illusion. In that year Percy B. St. John's *The White Canoe; or, the Spirit of the Lake,* a tale of Comanche hatred for and bitter warfare against the Texans, was issued as "Beadle's Dime Novels," No. 169. From that time on Beadle's contributions to Dime Novel Texas were great — after all, his opportunities were frequent since Beadle published some thirty different series of Dime and Nickel Novels between 1860 and 1900, as many as six or seven series at the same time.

George Munro, a former employee of Beadle, was Beadle's strongest rival for many years; Munro was the second publisher to enter the dime fiction field and was also second to issue a Dime Novel Texas item.

The success of Beadle resulted in many imitators, including Robert De-Witt, who went so far as to use an almost duplicating "yellowback" for his series, "DeWitt's Ten Cent Romances." "We require unquestioned originality" was one of the primary rules fixed by Beadle for the guidance of his authors, but De-Witt reprinted, rewrote, and perhaps "pirated" the works of some of the favorite writers of the day. At least six of the early Texas items in "DeWitt's Ten Cent Romances" were not written for that series. No. 20, *Jack Long,* quoted in the first paragraph of this article, illustrates the point.

Jack Long is an adaptation of the Charles W. Webber story which apparently was first issued in wraps in 1840 by H. W. Graham, Tribune Building, New York. It is included in that rare collection of Webber's short stories, *Tales of the Southern Border,* printed in Philadelphia in 1853. In the book Webber introduces the story with this statement:

The millions of copies of this story which have been circulated in this country through the daily and weekly press have all been from a mutilated edition which was impudently pirated in an English periodical under a new name. American editors, in copying, replaced a portion of the original title, to be sure, but took the text as they found it. I would, therefore, present it in book form for the first time, once for all pronouncing the following to be the only version authorized by me, of a narrative the facts of which are too nearly historical to justify their having been wantonly handled.

It is not clear whether or not Webber objected to the Graham issue, but, had he been alive in 1868, it is almost certain that he would have protested violently on the use of his title and story in DeWitt's No. 20, since the rewrite by Stoddard was rather poorly done and a superfluous love story was added.

Webber led a Dime Novel life. He spent some time in Texas as a Ranger, studied medicine and then theology, drifted into newspaper work, led an exploration party to the Colorado and the Gila rivers in 1849, wrote several books, and lost his life in 1856 in Nicaragua while on a filibustering trip with William H. Walker. *Old Hicks, The Guide* is probably his best book although his *Sam; or, the History of Mystery* was a popular history of our country with the readers of the 1850s.

DeWitt credited the item to Colonel Cris. Forrest, a pseudonym of W. O. Stoddard, later a prolific writer of highly respected historical juveniles — cloth bound, of course.

Nos. 45 and 46 of the same series were both taken from Captain Flack's *The Prairie Hunter*. No. 45, *Indian Jake; or, the Prairie Hunter*, covers essentially the first 120 pages of the C. H. Clarke, London, edition of *The Prairie Hunter*, while No. 46, *The Mountain Trapper; or, The Ranger and the Bear*, covers the rest of the story, pages 120 to 265. No. 45 is credited, properly, to Captain Flack, mystery author to Texana collectors, but No. 46 is credited to Lieutenant Henry L. Boone, one of the pseudonyms of Percy B. St. John.

Nos. 53, *The Texan Ranger; or, The Rose of the Rio Grande*, and 54, *The Mexican Bravo; or, The Fair Maiden's Rescue*, both issued in 1870, are from Professor J. H. Ingraham's *The Texan Ranger; or, The Maid of Matamoras*, which appeared in N. M. Curtis's *The Prairie Guide*, copyrighted 1847. No. 58,

Bel of Prairie Eden, is a brief version of George Lippard's Mexican romance of the same name published by Hotchkiss and Company of Boston in 1848.

Meanwhile, Munro was following his No. 28 with other Gerald Carlton items: in 1865, No. 34, *The Three Daring Trappers; or, Adventures Among the Indians and Beavers,* and No. 52, *Black Bill, the Trapper; or, Hunting Gold and Indians,* both involving the heroes of No. 28, Black Bill and Brose Martin. In No. 28 the enemies are the Navajos, in No. 34, the Pawnees, and in No. 52, Mexican outlaws and Comanches.

In 1866, Carlton wrote Munro's No. 75, *Old Norte, the Hunter; or, Adventures in Texas,* a real thriller, involving Pawnees, wicked Mexicans, and Navajos; in 1867, he wrote Nos. 102, *Old Zeke; or, The Wild Hunter of the Rocky Mountains,* and 107, *Red Rattlesnake, the Pawnee; or, Life on the Border,* two fast-moving stories of ranch life. In 1868, he added No. 131, *Mad Betsey; or, Fortune Hunting in Texas,* the story of a shipwreck in the Gulf, early days of Galveston, and ranching in East Texas.

Beadle's writers were rapidly adding to the Texas legend. Three new Texas novels in 1870 and six in 1871 appeared in the "Yellowback Series." In 1871, C. Dunning Clark, the historian, under his pseudonym W. J. Hamilton, wrote *The Prairie Queen; or, Tom Western, the Texan Ranger.* It first appeared as No. 232, "Beadle's Dime Novels"; it was reissued under the same title as No. 213, "Beadle's Pocket Novels" (a series of 272 issues published 1874 to 1884). It was again reissued as No. 72, "Beadle's Half-Dime Library" (a series of 987 issues,

1877 to 1904), this time with a new title, *Mad Tom Western, the Texan Ranger; or, The Queen of the Prairies*. Under the new title it also appeared as No. 56 of "Beadle's Pocket Library" (a series of 492 issues between 1884 and 1893).

Beadle had the reputation of keeping popular novels continually in print. A second printing within a week of the issue date was common. Many of them were reprinted several times in the original series before being reissued in one of the other series. The writer, owner of a copy of the scarce first edition of Duval's *Adventures of Big-Foot Wallace,* is almost as proud of his copy of the tenth edition of Buckskin Sam's *Big-Foot Wallace, the King of the Lariat; or, Wild Wolf, the Waco,* No. 204, "Beadle's (New York) Dime Library."

The double titles of the Dime Novels mentioned are not unusual but standard form. John Levi Cutler in the University of Maine *Studies,* Second Series, No. 31, "Gilbert Patten and His Frank Merriwell Sage," credits "Beadle's Dime Novels" No. 5, *The Golden Belt; or, The Carib's Pledge,* issued in 1860, with fixing the Dime Novel title form—double, with its parts separated by a semicolon and a comma.

The forty-year period, 1860 to 1900, of Dime Novel Texas should really be roughly divided into two parts, 1860 to 1884 and 1884 to 1900. From 1860 to 1884 was really the Dime Novel period, and from 1884 to the close of the century was really the heyday of the nickel novel. The first twenty-four years were characterized by novels of the booklet types of 4" x 6½", 5¾" x 7½", and 6" x 9½" in size that sold for ten cents. The paper on which they were printed was usually rag stock, and the books' wraps were either colored with a black line illustration or white with a vivid multicolored illustration. The best of the Dime Novel "hacks," plus a number of the popular writers of the day, wrote the real old Dime Novels.

Although some of the novels sold for five cents before 1884 and some were sold for ten cents as late as 1889, the real Dime Novel era ended when Beadle discontinued his last two booklet series, "Beadle's New Dime Novels" and "Beadle's Pocket Novels," in 1884. Munro and DeWitt had dropped their booklet series earlier. The nickel era was characterized by the larger format of the novels, 8½" x 12½", 8¼" x 11¼", and 8" x 11". They looked more like cheap magazines than books. The paper was of poor quality, often sulphite pulp. They were self-wrapped, with black and white front cover illustrations. The standard price was five cents. Another distinctive feature of the nickel era was the alliterative titles of many of the novels.

Sam Hall and Professor J. H. Ingraham contributed mightily to developing this last-named characteristic. Some of Hall's best were No. 318, *Ker-whoop, Kerwhoo; or, The Tarantula of Taos,* No. 634, *Cache Carl, the Chico Giant,* both in Beadle's Half-Dime Library," and No. 199, *Diamond Dick, the Dandy from Denver,* No. 221, *Desperate Duke, The Guadaloope "Galoot,"* No. 256, *Double Dan, The Dastard; or, The Pirates of the Pecos,* all in "Beadle's (New York) Dime Library."

Ingraham, so far as this writer is concerned, won the prize with the title to

"Beadle's Half-Dime Library," No. 702, *Blue Jacket Bill; or, the Red Hot Ranger's Red Hot Racket.* Oll Coomes concocted an occasional "nifty"; for example, *Tiger Tom, the Texas Terror,* the title of No. 218, "Beadle's Half-Dime Library." Badger was no "piker" in the contest. One of his best was *Daddy Dead-Eye, the Despot of Dew Drop,* the title of No. 474, "Beadle's (New York) Dime Library."

Much has been said about the "Bang! and another redskin bit the dust" opening paragraphs of Dime Novels. A casual survey of sixty novels about Dime Novel Texas in the writer's collection fails to bear out the contention that "action openings are the rule. For the sake of comparison, thirty novels that originally sold for ten cents and thirty that sold for five cents were used in the survey. Only three, or ten per cent of the ten-cent sellers used action openings while twelve, or forty per cent, of the five-cent sellers used action openings. The same writers appeared in both the five- and ten-cent series, but as the five-cent libraries were specifically written to appeal to the more juvenile readers, it is not strange that the action began with the first line.

The most frequent type of opening paragraph in the ten-cent sellers, appearing sixteen times out of thirty in the survey, was a description of the setting of the novel—a style introduced to the readers of sub-literature by J. H. Ingraham, father of Colonel Prentiss. A good example of this type of opening paragraph is found in *Indian Jake* by Captain Flack, "DeWitt's Ten Cent Romances" No. 45:

I am on the sea-shore: the sand under my feet is white and very firm. It has been made so by the wash of the waves. Sea weeds of various forms and shapes are tangled on the beach; beams from the West India Islands of strange shapes and chestnut colors are scattered just above the watermark, cast there by the waves. To the south and east the Gulf of Mexico, with its dark blue billows, indigo in color from the deep blue sky above, are by contrast white as the driven snow.

Not a redskin nor an outlaw was slain on the first page, much less in the opening paragraph.

While the early writers for the ten-cent libraries were under production pressure, it was but slight as compared to that of the stampede days that began about 1884 when the publishers of the various "five-centers" began their drives for popularity and readers. Literary pretentions were dropped, and openings changed materially. Colonel Prentiss Ingraham in *The Red Sombrero Rangers; or, Redfern's Last Trail,* No. 707 of "Beadle's Half-Dime Library," departs far from the example of his father and opens: "Hugh Hammond, you shall hang for this! You have killed him!" *Roaring Ralph Rockwood, the Reckless Ranger* by Harry St. George, No. 20 in "Beadle's Pocket Library," opens: "The sharp, whip-like crack of a rifle awoke a thousand echoes among the distant foothills, and broke the stilly silence of the night." Colonel Ingraham in *Buck Taylor, King of the Cowboys; or, The Raiders and the Rangers,* "Beadle's Half-Dime Library" No. 497, starts: "A cry of warning rung out from a man guarding a camp on a Texas Prairie." The three examples are all from the five-cent sellers and give a fair cross-section of the opening paragraphs of the twelve novels that used the direct action approach.

Whatever the openings and whatever the number of redskins, or "greasers," that "bit the dust," the narrow escapes of the hero and/or heroine, villains foiled and disguises removed, there seems to have been but little disagreement as to the proper ending for these "histories." J. Donald Adams, in his column "Speaking of Books" (*New York Times,* Book Review Section, September 5, 1943), says:

That was a comfortable, amiable practice indulged in by many of the Victorian novelists and some of the predecessors, of rounding off a tale by reassuring their readers as to what turn of fortune was the ultimate fate of the book's characters. They took it for granted that if they succeeded in the course of several hundred pages in engaging your interest in what befell their people, it was only fair that you should know everything worked out for everybody in the end.

This Victorian style was in common usage by the Dime Novel Texas authors. No less than fifty of the sixty novels surveyed have this type of ending. The other endings were evenly divided between "they married and lived happily ever after" and a "blurb" for the sequel. Major Sam S. Hall in his *Kit Carson, Jr., the Crack Shot of the West,* "Beadle's (New York) Dime Library" No. 3, outdoes the Victorians in informing his readers of the fate of his charaters — witness:

Col. John Ford (old Rip Ford) is now — at this writing — a member of the Texas Legislature, and can be seen any day on the avenue walking from his hotel to the State House, and ten to one you do not meet Ben Thompson (Fighting Ben) or Billie Thompson (Daring Bill) on the same street. . . .

Clown you will meet in San Antonio; everybody knows him by that name, and he is probably the only man on the continent who can say he whipped and drove off fifteen Indians, killing eleven of them singlehanded. . . .

Jack Hodge died at White Sulphur Springs, Arkansas, in consequence of the poisoned arrow wound received in the Nueces River fight. . . .

Joe G. Booth (Reckless Joe) does business in Dallas, Texas, but lives in Terrell, an adjoining town, where, if you choose to go to his cottage, you will be well treated by Mrs. Booth — none other but our friend, Martha Wells, or Rely; and a little Reckless Joe will show you how to ride a mustang, and two young fair Relys will gather wild flowers from the prairies for you. . . .

Tom Clark was killed in the public market in San Antonio shortly after returning from the Rio Grande by two desperadoes, but both were shot through the heart after Tom received his mortal stab. He died with his hands in mine, and as I closed his eyes I knew that one of my best friends on earth was dead. . . .

Jim Ransom is in New Mexico. Jim Bearfield ranches it on the Medina River. . . .

Big-Foot Wallace meanders about up and down the Nueces, or San Miguel, catching a mustang, or knocking a deer over, as he chooses; but his cat died from the wounds received in the Indian surprise-party, there being no one to take proper care of her when Big-Foot went to the big Cortina scrape. . . .

Kate Luby is now in Corpus Christi; teaching language and music to Texan girls, and takes great pride in her three sons, who are posted in all prairie knowledge. . . .

John G. Moore lives in Terrell, Texas, and

and owns thousands of acres of land, and more stock than he can estimate. . . .

Gen. Juan N. Cortina, once the bandit chief, accepted the cross of the Legion of Honor, through Emperor Maximilian, from Napoleon III, and afterwards turned over his numerous forces to Juarez. In his pretended submission to the French, he escaped the Scylla of Gen. Mejia's Legion, by which he was hemmed in in Matamoras, and the Charybdis of the many "Gringoes" or Americans who were watching for him on the other side of the Rio Grande. . . .

His release from the military prison of Vera Cruz, on $15,000 bail, last spring, is fresh in the memory of all, and its injustice maddening to Texans. . . .

His vagrant followers, even now, are lurking in the chaparrals, and not a week passes without the spilling of blood between Gringoes and Greasers. . . .

Clay Wells is in the Texas lunatic asylum, having never recovered from the blow given with the war club on the Nueces. . . .

Bill George (Texas Bill) is sheriff in Lancaster, Texas. . . .

Kit Carson, Jr., is around among us. . . .

Wild Will was as bad as represented. I saw him cut his horse to death myself on the ride through our camp, on Banketta Creek. . . .

P. S. Phil Cole was shot dead by Wild Bill in Ellsworth, Kansas, in 1875. He was standing in a bar-room door in the night shooting off his six in the air (as was his way, and as I have described in Fort Brown) when Bill shot him through the heart, and also his deputy sheriff by mistake, who was coming to his assistance — Bill thinking his aide was a pal of Phil's. . . .

This last spring Fighting Ben had a fight with roughs in Ellsworth and killed two. Sam . . .

Even Big-Foot Wallace's *cat* was remembered in the summary. To the writer, this is the most prized Victorian ending.

THE END OF AN ERA

With the new century came improvements in transportation facilities, moving pictures, and increased competition for the nickels and dimes of young America from the publishers of nickel novels about school and college life and detectives. Street and Smith's *Tip Top Weekly,* with Frank and Dick Merriwell, and the *New Nick Carter Weekly* had cut into the readers of the "westerns" printed by Beadle and Munro. They had sold entertainment, not literature, and the competition was too great. Erastus retired with a small fortune of some two or three million dollars while his former $16-a-week wrapping clerk, George Munro, quit with a mere ten million. The "Beadle Half-Dime Library" completed its run in 1904 and was the only one of the old series that created Dime Novel Texas to last into the new century — a "literary" era of the state was finished.

TEN THOUSAND PER CENT!

As a collector, the writer definitely feels that the "literature" of Dime Novel Texas should be preserved. Whatever it lacks in literary merit is offset by the knowledge that for forty years it was *the* written word on which the rest of the country interpreted Texas. The management of the University of Texas Library is to be congratulated on its wise and courageous move in buying for its Texas Collection the pertinent Dime Novels as they became available.

All Dime Novels are "scarce"; most

could, by all rules of the game, be called "rare." Not many copies of the numerous series and issues have survived. They vanished before their real interest and value were realized. They were so common and so absurdly cheap that no one gave a thought to their preservation.

Collectors are paying dearly for the oversight. The writer knows — in ten years he has secured less than half the Dime Novel Texas items pertaining to his particular little collecting segment of Texana — the Texas Rangers. But in the interest of spice and variety as well as completeness the search must go on until Ingraham's *Texas Charlie, the Boy Ranger,* Hall's *The Brazos Tigers; or The Minute Men of Fort Belnap,* Buffalo Bill's *Texas Jack, the Lasso King; or, The Robber Rangers of the Rio Grande,* Hall's *Raybold, the Rattling Ranger,* Major J. H. Robinson's *The Texas Rangers,* and all the other missing ones rest on the library shelf. Ten thousand per cent of the original price is a standard dealer quotation — whenever he has one to quote — and they are worth it.

CHAPTER XII

Books and Dealers

WRIGHT HOWES

THERE WERE FOUR COPIES of Alexander Major's memoirs, *Seventy Years on the Frontier,* on the shelf at Wright Howes's in Chicago recently. When you've collected Western Americana for twenty years you get to feeling like you know something, especially about such well-known books as Majors's memoirs — which is a mistake. You idly take a copy from the shelf to see how much the price is up over what you paid for a copy ten or fifteen years ago and there in Wright's neat backhand is the notation "2nd issue of ed 1." There are some vague stirrings of the mind as you try to recall the specs of the copy in the library of the little house on Guilford Road back home. So you reach for the other copies and you lay them out on the table and there by your side is the old maestro to explain his pencilings.

"This copy with the *gilt top,* the gilt lettering and front cover illustration and in the dark blue cloth with the beveled edges is the first issue — this copy (picking up another) has the gilt lettering and front cover illustration and beveled dark blue cloth binding but is nearly a quarter of an inch taller (he stood the copies side by side on the table); it is minus the gilt top and note the blurred

printing and dropped position of the "A" in RAND at the bottom of the spine so I figure it is the second issue. This copy (picking up still another) is obviously a later binding, the cloth is a shade lighter and the lettering and the illustrations are in yellow ink — however, the sheets may have been printed at the same time as the first two issues since the title page is dated 1893 so we'll call it the third issue." I can't recall what the master had to say about the fourth copy — certainly it was the third issue or later and of no concern unless you want to collect *all* issues of this particular book.

Personally, I'm satisfied with two, the one I had bought ten or more years ago (the third issue) and the one Wright had marked "1st issue of ed 1":

Seventy Years on the Frontier / Alexander Majors' Memoirs / of a / Lifetime on the Border / with a Preface by / "Buffalo Bill" (General W. F. Cody) / line / Edited by / Colonel Prentiss Ingraham / line / Chicago and New York / Rand, McNally & Company, Publishers / 1893 — dark blue cloth binding with beveled edges, spine and front cover lettering and illustration in gilt, brown endsheets, 325 pp. plus (3) pp. of advertising, gilt top, 7¾ inches tall, illustrated — frontispiece portrait plus fifteen full-page plates not included in the pagination.

Adding to my pleasure in owning the "1st issue of ed 1" is the fact that it is from the library of Colonel Eddie Wentworth, with his pictorial bookplate. Colonel Eddie, author, storyteller, and one of the best-loved men in the livestock industry, is a fellow Westerner and longtime friend.

It was a profitable visit but then all of the visits you pay the Dean of the Western Americana dealers are profitable in knowledge gained even if (as it occasionally happens) there is nothing new you can afford to add to your collection. The first collector's item I bought by mail was from a Wright Howes catalogue some twenty years ago and I have been learning about western books from him ever since. There is also a lesson in gracious living for those who visit the book apartment of Wright and Zoe Howes — you'll know more and feel better after a pleasant hour or so with them.

JERRY NEDWICK

FOR YEARS NOW the *New Arrivals* lists from Nedwick's in Chicago have mingled with slicks, fancy dans, pulps and other mimeographed and printed cats from dealers all over the world. List No. 272 came not long ago and with it, the sad announcement that after December 15, 1960, there will not be a Nedwick store in downtown Chicago. I discovered Nedwick's in 1938, and I followed Jerry from Wells Street to Michigan Avenue (two locations) to his cubbyhole back of the stock exchange to his now-closed store on South Wabash. Jerry's announcement says his doctor ordered him

to "slow down" and he adds (good news) that after a long vacation, he will issue some catalogs from his home. They will never quite take the place of those *New Arrivals* lists, however. They were in double-columns and not easy to read but read them you did — if you were a collector, you simply couldn't take a chance on missing a real gem. I dropped by Jerry's one day as the list was being assembled for mailing. Jerry gave me a copy and said, "You'd better look this over," but I stuffed it in my pocket (who wants to look at a catalog when you can look at books). On the train that night, I did read it and the following morning I wired Jerry for a book on the list. I fidgeted until the book came because it had been on my want list for ten years — ever after when Jerry offered me an advance copy I sat down and read it through. The book in this case was Will C. Barnes's *Western Grazing Grounds and Forest Ranges* (Chicago, 1913). It eluded me for years and certainly deserves to be rated as "scarce" although it is not a rare book.

The only book of poetry included in Ramon F. Adams's bibliography *The Rampaging Herd* (Norman, Oklahoma, 1959) is F. W. Lafrentz's *Cowboy Stuff* (New York, 1927). The edition was limited to 500 numbered copies signed by the author, the illustrator (Henry Ziegler) and the publisher (George Haven Putnam). It was never really offered for sale and is now rare and much sought by cowboy and cattle collectors. I bought a copy from Jerry when his store was on North Michigan.

Lafrentz's handsome book had a very interesting history. As secretary of the

Swan Land and Cattle Company of Wyoming, Lafrentz learned firsthand about *Cowboy Stuff*. Later as Chairman of the Board of The American Surety Company of New York he became very much interested in Lincoln Memorial University at Cumberland Gap, Tennessee. In considering ways and means of getting his wealthy friends to contribute the funds needed to build a new girls' dormitory, he hit upon the happy idea of writing and publishing *Cowboy Stuff* and of giving each contributor a numbered and signed copy. Copies one to ten went to contributors of $5,000 each and copies eleven to twenty to those who gave $1,000 each. The contributors of $500, $250 and $100 received the copies with higher and higher numbers. In total the five hundred contributors gave $125,000, all of which went to building the dormitory. From the number of my copy, I feel that the original owner contributed $250 to the worthy cause. The Lafrentz Poole Dormitory (named for his mother Doris, and for his wife's mother Elizabeth), was dedicated on November 3, 1929. *An Address,* a thin booklet containing Lafrentz's remarks on this occasion, is rarer than *Cowboy Stuff.*

BILL SMITH

WILLIAM C. (BILL) SMITH retired from bookselling in 1955 but not for long. His Smith Book Co., high in the Union Central Building in Cincinnati, was always a port-of-call when I was in the Queen City. Not long ago, I had a brief letter from him warning me not to wait too long before stopping by Fort Thomas, Kentucky, where he issues an occasional catalog from his home, to split a bottle with him — he reminded me that he was eighty-seven. However, in today's mail there arrived from the publisher, R. E. Banta of Crawfordsville, Indiana, a most spritely booklet of sixty-six pages entitled *Queen City Yesterdays: Sketches of Cincinnati in the Eighties,* written by this same William C. Smith. It is the story of his boyhood in Cincinnati and mighty fine social history of a period worth remembering. I think he will be there when my travels next put me in reach of Fort Thomas.

My trips to Cincinnati were few and far between, but Mr. Smith (I could never quite bring myself to calling him "Bill," though that was his name to the trade — and affectionately spoken always) bridged that gap very effectively with his frequent catalogs. I remember my first visit — I introduced myself as "Jeff Dykes of College Park, Maryland" and without hesitation he said, "And formerly of Fort Worth, Texas." I was on his mailing list before I moved East and he remembered it. His catalogues did not often contain lengthy descriptions, and the selling "blurbs" were completely absent yet they got the job done. His customers will doubtlessly remember the quotation on the front cover of each catalog — "Rare books are getting scarce."

I bought a number of good books from Mr. Smith and a few great ones. There comes to mind one in particular which is a key book in my Range Life collection — Dr. Hiram Latham's *Trans-Missouri Stock Raising.* It was issued by the Daily Herald Steam Printing House in Omaha, Nebraska, in 1871. It was the first book to survey the stock-raising potentials of any major section of our great western range area. It was issued in wraps and had just eighty-eight pages. It is said that the Union Pacific Railroad distributed thousands of copies of this booklet in the East to encourage settlement along its rails. If this is true, folks evidently thought that they got the booklet too cheap to keep. I have located only two other copies although there is a rumor that another copy was purchased recently by one of the great institutional libraries from a New York dealer at a very high price. Mr. Smith did not overcharge me for Dr. Latham's booklet or for any other book I ever bought from him. In fact, he would have been justified in charging me more for it as it is one of the really rare cattle items. Such well-known students of cattle books as J. Frank Dobie and Louis P. Merrill are still seeking copies to round out their collections. It is good to have friends in the trade, and when I make that trip to Fort Thomas, I'll take the bottle!

THE PASSING
OF A WESTERNER
BILL RAINE

WILLIAM MACLEOD ("Bill" to his legion of friends) Raine's ticker failed him and he passed on at St. Luke's Hospital in Denver on July 25, 1954. I saw Bill for the last time in May. When I called him to invite him to stop by my hotel for a drink and to guide me to the monthly dinner of the Denver Westerners he rather apologetically said, "Sorry, but the old heart isn't what it used to be and won't stand the walk from the Shir-

ley-Savoy to the Press Club." On the promise of a taxi to finish the journey he did stop off along with some other members of the Denver Posse for an hour or so. And don't think he didn't hold the center of the stage — in a big easy chair with a short one in his hand, he told tales of the West that was part wild and part civilized when he went there to die more than fifty years ago. As a young newspaper reporter in Denver at the turn of the century, as a seeker for the truth hidden in legends and campfire tales in out-of-the-way places, as a rider with the Arizona Rangers and as a foe of the phony or legend-ridden badman, gunman and peace officer, he reached back in his memory to entertain us. Far too soon we had to break up the session and adjourn to the Press Club for a fine meeting of the Westerners. Bill hadn't been to a meeting of the Westerners for some time (and the May meeting which I prodded him into attending may have been his last) and it was heartwarming to see and hear the welcome he got from the Posse of which he was, I believe, a charter member.

Yes, Bill Raine was a Westerner. The fact that he was London-born (1871), Arkansas-raised and Ohio-educated (Oberlin College) does not seem important when you think about the wiry little cuss who wouldn't die, but lived on for more than fifty years in his beloved West and made it his. For make it his he did in four-score novels, narratives and historical volumes. Bill was eighty-three when that failing heart finally quit on him, and he told us in May that he had written a book for every year of his life. His western novels were middle-of-the-road in my classification scheme — not as much shooting as some, not as many trite situations as most, not as many luscious heroines as most, and with authentic, well-drawn backgrounds based on Bill's intimate knowledge of the people and ways of the West. I read Bill's *The Texas Ranger* more than forty years ago and later most of his other novels. More than fifty of them, personally inscribed to me, rest in the little house on Guilford Road, and they are not for sale or lending.

Cattle (1930) is Bill's best-known historical work. J. Frank Dobie calls it "a succinct and vivid focusing of much scattered history." Will C. Barnes is listed as the joint author but Bill told me the story of their "collaboration" over a luncheon table a good many years back. It is carefully recorded in the diary which I was keeping at the time but is much too long to repeat here. Suffice it to say that Bill stated emphatically that he wrote every word of *Cattle*. *Famous Sheriffs and Western Outlaws* (1929), *Guns of the Frontier* (1940), and *45-Caliber Law* (1941) are well-known items of Americana that are eagerly sought by the collector. A long time ago, in 1908, in fact, Bill wrote "Billy-the-Kid" for *The Pacific Monthly*. In this article he repeated some of the errors made by Hough and others in writing about the little outlaw. I felt that I had to say just that about the article in my *Kid Biblio* and I sent a copy of what I planned to say to Bill for his remarks. His reply was prompt and characteristically to the point — "It is a little annoying to have pointed out the errors of an early story, written on a magazine order before I had time to test the tales

and rumors about Bonney that were current. . . ." I also sent along the proposed comments on his other books that included material on the Kid (in these he corrected many of the errors of the earlier article), so Bill closed by saying, "However, I appreciate the fact that you are quite fair to me." And when the biblio was finally issued his letter of commendation was among the first to arrive. That was Bill!

A number of Bill's novels have become western movies, and in recent years the 25¢ pocket reprint houses have used many of his novels. One to half-a-dozen of his reprints can usually be found at any well-stocked newsstand. Bill was Honorary President of the Western Writers of America at the time of his death. This organization of free-lance western novelists aims at the goal of honest, realistic and convincing fiction about the West. Bill was the dean of that school of writers. As Douglas Branch says in *The Cowboy and his Interpreters,* Bill belonged to "The Aristocracy of (Western) Novelists."

WALTER LATENDORF

THE MANNADOS BOOKSHOP was a Western Oasis in the heart of New York City—complete with western paintings, bronzes, books, good whiskey, genial companions, and a knowing host, the late E. Walter Latendorf. Here gathered such displaced Westerners as Harold McCracken, author of *Frederic Remington* (New York, 1947), *The Charles M. Russell Book* (Garden City, 1957) and many other books of western interest; the late Mahonri Young, artist and sculptor, the grandson of the famous Brigham; Nick Eggenhofer, one of the best of our present-day western illustrators and others too numerous to mention. Here, too, you were apt to find a little old man chatting brightly to Walter or sitting silently while the western talk flowed, for Walter had once managed and was always loved by the Singer Midgets.

At Mannados, you met the Western Americana collectors from everywhere for all the lovers of western books and art do not live west of *the river*. Walter had a good all-around stock of western books but specialized in those illustrated by Remington, Russell, Tom Lea, Will James, Ross Santee, Frank Tenney Johnson, Buck Dunton and other well-known western painters. He dealt in paintings, drawings, prints, and bronzes of these same artists and others. His catalogues were bibliographical gems and are eagerly collected by those interested in western art.

I bought quite a number of books from Walter, and since it was our mutual interest in the art of the Old West that first drew us together, it seemed only justice for him to find for me one of the real Remington-Russell rarities — Owen Wister's *The Virginian* issued in 1911 in a limited, signed edition of 100 copies. My copy is number thirty-one and as with nearly all the books I bought from Walter, the condition is very good to fine. The limited edition is in parchment and boards, 506 pp., on Japan vellum, gilt top, with a "Re-Dedication and Preface," dated October, 1911. The frontispiece by Russell is in color; there are ten full-page plates by Remington, and scattered through the text are forty-two drawings by Russell.

I saw Walter for the last time on November 6 — he was a sick man though full of hopes and plans (particularly for a Will James catalogue for which he had been accumulating material for many months). My wife, Martha, correctly appraising the situation, pleaded some shopping and said goodby to Walter. After she left, he stretched out on the big divan in the back of the store and after he made sure the whiskey was easy to my hand, we talked our last hour together — neither of us knew that then, but I doubt that it would have been much different if we had. Walter praised Tom Lea's *King Ranch,* and Harold McCracken's *The Charles M. Russell Book* but decried Doubleday's rationing of the 250 copies of the limited, signed edition of it (he had many orders and was wondering how he could ever explain to his good customers his failure to supply them after accepting their orders many months before — *this he was spared*). But mostly we talked about the James catalogue — his pet project for 1958. A dentist friend came to drive him home to New Jersey and so we parted. He died on November 17 — the oasis is no more!

USHER L. BURDICK
(1879–1960)

USHER L. BURDICK served the Potomac Corral as His Honor, The Judge, the first year of our existence. Westerners have missed him from our meetings the last couple of years and now we have accepted the fact that he will not be back.

Usher Burdick died August 19, 1960, at the age of eighty-one.

He was a native of Minnesota, but the family moved to North Dakota when he was quite young. He grew up on Graham's Island where he became an expert horseman and formed lasting friendships with the Sioux. He went back to the University of Minnesota to study law and played end on the championship football teams of 1903 and 1904.

He was a member of the North Dakota legislature, lieutenant governor, rancher, publisher, and author. He was elected to Congress in 1934. I met him first in 1938. He owned a bookstore on G Street in Washington, and after I had selected several books and was waiting, rather impatiently, for the clerk to finish with another customer, I was suddenly confronted by a quite large gentleman who had bounced out from behind a desk in the back of the store. He told me who he was and commented on my judgment in the selection of the books. This was the beginning of an enduring friendship. Mr. Burdick was one of the great collectors of Western Americana and one of the best book scouts this country ever had. He told me that twice, when times got tough, he had to "eat" his books but that as soon as he got on his feet again he bought more and better ones. He bought, sold, traded, and treasured books. I spent several hours with him last February and we roughly estimated that he owned about 25,000 books and pamphlets at that time. My own collection is immeasureably richer because I knew Usher Burdick.

He was a prolific writer about the West. Perhaps the best thing he wrote was *Recollections and Reminiscences of Graham's Island,* the story of his boyhood experiences. It appeared first in *North Dakota History* and was later reprinted as a separate. His last book, *Some of the Old-Time Cowmen of the Great West* (Baltimore, 1957), was part of the manuscript (I was once privileged to examine it) of a great history of the range livestock industry that Mr. Burdick felt would be his crowning historical achievement. His contributions to the preservation of local North Dakota history are sure to be recognized in the not too distant future. I own about twenty of his books and pamphlets in this field of local history and they are indeed worthwhile.

In many ways Usher L. Burdick was a maverick — the party yoke did not set well on his broad shoulders. Last fall, while I was visiting in North Dakota, I was introduced to an elderly citizen as being from Washington, D.C. He immediately asked me if I knew their congressman, Mr. Burdick. I told him that I did and then he leaned over to tell me quite confidentially, "You know, the damnfool Republicans wouldn't nominate him for another term in Congress, but, by God, we fooled them — we nominated him on the Democratic ticket and elected him!" Of course, it was his son, Quentin, who had been elected but I didn't parade my own knowledge of the event and just laughed with the old gentleman. Mr. Burdick told me that North Dakota politics being what they were, he did not completely approve of his son, Quentin, entering the Senate race (for the seat vacated by the death of Senator Langer). Mr. Burdick was elected to the

House ten times but lost his only try for the Senate by a handful of votes. He said that if Quentin did go in that he would go home to do what he could for him. Quentin won the seat and thus achieved a place in the Congress that his father had aspired to but had failed to gain.

But son Quentin will have to go some to achieve the place in the hearts of his fellow North Dakotans that his father had for so many years. What a man — politician and statesman, horse lover, book lover, big and hearty, author, friend of the farmer, critic of all those he felt wanted to step on the neck of John Q. Public, gruff and powerful, yet strangely gentle in many ways — they're not sending us many from the Usher L. Burdick mold from the West any more — what a pity!

WHO WAS CAPTAIN FLACK?

THIS HAS BEEN one of the literary mysteries which has intrigued me for most of the past twenty years. Captain Flack evidently spent some time in Texas and the Southwest since he wrote about the country and its flora and fauna with considerable fidelity. He almost certainly was English as all his books were printed in England after the material from which they were compiled had appeared in an English sporting journal, *The Field*. He used the nom de plume "The Ranger" and on the title page of *The Texan Rifle-Hunter* following his name are the words "Late of the Texan Rangers."

Four of his six books were issued in 1866 by four different English publishers:

1. A Hunter's Experiences / in the / Southern States of America / being an account of the natural history of the various / quadrupeds and birds which are objects / of chase in those countries / by / Captain Flack / ('The Ranger') / London / Longmans, Green and Co. / 1866. This book is bound in blue cloth and is a volume of 359 pp., 7-15/16″ tall.

2. The / Texan Rifle-Hunter / or / Field Sports on the Prairie / by / Captain Flack / ("The Ranger") / Late of the Texan Rangers / publisher's symbol / London / John Maxwell and Company / 122 Fleet Street / MDCCCLXVI. / (All rights reserved.) This book is bound in red cloth, contains 333 pages and is 7-9/16″ tall.

3. The / Texan Ranger / or / Real Life in the Backwoods / by / Captain Flack / author of "The Prairie Hunter," etc., etc. / publisher's symbol / London / Darton & Co., 42, Paternoster Row. The preface is dated 1866. This book is gilt decorated on the spine and front cover, is 6-11/16″ tall, with 319 pp., with all edges gilt.

4. The Prairie Hunter / by / Captain Flack / author of "The Texan Ranger," etc., etc. / London: / C. H. Clarke, 13, Paternoster Row. The preface of this book is dated 1866. It is 6-5/16″ tall and is bound in cloth with a morocco title label on the spine. The book contains 309 pages.

The texts of these four books are all different although all four are concerned with hunting and with pioneer life in the Southwest.

I corresponded for some years with a Dime Novel collector in Liverpool who had it from an eighty-five-year-old friend (in 1947) that Captain Flack was Percy Bolingbroke St. John of the famous writing family. The evidence presented was not convincing.

When J. Frank Dobie went to England in the forties to teach a year at Cambridge, I asked him to solve the mystery. He admitted to sharing my curiosity concerning Captain Flack but on his return home wrote to admit failure. Longmans, Green and Co. searched their file for Pancho and found the check with which they had paid for book No. 1 listed above. The check was made out to "Captain Flack" and was endorsed "Captain Flack" — no more, no less.

SHOULD I BUY
REMAINDERS?

IT IS PERHAPS natural for a young collector to seek the advice of an old hand on the subject of buying Western Americana remainders. This is particularly true when the old collector is also a book reviewer who had, on occasion, praised the book when it was first issued.

Some of the new collectors who have contacted me feel that the remaindering of a book is a sure indication of its lack of merit. It is sometimes hard to explain to them how it is that good books are occasionally remaindered. It should be noted here that in speaking of remainders we are referring to the selling *at below the published price of new copies of first printings* by book dealers who have bought them at reduced prices from the publisher. Several large wholesalers specialize in handling remainders and relieve the publishers of dealing with a large number of retailers. Some of these wholesalers also sell remainders direct to the public by mail or through their own retail outlets. Many book dealers have a table of remainders part or all of the time or have special well-advertised remainder sales to get customers into their stores.

A remainder, in simple terms, is a book on which the publisher made a mistake. The mistake may have been in publishing the book or in printing more copies than the buyers were willing to take at the published price. To be sure, not all remainders are good books and in such cases, the publisher's mistake may have been in issuing it. But many worthwhile books also show up on the remainder tables and lists. When such books are also solid bits of Western Americana my advice is to buy.

This advice is based on nearly half a century of book buying—the last twenty as a serious collector of Western Americana. I am not, of course, qualified to arbitrate the general question of remainder buying but insofar as Western Americana is concerned it has worked out quite satisfactorily for me. For example, in February, 1942, I bought five new copies of Fairfax Downey's *Indian-Fighting Army* (New York, 1941) from a sale table in a Fort Worth, Texas, department store at seventy cents a copy. Unfortunately, through the years I have traded away four of the copies — I say unfortunately because while I was satisfied with each swap I made at the time, if I had those four extra copies now they would bring me fifty dollars worth of good western books in trade. Of course, we like to remember our successes and not all remainders have gone up in price as rapidly as Downey's very good book.

On the other hand, I cannot recall a single Western Americana remainder over ten years old that has not reached and passed its original published price. In 1938, *The Phantom Bull* (Boston, 1932) by Charles E. Perkins and illustrated by Ed Borein, cost me four bits a copy from a big New York remainder house. The same dealer charged me seventy-nine cents a copy for Charles A. Guernsey's *Wyoming Cowboy Days* (New York, 1936), which contains three illustrations by Charlie Russell plus a photo of him. Needless to say, both these remainders came in right handy when a trade was in the wind.

Among the other remainders that I recall buying are *The Last of the Seris* (New York, 1939) by Dane and Mary Coolidge; James B. O'Neil's *They Die But Once* (New York, 1935); Charles J. Brill's *Conquest of the Southern Plains* (Oklahoma City, 1938); *Caspar Collins* (New York, 1927) by Agnes Wright Spring; *Villains and Vigilantes* (New York, 1936) by Stanton A. Coblentz; *Dave Cook of the Rockies* (New York, 1936) by Collier and Westrate; Colonel Dean Ivan Lamb's *The Incurable Filibuster* (New York, 1934); James A. McKenna's *Black Range Tales* (New York, 1936), and Grant Shepherd's *The Silver Magnet* (New York, 1938). One copy of each now has a place of honor in my collection although the nine cost me less than ten dollars.

One of the great remainder stories is told by William A. Keleher of Albuquerque, New Mexico, author of *The Fabulous Frontier* (Santa Fe, 1945), *Maxwell Land Grant* (Santa Fe, 1942) and other entertaining and scholarly books on New Mexico. The book that was remaindered is the now extremely rare Pat Garrett's *The Authentic Life of Billy the Kid* (Santa Fe, 1882). Keleher says the book sold first for one dollar, then for seventy-five cents and finally the remnant of several dozen copies was sold to an early Billy the Kid enthusiast for twenty-five cents a copy and that the purchaser hauled them away in a wheelbarrow. Another friend reports that he was a lucky purchaser at the two-bit price and states, "there was a bushel basket full of copies in front of the newspaper office in Santa Fe when I first arrived there." A copy seldom turns up today and the price is accordingly high.

It is my opinion that nearly, if not all, the Western Americana remainders on the sales tables or lists today are good buys. (I'm laying by a few.) If history repeats (and it does), each of them will slowly inch up to the published price and as the supply is exhausted (books that are remaindered are hardly ever reprinted) the price keeps rising. There may not be a Garrett or even a Downey in the present crop but at a fourth or a third or a half of the published price the collector has a real bargain. If perchance you bought one of the remainders at the time of issue at the full retail price, don't give it away or discard it — buy another copy or two at the reduced price to protect your original expenditure. Truly some of the best Western Americana of the past five years can now be found among the remainders — this is your opportunity to profit by the mistakes of the publishers. Buy!

CHAPTER XIII

Dobie Rarities

THE QUESTION I am asked most often by my friends interested in Dobie is "What is your rarest Dobie book?" Sometimes I take down a copy of Fred Lambert's *Bygone Days of the Old West* for which Pancho wrote the foreword — one of two copies bound by Bayntun of Bath, England. I bought my copy from the late Frank Glenn of Kansas City, one of the great bookmen of the mid-country, whose charming wife, Peggy, still operates Glenn Books there. I got the story of this binding from Frank Glenn. Lambert, who lived at Cimarron, New Mexico, wanted a limited, numbered and signed edition of 200 copies in a fine binding — "the best," he said. Burton Publishing Company of Kansas City was his publisher (perhaps "printer" would be more accurate — at least, I've always suspected that Fred picked up most or all the printing bill) and Glenn was called in to suggest a binder and help with the design. Two sets of the sheets of the book were sent to the famed British binder, Bayntun of Bath. They were bound in brand-decorated horsehide with the hair side out. Marbled end sheets and gilt on all the edges were added and the result was a handsome volume indeed. I made one mistake the night I bought my copy from Glenn in his shop off the lobby of the cattlemen's favorite Kansas City hotel, The Muelbach — I should have bought both copies. When I sent mine to Pancho to be autographed, he greatly admired the Bayntun binding and wanted it for the Dobie Collection then destined for the J. Frank Dobie Room in the Humanities Research Center at The University of Texas. I had to say "no" but I did try to run down the other copy for him without success. "The best" that Fred Lambert wanted (and got) proved to be too expensive for Burton (or Fred) and the limited edition of 200 copies that was finally issued by Burton is bound in brown leather with four of Fred's illustrations on the front cover — one pressed in each corner. It is good but suffers greatly by comparison with the Bayntun design. (Bayntun operates a bookshop, too, and we had the pleasure of buying a few good Texas books there when we visited Bath in 1970.)

Incidentally, Frank pulled out all the stops in his foreword — for example, "... his rhythm is as natural and regular as a hound dog's elbow thumping on a ranch gallery floor after dark when the fleas get into action" and ... "Wild Hoss Charley ... deserves to stand up beside Pecos Bill and Paul Bunyan." In another copy of Lambert's book on June 7, 1959, Frank wrote "I had not read this since I wrote it a long time ago — a long time before 1948 — copyright date on book. I could not write that way now . . ." Neither Lambert nor the publisher had bothered to send Frank a copy of any edition.

Copies of the limited signed edition of 200 copies of *Bygone Days of the Old West,* each with one of Lambert's illustrations laid in, are very difficult to find indeed (your writer has seen just one copy). As for the fabulous Bayntun trial binding, there is one of two copies still unaccounted for, so far as your writer knows. The limited is not mentioned by McVicker or Cook and even Frank did not know about the Bayntun "trial" limited. The way Frank's cousin Dudley Dobie tells it, when Frank got a box of his books from me for autographing in 1959 he called Dudley at San Marcos and said, "Dudley get on over here — you've got to see the Dobie items that Jeff has found." Dudley went. I don't remember all the items in that lot but the most important was the Lambert book in the Bayntun binding.

Sometimes I take Dobie's own *Hacienda of the Five Wounds* from the shelf — that is, all that is left of it, a salesman dummy. While I was appraising the Dobie Collection for The University of Texas I found the dummy (a cloth covered stiff board folder with one page announcing the book with a facing page of text . . . page 3 from the book) not with the Dobie items but being used as a protective cover for the rare little Jim Hinkle booklet *Early Days of a Cowboy on the Pecos* (Roswell, New Mexico, 1937) on the shelf of cattle books. The dummy had been hand lettered HINKLE in ink

on the backstrip (but up-side-down) by Frank. As soon as I found it in his bookroom I took it downstairs to Frank for an explanation. There was a real merry twinkle in his eyes as he told the story — but here are his own words as he wrote them out on October 26, 1959: "Harry Maule was editor of Doubleday. He wanted a book from me bad — though in the end it never sold much. I called it *The Hacienda of the Five Wounds.* After it was set up I wrote to him to change (the) title to *Tongues of the Monte.* He didn't like the 1st title & changed with alacrity. This was a kind of dummy sent me before (the) change was made. For a long time I used it to protect a pamphlet by ex-Gov. Hinkle of N.M." The one important thing about the story that he didn't write (not much space was available) was where the idea for the change originated. Frank and Miss Bertha were driving back to Austin from a meeting in San Antonio where Frank had been one of the speakers when she said, "Frank, you used a term in your talk tonight that should be the title of your book," and when she mentioned *Tongues of the Monte* Frank was quick to agree. He contacted Maule and the change was made, despite the fact that the book was in type and announced for release on October 4, 1934 — with the new title Doubleday released the book in 1935. Doubleday let the book go OP, and it was reissued by the University Press in Dallas (S.M.U.) in 1942 with a new title, *The Mexico I Like.* Frank wrote in my copy "And I like the title better than *Tongues of the Monte* which puzzled instead of drawing book buyers." But that was not the end of title changes for the book, and Frank tells the story in the last paragraph of the preface of the 1947 issue: "Settling on a title for this book has made me waver worse than Coleridge trying to decide which side of the road to walk on . . . Now that my much-liked publishers, Little, Brown and Company, are issuing the book, I have decided to revert to *Tongues of the Monte*. That title says something to me. The three editions plus the first British issue with the title *Tongues of the Monte* (London, 1948) are all in the collection with the original sales dummy—I was greatly surprised when Frank sent it to me to complete one of our complicated trades. Frank and I traded many times but we swapped books only once that I recall. There was none of the usual hoss tradin' bickering in a Dobie-Dykes trade—rather we tried to out-do each other in giving not getting. Perhaps I used the wrong word when I said "complete"—our trades were never really finished—only interrupted from time to time. I had sent Frank a copy of Jenkins's *Olive's Last Roundup,* a very good little cattle book issued in Loup City, Nebraska, and rated "rare" by my old friend Ramon Adams in *The Rampaging Herd*. Frank Glenn found a small cache of the Jenkins and sold me a copy for $35. Later I bought a copy at an auction in New York so I had a spare to give to Frank. Yet I was mighty happy with the "trade"—I got the only copy of the salesman's dummy known to me. There may be others but it is certainly rare and surely of bibliographic importance.

Some of my friends are surprised when I say the salesman's dummy of *The Hacienda of the Five Wounds* and

Bygone Days of the Old West in the Bayntun trial binding are my rarest Dobie items. Almost always they come back with the question as to the rarest of Frank's own books. Despite the claim of one of my young colleagues in a recent catalog that the Rawhide Edition of *The Longhorns* is the rarest of all Dobie books, I am just as sure that the Pinto Edition of *The Mustang* is the rarest. The limited edition (Pinto) of *The Mustangs* consists of 100 copies while the limited (Rawhide) edition of *The Longhorns* totals 265 copies. To be sure *The Longhorns* was published in 1941, eleven years before *The Mustangs,* but as Frank once said—he doubted that a single one of the 265 copies of the Rawhide edition had been destroyed. Since rarity is determined by supply and demand and my own observations over the years indicate that despite the impact of the Tom Lea collectors in the case of *The Longhorns, The Mustangs* (Pinto edition) is just as avidly sought as the Rawhide edition of *The Longhorns*. In fact, with only 100 copies available the scramble was on the very day of issue and I was happy even with copy no. 99. One more small bit of evidence—three copies of the Rawhide edition of *The Longhorns* have been offered for sale in the catalogs of my fellow dealers in the past few years while in the same period only a single copy of the Pinto edition of *The Mustangs* has been listed. That seems about the right ratio: totals available: 265 to 100—offered: 3 to 1.

As a matter of fact, I consider the salesman's dummy of *The Longhorns* to be rarer than the Rawhide limited. The dummy is bound in full calf (the Raw-

One of the very rare horsehair-bound copies of J. Frank Dobie's Bygone Days of the Old West, *created by Bayntun of Bath*

hide binding) and has the double title page in color, the text of pages 3 and 4 and the photographic record section. The copy in my collection is the only one I have ever seen. It is, of course, much less desirable and not as costly as the limited but it is rarer.

The Sierra Madre edition of *Apache Gold and Yaqui Silver* is limited to 265 and since it, like *The Longhorns,* was illustrated by Tom Lea there is competition from the Lea collectors for the occasional copy that appears on the market. It is rare.

Tales of the Mustang was beautifully printed by the Rein Company of Houston for the Book Club of Texas in 1936 in a limited edition of 300 copies. It may be as difficult to find as any of the other Dobie limiteds except *The Mustangs.*

Of Frank's own books that were not issued in limited (300 copies or less) editions there are two that I rate as rare: *On the Open Range* (Dallas, 1931) and *The Flavor of Texas* (Dallas, 1936). Frank wrote in my copy of *On the Open Range,* "Dear Dykes — I am delighted that you have a copy of the first edition of this book. Only 750 copies were printed as I recall in that edition though 15 or 20 M were printed in the school edition — 9/1/43." It is seldom that a copy of the first reaches the market. So far as I know *The Flavor of Texas* is the only Dobie book that was never reprinted — it is hard to find and expensive. To be sure, the *Tales of the Mustangs* was not reprinted under that title but in my copy Frank wrote: "About everything in this beautifully made little book is now in *The Mustangs.*"

The first printing of *A Vaquero of the*

Brush Country (Dallas, 1929) with the words "Rio Grande River" on the map on the end sheets is scarce. So is the first printing of *Coronado's Children* (Dallas, 1930) with the publisher-altered dedication that upset Frank. He wrote in my copy (re the dedication) *"a clean cowman of the Texas soil* was what I wrote & some unclean fool cut the *clean* out. Restored in later printings."

John C. Duval, First Texas Man of Letters — His Life and Some of His Unpublished Writings (Dallas, 1939) was issued in an edition of 1,000 (950 for sale) copies. Tom Lea illustrated the book with some of his best drawings and naturally the Lea collectors compete when an occasional copy appears for sale. I rate it very scarce.

Of the books edited by Dobie I regard *Legends of Texas* (Publication No. III of the Texas Folk-Lore Society), Austin, 1924, as the hardest to find and apt to be the most expensive. Frank wrote in my copy on March 2, 1943: "How proud I was of this book — my first. How proud we both were, for it seems to me that my wife Bertha did as much as I on it. A rare book now." Twenty-eight more years have added to the problem of finding a copy.

The other Folk-Lore Society Publication that I rate as rare is No. XVI, *Mustangs and Cow Horses,* Austin, 1940. Add to the Dobie fans those seeking the book for its illustrations, the horse book buffs, and the range life collectors and, pardon the pun, you have a hoss race anytime a copy appears on the market. The competition is unusually strong from the Charles M. Russell collectors, probably the most avid of the breed.

Tom Lea may not have the following of Russell but his fans are just as dedicated. Ross Santee, Will James, John W. Thomason (the fighting Texas Marine), Harold Bugbee (my classmate at Texas A & M), and William R. Leigh are among the other illustrators represented in the book and each has his share of fans.

A Tenderfoot Kid on Gyp Water by Carl P. Benedict was designed and printed in an edition of 550 copies by the typographical maestro Carl Hertzog of El Paso. It is Volume Three in the Range Life Series edited for the Folk-Lore Society by Dobie. My copy is inscribed by Frank who wrote the introduction — I think from what he wrote and said he liked it best of the series and copies are scarce to rare.

A number of the Dobie booklets and broadsides are fully as scarce or rare as his books. There are two very good reasons for this — one, most of them were printed in small editions and second, they were not issued for sale — Frank gave them away to his friends. From the small number that have reached the market those friends have been most reluctant to part with them. Some of the best were used as Dobie Christmas remembrances and it was a mark of distinction to be on the Dobie list. It was a proud moment for us when we got our first Dobie Christmas remembrance sometime in the early fifties. Later Frank dug deep into his files to supply many of the early Christmas booklets needed to give me an almost complete set.

From my experiences in finding and buying them and from studying the cata-logs of my fellow dealers I consider the following to be among the scarce and rare Dobie booklets in my collection: *Texas-Mexican Border Broadsides and La Cancion del Rancho de Los Olmos* (1923); *Andy Adams, Cowboy Chronicler* (1926); *Mustang Gray: Fact, Tradition and Song* (1932); *Juan Oso, Bear Nights in Mexico* (250 numbered and signed copies, Christmas, 1933); *Bigfoot Wallace and the Hickory Nuts* (300 numbered and signed copies, Christmas, 1936); *Mesquite* (1938); *Picthing (sic) Horses and Panthers* (1940); *Bob More, Man and Bird Man* (Christmas, 1941); *Divided We Stand* (Detroit, 1943); *The Seven Mustangs* (Christmas, 1948); *Babicora* (1954) and *The Mezcla Man* (designed and printed by Carl Hertzog, Christmas, 1954). I am sure that some Dobie buffs will disagree with my choices and perhaps there are other Dobie booklets just as rare. As for the broadsides, I consider all those fragile items that are so hard to protect to be very scarce to rare.

Several of the books with Dobie contributions, in addition to Lambert's *Bygone Days of the Old West,* were issued in limited editions and must be rated rare. For example, The Texian Press, Waco, issued the limited edition of the *Heroes of Texas* (late in his life Frank wrote or rewrote "James Bowie" for it) in 1966 in an edition of 50 copies, signed by eleven of the contributors and bound in full leather. With only 50 copies and contributions by a number of talented Texas writers the supply was quickly exhausted. Bob Denhardt's *The Quarter Horse* (Fort Worth, 1941) with Dobie's "Billy Horses and Steel Dust," was issued in a limited numbered edition of 125 copies — if you think thirty years doesn't make a difference, try to find a copy today.

While the *1952 Brand Book* of the Denver Westerners with "Trail Driving a Hundred Years Ago" by Dobie does not qualify as a limited edition — it was issued in an edition of 500 copies — it is long OP and much sought (and expensive). *The 1962 Brand Book of the Denver Posse of the Westerners,* edited by my old friend the late John J. Lipsey, includes "Out of the Original Rock" by Dobie. The Contributors' Edition was limited to 39 copies — my copy is no. 22. There also was a Posse Edition of 61 copies and a Regular Edition of 550 copies. The Contributors' and Posse Editions are rare and expensive. Apt to be even more expensive and harder to find despite a printing of 1,000 copies is Eugene Manlove Rhodes's *The Little World Waddies,* designed and printed by Carl Hertzog, illustrated by Harold Bugbee, edited and published by W. H. Hutchinson, my California historian friend, and Frank contributed "My Salute to Gene Rhodes" as the foreword. Frank often got a lot of mileage out of the articles or essays he wrote and this tribute to Gene Rhodes is a good example. In my copy of *The Little World Waddies* Frank wrote: "My preface to this book has a history. Frank Dearing and J. W. (*sic*) Hutchinson asked me to write it. It was understood that all money taken in above the cost of printing was to go to May Rhodes. Following the publication of the book I got Carl Hertzog to run off a reprint of the 'Salute to Gene Rhodes' for sending out as a Christmas remembrance

by Bertha Dobie and myself. I made a few corrections. Some time afterwards the editor of Houghton Mifflin Company asked me for a preface for *The Best Novels and Stories of Eugene Manlove Rhodes.* I told him I had already written it. I made a change or two and it was used; also I got a check for $250. The editor showed it to Weeks, editor of the *Atlantic Monthly* and the *Atlantic* published a good part of it — for another check — small. Thus charity was rewarded — 12/28/53."

Jack Potter's *Lead Steer and Other Tales* (Clayton, New Mexico, 1939) was privately printed by the author. He was a great storyteller, and it was my pleasure to listen to him many hours as we both made the Panhandle-Plains fairs and fat stock shows in the early thirties. Frank wrote "Belling the Lead Steer" as the introduction and the booklet was illustrated with drawings by Harold Bugbee and with photos (one of Frank). It is a dandy and very scarce to rare.

Even some of the school readers are scarce. *Mustang Gray* (Southern Life and Literature, Book One — St. Louis, etc., 1941) with three contributions by Dobie is not listed by McVicker or Cook. Frank wrote in my copy: "Friend Dykes — This is the first copy of this book I have seen — so far as my recollection goes . . ." I am reasonably sure I found a copy later for Frank to include in the Dobie Collection at The University of Texas.

Another limited edition that must be rated rare is *Cowboys and Cattlemen* (New York, 1964), selected and edited by Michael S. Kennedy. Mike selected Frank's "Snowdrift, Lonest of All Lone

Rarities by renowned Texas author J. Frank Dobie

Wolves" for this anthology. The limited is an edition of 199 numbered and signed copies bound in horsehide with the hair on, and there is an original watercolor or drawing by one of the several contributing contemporary artists in each copy. It is a beautiful book and quite expensive now.

The Limited Editions Club issue of Helen Hunt Jackson's *Ramona* was beautifully printed by Saul and Lillian Marks at the Plantin Press, Los Angeles, in 1,500 numbered copies, signed by illustrator Everett Gee Jackson. Frank wrote the introduction and in my copy says: "Reading *Ramona* was not dull, as I feared it might be . . ." Despite the size of the printing, very few copies have appeared on the market since it was released in 1959 — it is scarce and expensive now.

There are limited editions among the books that include information about Frank and his writings. Winston Bode's *A Portrait of Pancho* (Austin, 1965) was issued in a limited edition of 150 copies numbered and signed by the author and the publisher, John H. Jenkins. It is bound in full leather and slipcased. It was bringing a premium in weeks.

José Cisneros at Paisano — an exhibit: *Riders of the Spanish Borderlands* was designed by Bill Wittliff of The Encino Press for the Institute of Texan Cultures at San Antonio. It was issued in an edition of 300 copies and was OP in days. It includes "The Dobie-Paisano Project" by Bertha McKee Dobie and the illustrations by Cisneros are great.

Larry McMurtry's *In a Narrow Grave — Essays on Texas* (Austin, 1968) was issued in a limited edition of 250 numbered and signed copies, printed on art-laid paper and bound in leather and boards. There is much on Dobie (Bedichek and Webb) in the essay "Southwestern Literature?" As indicated by the question mark following the title, Larry seems to doubt there is much Southwestern literature. After the beautiful job erudite Margaret L. Hartley, editor of *Southwest Review,* did in "reassuring" Larry it hardly seems necessary for this old Texan to take a hand.

Zamorano Choice (Los Angeles, 1966) was compiled by historian W. W. Robinson and includes "Hill on Dobie" by Don Hill. It was issued in a limited edition of 300 copies — four of the great printers in Southern California cooperated in producing a lovely volume for the Zamorano Club: Grant Dahlstrom (The Castle Press), Ward Ritchie, Saul Marks (Plantin Press) and Richard Hoffman (California State College at Los Angeles). It was issued on the occasion of a joint meeting on September 24–25, 1966, of The Roxburghe Club and The Zamorano Club of Los Angeles. The members of the two clubs seem to hold tight to their copies — the occasional copy is certain to be expensive.

Senator Ralph W. Yarborough's *Frank Dobie: Man and Friend* (Washington, D.C., November, 1967) was issued by the Potomac Corral, The Westerners, in a limited, numbered edition of 250 copies signed by the Senator and by your writer — I got in on the act by writing the foreword, "Pancho's Friend Ralph." I don't recall the exact words but in a copy I inscribed for a friend I said about this: "All I did was nag the Senator in agreeing to write this paper to present at a dinner meeting of The Westerners (we were both members) — reassure him from time to time as he wrote it and introduce him when he gave it." It was OP in days and bringing sizeable premiums in weeks — it is costly now.

The size of the printing makes it appropriate for me to include my own *A Dedication to the Memory of James Frank Dobie, 1888–1964* that first appeared in the Autumn, 1966, issue of *Arizona and the West*. The only separate printing was limited to 25 copies — it was rare on the day of issue.

While far over the number accepted as limited, the Special Edition of Ed Ainsworth's *The Cowboy in Art* (New York and Cleveland, 1968) is now quite scarce to rare — some of my colleagues are asking $100 to $150 for a copy. The special 1,000 copies were bound in full leather and all edges were gilt — they were slipcased and would have been signed but for the untimely death of dear old Ed. The chapter "The Vanishing Mustang" has much on the help Ed gave his fellow Texan, Pancho, in finding an authentic mustang — Dobie was writing *The Mustangs* at the time.

Bertram Rota's *The Night of the Armadillos* was printed in London and used by Bertram and his son, Anthony, the well-known London book dealers, as their Christmas remembrance in 1960. Bertram spent a night at Paisano with Frank during one of his visits in Austin — and he evidently saw an armadillo or two. Frank wrote in my copy: "For my paisano and amigo Jeff Dykes, who understands poetic license — 14 March 1961." After I became a book dealer I

tried to buy copies to supply to some of my avid Dobie customers — there were none for sale and I was told none had ever been sold. On my 1968 visit to London I called on Tony Rota (Bertram, like Frank, was gone) — after some searching Tony found six copies of *The Night of the Armadillos*. He gave them to me with the understanding that I would give, not sell, them to real Dobie buffs. I did. Bertram gave Frank a few — Tony gave me six and, so far as I know, no others have crossed the Atlantic.

Frank H. Wardlaw's *I Have That Honor* (tributes to J. Frank Dobie) was beautifully produced for him by the Meriden Gravure Company, Meriden, Connecticut, in 1965 in an edition of 500 copies. It is illustrated with Tom Lea's portrait of Dobie and with photos of Frank and his friends. Despite the 500 copies, I know a number of Dobie buffs who are still trying to acquire it — none were offered for sale.

The reprint of *Bob More* and the delightful *Carl Sandburg & Saint Peter at the Gate,* both published after Frank's death by Bill Wittliff at the Encino Press in small editions, are certainly scarce. Lon Tinkle's *J. Frank Dobie, The Making of an Ample Mind,* also published by the Encino Press, and Herbert Faulkner West's *Notes from a Bookman* are just as hard to find now.

The weakest link in my Dobie Collection is the magazine section. For lack of shelf and storage space I did not make an all-out effort to collect the magazines in which Frank's articles and stories appeared. The day I walked into the room at the University where the Dobie magazines were stored (Frank ran out of room at home) I was glad that I had used restraint. The room (it was small) seemed to be overflowing and it took me more than a day to put a value on the lot. McVicker lists over 500 magazine articles but it seems to me that there were more in that room. There could have been — in the list "Supplementing McVicker and Cook" I have listed some forty additional magazines with Dobie contributions.

I have listed a number of the catalogs of my fellow booksellers in the section "Supplementing McVicker and Cook." I am not sure that any of them can be rated as really rare but I would not accept a commission to acquire the lot for a customer. I have looked for another copy of my old friend Otto Claitor's no. 40 for over thirty years without success — any order including it would be just about impossible to fill. Most of the others are much more recent but I would still not agree to assemble a set — particularly if there was a time limit.

SUMMARY

Exceedingly Rare

1. *The Hacienda of the Five Wounds* (salesman's dummy), *unknown
2. Lambert—*Bygone Days of the Old West* (Bayntun of Bath trial binding), 2
3. *The Longhorns* (salesman's dummy), unknown
4. *The Mustangs* (Pinto edition), 100

Rare

5. *The Longhorns* (Rawhide edition), 265

*Number of copies

6. *Apache Gold and Yaqui Silver* (Sierra Madre edition), 265
7. *Tales of the Mustangs,* 300
8. *Legends of Texas* (1924 edition), unknown
9. *Mustangs and Cow Horses* (1940 edition), unknown
10. *On the Open Range* (1931 edition), 750
11. *The Flavor of Texas,* unknown
12. Lambert — *Bygone Days of the Old West* (limited edition), 200
13. Rhodes — *The Little World Waddies,* 1,000
14. *Juan Oso, Bear Nights in Mexico,* 250
15. *Bigfoot Wallace and the Hickory Nuts,* 300
16. *Bob More, Man and Bird Man,* unknown
17. *Babicora,* 200
18. Loftin *et al.* — *Heroes of Texas* (limited and signed edition), 50
19. Denhardt — *The Quarter Horse* (limited edition), 125
20. Kennedy (editor) — *Cowboys and Cattlemen* (limited edition), 199
21. Rota — *The Night of the Armadillos,* unknown
22. Yarborough — *Frank Dobie, Man and Friend* (limited and signed edition), 250
23. Robinson (compiler) — *Zamorano Choice,* 300
24. Lowman *et al.* — *José Cisneros at Paisano,* 300
25. Lipsey (editor) — *The 1962 Brand Book of the Denver Posse of The Westerners* (Contributors' edition), 39
26. Bode — *Portraits of Pancho* (limited and signed edition), 150
27. Dykes — *A Dedication to the*

Memory of James Frank Dobie (only separate edition), 25

28. McMurtry — *In a Narrow Grave* (limited edition), 250

Very Scarce to Rare

29. Benedict — *A Tenderfoot Kid on Gyp Water*, 550

30. *John C. Duval, First Texas Man of Letters*, 1,000

31. *A Vaquero of the Brush Country* (first issue), unknown

32. *Coronado's Children* (first issue), unknown

33. *Texas-Mexican Border Broadsides and La Cancion del Rancho de Los Olmos*, unknown

34. *Andy Adams, Cowboy Chronicler*, unknown

35. *Mustang Gray: Fact, Tradition and Song*, unknown

36. *Mesquite*, unknown

37. *Picthing (sic) Horses and Panthers*, unknown

38. *Divided We Stand* (Detroit, 1943 issue), unknown

39. *The Seven Mustangs*, unknown

40. *The Mezcla Man*, unknown

41. Howe (editor) — *1952 Brand Book, The Westerners, Denver*, 500

42. Potter — *Lead Steer and Other Tales*, unknown

43. Stone *et al.* — *Mustang Gray*, unknown

44. Ainsworth — *The Cowboy in Art* (special edition), 1,000

45. Wardlaw — *I Have That Honor*, 500

46. Jackson — *Ramona* (The Limited Editions Club issue), 1,500

47. Tinkle — *J. Frank Dobie, The Making of an Ample Mind*, 850

48. *Bob More, Man and Bird Man* (Encino Press edition), 550

49. *Carl Sandburg & Saint Peter at the Gate* (Encino Press edition), 750

50. West — *Notes from a Bookman*, 399

Note: Forty-nine of the fifty rarities listed above are in the Dykes Collection — the exception is no. 12.

CHAPTER XIV

Remington Rarities

RARITY IS A simple matter of supply and demand. If the demand for a particular book in a certain edition (usually the first but not always so) is greater than the supply, the price goes up and dealers list it as scarce or rare. The size of the edition is not always the key to a rarity — a small printing may go begging because no one is interested in it. A small printing of a wanted book is almost sure to result in it becoming scarce, and, as time goes by, rare. In a few cases, demand is primarily the result of the illustrations in a book. Remington illustrations have been influencing book buyers for a long time. Most of the books illustrated by Remington during his lifetime (he died in 1909) are no longer common, but some of the hardest to find now were later issues.

What is the rarest of all Remington illustrated items? Everyone seems to have an answer — a different one! Merle Johnson, bibliophile who put together the big Remington reference collection for the New York Public Library in the twenties and author of *American First Editions* (New York, 1929), was probably the first of the serious Remington scholars and is said to have left a note among his papers stating *A Rogers Ranger in the French and Indian War, 1757–1759* is "probably the rarest of all Remington books." Helen L. (Teri) Card disagrees with Johnson. In *The Collector's Remington,* that she had privately printed in 1946, she seems to pin the *rarest* title on Fry's *Army Sacrifices* with the cover title *Indian Fights, Illustrated 1887.* Incidentally, Teri's little booklet is mighty scarce to rare — she had only 100 copies printed which wasn't enough to go around — so numerous are the Remington buffs. Teri was, on occasion, one of the Remington scholars who gathered at the round table in the old Mannados Bookshop in New York City. Presiding over such gatherings was sure to be the genial proprietor, Walter Latendorf, dispenser of book knowledge and good whiskey, and authority on New York eating places. Walter's Catalog no. 17, *Frederic Remington* (1947), has become a standard reference volume, and he had the help of Teri in compiling it. Harold McCracken, another member of Walter's Round Tablers and author of *Frederic Remington, Artist of the Old West* (Philadelphia and New York, 1947), also lent a hand on Walter's Catalog 17. Of course, Harold has a candidate for the rarest — *A Dinner on the Occasion of the Tenth Anniversary of Collier's under the Guidance of Mr. Robert F. Collier.* I saw it first at Mannados, where I tried to persuade Walter to sell it to me, but he had already promised it to Harold. I examined it again at Cody in May, 1965, in Harold's great Remington collection at his home.

Doug Allen was another Remington buff that I met at the Mannados. Doug had his choice, Walter had his, although he was inclined to agree with Harold on the little Collier item most of the time. Walter sold me the limited Remington-Russell edition of *The Virginian* and from his sales talk I was sure I was buying the rarest Remington item. It is a beautiful job and limited to 100 numbered and signed copies. I am proud to have a copy and, while it is rare, it is not my choice of the rarest. On another of my visits to New York, Walter sold me a copy of the *Star Gambol of the Lambs* and a couple of *Squadron "A" Games Programmes,* each quite rare but still not my choice.

Actually the item that was on my want list the longest is not even considered to be a rarity by my Remington-collecting friends — Seely's *The Jonah of Lucky Valley.* I missed the copy listed in Walter's Catalog 17 and waited until the summer of 1963 — sixteen long years — for another chance to buy it. It was issued as no. 719 in Harper's Franklin Square Library to sell at fifty cents. Perhaps thousands were printed—few have survived — another case of "too cheap to keep"? It may not be rare in the opinion of any one else, but it has that rating with me. I waited a long time for a first of Jones's *Quivira,* although the second printing is quite common. I saw the first British printing of *Crooked Trails* in the Everett Graff collection in the late forties. It took me more than a dozen years

to find a copy. *The Gridiron '82* was on my want list at least as long.

My nomination for the rarest Remington illustrated item is not in my own collection. It is the little Kansas City DAR booklet on the Santa Fe Trail. The only copy that I have ever seen is in the Kansas Historical Society collection at Topeka. I haven't given up on this one, but after twenty-five years I am beginning to have doubts. I have never heard of a copy being offered for sale anywhere at any price.

Several of the items included in the check list also were offered in limited signed editions. A surprisingly large number of them have been offered for sale, "mint in original box," at extremely high prices in recent years. I have not included all such items in my list of Remington Rarities — I cannot deny that they should be, and probably are, rare — but they do keep appearing. About the only real difficulty in securing some of them would seem to be a lack of cash — not a valid reason for tabbing an item with a rarity label.

In the following list the selections are mine. To be sure, what I learned at the round table in the old Mannados from Walter, Teri, Harold and Doug has influenced the choices. A recent visit with Harold at the art museum that he so ably directs and at his home where his personal collection is shelved certainly backstopped some of my selections.

My old friend and the dean of the Western Americana dealers, Wright Howes, in his great bibliography, *US-IANA* (New York, 1954, revised and enlarged, Chicago, 1962), considers four degrees of rarity: *mildly rare,* obtainable only with some difficulty; *quite rare,* obtainable only with considerable difficulty; *very rare,* obtainable only with great difficulty; and, *superlatively rare,* almost unobtainable. I have attempted no such classification of the Remington Rarities. It is simply my belief that the following items should be included in any compilation of Remington Rarities.

Note: Complete descriptions of the Remington Rarities listed below appear in *Fifty Great Western Illustrators* (Northland Press, 1975). For easy reference the D-Remington numbers in that book follow the entries.

1. Remington, Frederic. *A Rogers Ranger in the French and Indian War, 1757–1759.* New York, 1897. (Merle Johnson says this is the rarest Remington illustrated item — this reprint from *Harper's Magazine* was probably limited to 100 copies.) D-Remington 308.

2. ———. *Crooked Trails.* London and New York, 1898. (The first American printing is no longer common, but this first British printing is very difficult to find on this side of the ocean.) D-Remington 309.

3. ———. *The Way of an Indian.* New York, 1908. (The first printing of this highly praised novel is quite scarce to rare.) D-Remington 318.

4. ———. *Drawings.* New York, 1897. (This edition was limited to 250 copies — seldom seen these days.) D-Remington 325.

5. *Done in the Open.* New York, 1902. (Very few copies with the added "k" were released prior to the discovery of the error.) D-Remington 333 or 334.

6. *Ibid.* (The *de luxe* edition is quite difficult to obtain.) D-Remington 336.

7. *Blätter und Blüten.* St. Louis, (1907). (This book in German is unknown to most Remington collectors.) D-Remington 411.

8. Brady, Buckskin. *Stories and Sermons.* Toronto, 1905. (I searched for this book for years for my Range Collection and, when I finally found a copy, the Remington illustration was an unexpected dividend. Not in many of the great range collections and not in Howes's *US-IANA.* Quite rare.) D-Remington 421.

9. Brown, Jennie Broughton. *Fort Hall on the Oregon Trail.* Caldwell, Idaho, 1932. (The trade edition of this fine history is no longer common, but just try to find a copy of the limited edition at any price.) D-Remington 439.

10. Burke, John M. *Buffalo Bill's Wild West and Congress of Rough Riders of the World.* New York, (1900). (Thousands of these souvenir booklets were sold at the show during the season, but few copies seem to be extant.) D-Remington 443.

11. (Collier.) *A Dinner on the Occasion of the Tenth Anniversary of Collier's under the Guidance of Mr. Robert F. Collier.* New York, 1908. (Harold McCracken's choice of the rarest Remington illustrated item. He owns the only copy I ever saw.) D-Remington 480.

12. Freeman, James F. (President). *Prose and Poetry of the Livestock Industry of the United States.* Denver and Kansas City, (1905). (One of the so-called "Big Four" of all range life books. It is said that the publication broke two printers and almost bankrupted the National Livestock Historical Association.

All the copies I have seen — not very many — have had the name of a member on the front cover in gold. The information provided by the oldtimers in the association is that only enough copies were issued to fill the advance orders of members. Quite rare and expensive.) D-Remington 581.

13. French, Dr. L. H. *The Desertion of Sergeant Cobb*. New York, n.d., (1901?). A very elusive Remington item — it took me years to find this one.) D-Remington 584.

14. Fry, James B. *Army Sacrifices,* but with the cover title, *Indian Fights, Illustrated, 1887*. New York, 1879, (1887). (Teri Card's nomination of the rarest Remington illustrated item — and it is very difficult to obtain.) D-Remington 590.

15. Irving, Washington. *Astoria*. New York, 1910. (An unreported Remington illustrated edition of this classic. I have seen only one copy of this book.) D-Remington 697.

16. Judd, Mary Catherine. *The Story of Fremont and Kit Carson*. Dansville, New York, and Chicago, 1906. (This little booklet is just about unknown to Remington collectors.) D-Remington 719.

17. Kemble, Edward, *et al.* (Programme Committee). *Lambs All Star Gambol*. New York, 1909. (Remington was a member of the Lambs and he illustrated other Gambol programmes — all quite scarce to rare. The choice of the 1909 programme was arbitrary on my part — it was the year Remington died.) D-Remington 728.

18. Lovett, Richard. *United States Pictures Drawn with Pen and Pencil*. (London), 1891. (One of the first uses of a Remington illustration in a British book. Unknown to most Remington collectors, but in the collections of Harold McCracken and this compiler.) D-Remington 794.

19. Pollock, J. M. *The Unvarnished West*. London, n.d., (1911?). (This book of reminiscences of sheepraising in Southwest Texas is much sought by Range Life collectors. The Remington illustrations, without credit to the artist, were a pleasant surprise when I finally found a copy.) D-Remington 918.

20. Rich, Lawson C., et al. *The Gridiron '82*. (Canton, New York), 1882. (Probably the first use of Remington illustrations in a publication that can be called a book. Very difficult to come by at any price.) D-Remington 944.

21. Seely, Howard. *The Jonah of Lucky Valley*. New York, 1892. (When I wait sixteen years for a second chance to buy a copy of a book I want, it is rare.) D-Remington 987.

22. Throop, George E., *et al.* (Programme Committee). *Squadron "A" Games, Souvenir Programme, Feb. 18th, 1897*. New York, (1897). (Walter Latendorf sold me programmes of these "Games" for several years — all rare. I chose the 1897 programme to include in this list because of the eight Remington illustrations.) D-Remington 1052.

23. U.S. Information Service. *An Outline of American History*. (Washington, D.C., 1952.) (Prepared for use abroad and never released in this country. When one of my traveling compadres spotted the Remington illustration in this book and reported it to me on his return from overseas I immediately sought a copy in

Washington. It seemed that it was practically a heinous offense for me to know that such a book existed — to aspire to ownership of this history printed at the expense of the American people and doubtlessly distributed free by the thousands overseas was unheard of. I finally got a copy, but it wasn't easy.) D-Remington 1062.

24. Van Brunt, Mrs. John (chairman), et al. *The Story of a Great Highway,* but with the cover title *The Old Santa Fe Trail.* Kansas City, Missouri, n.d. (This fragile little booklet is known in only one copy.) D-Remington 1067.

25. Watson, Douglas Sloane. *West Wind.* Los Angeles, 1934. (Printed for presentation only — small edition and much sought by the Fur Trade collectors and the fine printing buffs. Rare and expensive.) D-Remington 1089.

26. Wister, Owen. *The Virginian.* New York, 1911. (At one time Walter Latendorf's selection as the rarest Remington illustrated item. Also a Russell Rarity. If anything, Russell collectors are more avid than Remington buffs and they provide some real competition when a very occasional one of the 100 copies is offered for sale.) D-Remington 1127.

27. Woodstrike, Frank. *Great Adventure.* New York, (1937). (Also a Russell Rarity — see citation above. A few copies were winnowed out of their poetry sections by enterprising dealers following the publication of the Renner-Dykes article, but it is still mighty hard to find.) D-Remington 1140.

28. *5th U.S. Cavalry — 92d Organization Day, 1855–1947.* Honshu, Japan, (1947). (How many of these folders came home from Japan? One is known to this collector. It is a highly desirable bit of Remington ephemera.) D-Remington 1266.

Note: After the publication of the above list in April, 1966, some dealers and a few of my collecting friends insisted that it was too short. They usually followed by suggesting additions. Eleven years as a dealer convinced me that my friends were right. There are other Remington items that are very difficult to obtain for my customers. I am not sure that I believe that the following items are as rare as those above but I do know that they are:

VERY SCARCE TO RARE

29. Remington, Frederic. *Pony Tracks.* New York, 1895. (Remington's first book and a *Merrill Aristocrat* — much sought by Range Collectors.) D-Remington 305.

30. ———. *Crooked Trails.* New York and London, 1898. (Not as difficult to find as the British edition, no. 2, but far from common — as a *Merrill Aristocrat* coveted by Range Collectors.) D-Remington 309.

31. Carter, M. H., ed. *Panther Stories Retold from St. Nicholas.* New York, 1904. (An elusive juvenile—particularly in decent collecting condition.) D-Remington 460.

32. Gable, Thomas P. *First Report of Game and Fish Warden for New Mexico, 1909–1910–1911.* Santa Fe, 1912. (Distributed free and few have survived — too cheap to keep?) D-Remington 592.

33. Godfrey, General Edward S. *General George A. Custer and the Battle of*

Little Big Horn. New York, (1908). (The first separate printing and much sought by the Custer buffs — more dedicated than the Remington collectors.) D-Remington 605.

34. Gunnison, Alman. *Wayside and Fireside Rambles.* Boston, 1894. (In forty years as collector and dealer I've seen less than half-a-dozen copies for sale.) D-Remington 622.

35. Howard, Major Gen. O. O. *My Life and Experience Among Our Hostile Indians.* Hartford, (1907). (The Indian Fighting Army fans compete for this one.) D-Remington 682.

36. Humfreville, J. Lee. *Twenty Years Among Our Savage Indians.* Hartford, 1897. D-Remington 690.

37. Barnum, Frances Courteney (Baylor). *Juan and Juanita.* Boston, 1888. (A *Peter Parley to Penrod* choice and the Remington buffs compete with the collectors of Jake Blanck's famous list of best-loved juveniles for this book.) D-Remington 388.

38. Janvier, Thomas A. *The Aztec Treasure House.* New York, 1890. (Included in Blanck's *Peter Parley to Penrod* as a borderline selection and much sought.) D-Remington 704.

39. Lewis, Alfred Henry. *Wolfville.* New York, (1897). (The first issue with "Moore" in perfect type line 18, page 19 is seldom available.) D-Remington 764.

40. Longfellow, Henry Wadsworth. *The Song of Hiawatha.* Boston and New York, 1891. (The 250 numbered copies in vellum is the most sought.) D-Remington 786 and 787.

41. Page, Thomas Nelson et al. *Stories of the South.* New York, 1893. (An elusive little book.) D-Remington 883.

42. Pennell, Joseph. *Pen Drawings and Pen Draughtsmen.* London and New York (but printed in Edinburgh), 1889. (One of the first appraisals of Remington's art.) D-Remington 901.

43. Ralph, Julian. *On Canada's Frontier.* New York, 1892. (The London edition also published in 1892 and issued in a half-calf binding is scarcer than the American.) D-Remington 934.

44. Roosevelt, Theodore. *Ranch Life and the Hunting Trail.* New York, (1888). (The Range collectors compete for this book — it is a *Merrill Aristocrat.*) D-Remington 956.

45. Squires, Henry C. *Catalogue of Sportsmen's Supplies.* New York, 1891. (A handsome catalogue but with a full leather binding, marbled end sheets, 204 pages and numerous illustrations, the edition had to be small.) D-Remington 1,022.

46. Walworth, Jennette. *History of New York in Words of One Syllable.* Chicago, etc., 1888. (The only copy of this book I ever owned was pretty well beat up — I'm still looking for a copy in collector's condition.) D-Remington 1,080.

47. Whitney, Caspar W. *On Snow-Shoes to the Barren Grounds.* New York, 1896. (The London issue also in 1896 is more difficult to find.) D-Remington 1,102.

48. Barns, W. E. et al. *Souvenir Program of the Thirteenth Annual Meeting of the Concatenated Order of Hoo-Hoo.* Saint Louis, September 9, 1904. (Did any of you ever see this one?) D-Remington 1,147.

49. Bates, Col. Charles Francis. *Custer's Indian Battles.* Privately printed,

Bronxville, N.Y., (1936). (A Luther Custer High Spot.) D-Remington 1,148.

50. Card, Helen L. *The Collector's Remington*. Privately printed, Woonsocket, Rhode Island, (1946). (Two volumes, limited to 100 of each, increasingly difficult to obtain.) D-Remington 1,367 and 1,368.

CHAPTER XV

Russell Rarities

WHAT MAKES a book "rare"? Obviously, there are several factors including supply and demand that determine whether or not a book or other document becomes a rarity. Time is certainly another one of these and the older the book, the more likely it is to be difficult to find. The number of copies printed is also significant and after a few years any strictly limited edition is bound to be scarce. Not the least of the things that influence rarity is the quality of the bookmaker's art — relatively few books that are poorly printed and bound are likely to be preserved.

Significance of the contents isn't necessarily important. A book may be scarce because its content is treasured and so long as this is true, all such books are likely to be closely held by their owners. On the other hand, tastes change and even books once considered classics may later be discarded and reach the dealers' shelves in considerable numbers.

Judgment as to what is or is not important also varies at any particular time. Many ephemeral items, for example, were made to be thrown away after their first use and later became treasures avidly sought by the dedicated collector. Such Russelliana include illustrated handbills and other advertising booklets, gallery catalogs, programs for some particular affair, obscure magazine articles, and a host of others.

In the final analysis, opinions on the degree of rarity of a particular book depends on the individual's knowledge and experience. The authors make no claim to infallibility in this respect but in their experience the following books would have to be included among the Russell Rarities. As nearly as it is possible to do so, these are arranged in the order of their scarcity.

RUSSELL RARITIES

Note: Complete descriptions of all except two of the rarities listed below appear in *A Bibliography of the Published Works of Charles M. Russell,* compiled by Karl Yost and Frederic G. Renner, University of Nebraska Press, Lincoln, (1971). For easy reference the Y-R numbers follow the entries. (The list was revised by the authors in September, 1976).

1. *The Blazed Trail on the Old Frontier* by Agnes C. Laut. 271 pp., illus., gilt decorated morocco with brown linen end sheets. Robert M. McBride and Co., New York, 1926, words "Published 1926" on the copyright page. Y-R I-40. (A unique copy presented to Ralph Budd on the occasion of the Columbia River Historical Expedition in the year 1926 with an inserted hand-lettered pre-

sentation sheet and with the "Invocation" by Reverend T. F. Gullixon hand lettered in red and black on two pages in lieu of the one page printed Invocation in the first edition, plus an original watercolor signed by Russell and dated 1925 on the half-title. This presentation copy is now in the Renner Collection.)

2. *The Round-Up.* Pendleton, Oregon, September 14–15–16–17, 1927. Leaflet folded to size 3⅜ x 6¼. Y-R X-92. (The only copy known to the authors is in the Renner Collection.)

3. *Pictures in Color* by Famous American Artists. Charles Scribner's sons, New York, (1905). Pictorial cloth-backed folder, size 5¼ x 8, one print, *A Bad Hoss,* by Russell. Y-R V-4a. (The only copy known to the authors is in the Renner Collection.)

4. *Rhymes from the Roundup Camp* by Wallace D. Coburn. 147 pp., illus., olive green cloth. W. T. Ridgely Press, Great Falls, 1899. First edition, first issue of Y-R I-8. (In all other editions, "a" replaces "the" in the title. Two copies only known to the authors. The deluxe edition in full red leather of *Rhymes from a Roundup Camp* also issued by Ridgley in 1899 is exceedingly rare.)

5. *Early Days.* Noted occurrences on the line of the Colorado Midland Railway. Unpaged (44), illus., size 11 x 9, colored pic. wraps. Published by the Colorado Midland, (1901). Y-R XV-2. (The only copy known to the authors is in the Renner Collection.)

6. *Western Life for Eastern Boys.* 24 pp., illus., wraps, punched and tied. Published by Flying "D" Ranch, Gallatin Valley, Montana, Anceny & Child, Proprietors, but printed by Poole Bros., Chi-

cago, January 24, 1912. Y-R XI-19. (The only copy known to the authors is in the Renner Collection.)

7. *Illustrated Souvenir of Great Falls Fire Department.* 130 pp., illus., size 6 x 8¾. Published by the Department, August, 1912. Y-R I-27. (Two copies only known to the authors.)

8. *Montana's Capitol Dedicated at Helena, Montana, July 4, 1902.* 24 pp., illus., wraps. Souvenir published by W. T. Ridgley Printing Co., Great Falls. Y-R X-79. (Two copies only known to the authors.)

9. *Russell Post Cards Reproduced from Original Paintings of C. M. Russell.* Unpaged (40), illus., wraps. Published by the W. T. Ridgley Calendar Company, Great Falls, (1908). Y-R XIII-106. (Two copies only known to the authors.)

10. *Reproductions from Works of C. M. Russell.* Unpaged (12), illus., wraps. Published by the W. T. Ridgley Calendar Co., Great Falls, (1906). Y-R III-105. (Two copies only known to the authors.)

11. *Pen Sketches* by Charles M. Russell. Twelve plates, 14 x 11, various bindings. Published by W. T. Ridgley Printing Co., Great Falls, 1899. Y-R I-6. (The first issue has a camping scene on the fly-leaf above the publisher's imprint and the brown suede binding is the rarest.)

12. *Mrs. Nat Collins, The Cattle Queen of Montana* compiled by Charles Wallace. 249 pp., illus., pic. wraps. C. W. Foote, Saint James, Minnesota, 1894. Y-R I-2. (The authors know of only one copy offered for sale in the last forty years.)

13. *Then and Now, or Thirty Six Years in the Rockies* by Robert Vaughn.

461 pp., illus., deluxe edition in full calf inscribed by the author. Tribune Publishing Co., Minneapolis, 1900. Y-R I-11. (Two copies only known to the authors.)

14. *Charley Russell's Sentiments.* Broadside, size 10½ x 15⅜, 47 lines plus 11 stanzas of verse (written by Russell in response to a toast delivered by Robert Vaughn). Printed at Great Falls, November 15, 1911. Y-R X-16.

15. *Butte and Its Copper Mines* (The Greatest Copper Mining District in the World). 24 pp., illus., size 8-9/16 x 6½, pic. wraps. Issued by The Thompson Investment Company, Butte, 1899. Y-R I-7. (The only copy known to the authors is in the Renner Collection.)

16. *Meek's Dude Ranch* by Otto Meek (President) *et al.* 47 pp., illus., wraps. Meek Ranch, Baker, Nevada, n.d. (1925?). (Two copies only known to the authors — it is not in Y-R.)

17. *Semi-Annual Report of State Game and Fish Warden, State of Montana, 1902.* 64 pp., illus., wraps. Helena, 1902. (Two copies only known to the authors.)

18. *Chip of the Flying U* by B. M. Bower, pseud. of Bertha M. Sinclair-Cowan. 264 pp., illus., red cloth. Street & Smith, New York and London, (1906). Y-R I-21. (Four copies only are known to the authors—not to be confused with the later Dillingham edition.)

19. *The Range Dwellers* by B. M. Bower. Street & Smith, New York and London, (1907). Y-R I-22. (Four copies only are known to the authors—not to be confused with the later Dillingham edition.)

20. *Studies of Western Life* by Charles M. Russell. Unpaged (26), illus., size 9¼

x 6⅞, red cloth with three-punch silk tie. The Albertype Co., New York, for Ben R. Roberts, Cascade, Montana. Y-R I-1.

21. *The Open Range* by Oscar Rush. 263 pp., illus. deluxe edition of ten signed and numbered copies in morocco. The Caxton Printers, Caldwell, Idaho, 1936. Y-R XVI-49.

22. *The Pronghorn Antelope and its Management* by Arthur S. Einarsen. 238 pp., illus., twenty copies specially bound in cloth and antelope hide. Wildlife Management Institute, Washington, D.C. 1948. Y-R I-55. (Presentation copies, never offered for sale.)

23. *Riding the High Country* by Patrick Tucker. 210 pp., illus., deluxe edition of twenty-five signed and numbered copies in morocco. The Caxton Printers, Caldwell, Idaho, 1936. Y-R XVI-52.

24. *The Great Northern Country: Being the Chronicles of the Happy Travellers Club from Buffalo to the Pacific Coast.* 169 pp., illus., cloth. Passenger Department, Great Northern Railway and Northern Steamship Co., (Saint Paul, 1895). Y-R XVI-1.

25. *Great Falls City Directory 1900.* 366 + 2 pp., illus., buckram. R. L. Polk & Co. and W. T. Ridgley, Great Falls, 1900. Y-R I-10.

26. *How the Buffalo Lost His Crown* by John H. Beacom. 44 pp., illus., size 12½ x 10, cloth. (Forest and Stream Publishing Co., New York, 1894.) Y-R I-2. (In addition to the exceedingly rare edition in cloth, one copy only in a one-quarter morocco deluxe binding is known to the authors.)

27. *Adventures Afloat and Ashore* edited by Katherine Newbold Birdsall. 435 pp., illus., cloth. G. P. Putnam's Sons,

New York and London, (1911). Y-R XVI-25. (A volume in The Young Peoples Bookshelf and most sets must still be intact as only two copies of this volume are known to the authors.)

28. *Progressive Men of Southern Idaho.* 952 pp., illus., full morocco. A. W. Bowen & Co., Chicago, 1904. Y-R XVI-9.

29. *Progressive Men of Western Colorado.* 876 pp., illus., full morocco. A. W. Bowen & Co., Chicago, 1905. Y-R XVI-12.

30. *Progressive Men of Bannock, Bear Lake, Bingham, Fremont and Oneida Counties, Idaho.* 664 pp., illus., full morocco. A. W. Bowen & Co., Chicago, 1904. Y-R XVI-8.

31. *Progressive Men of the State of Wyoming.* 965 pp., illus., full morocco. A. W. Bowen & Co., Chicago, 1903. Y-R XVI-7.

32. *Progressive Men of the State of Montana.* 1,886 pp., illus., full morocco. A. W. Bowen & Co., Chicago, (1902). Y-R I-14. (This one is a mug book that became a rarity—the Russell illustration in it was used in Rarities 28, 29, 30 and 31.)

33. *The Souvenir of Western Women* edited by Mary Osborn Douthit. 200 pp., illus., colored pic. wraps and an unknown number of presentation copies in full limp leather. Anderson and Duniway, Portland, 1905. (Four other editions, that are almost as hard to find.)

34. *Seventh Report of the Bureau of Agriculture, Labor and Industry of the State of Montana for the Year ending November 30, 1900,* J. H. Calderhead, Commissioner. 613 pp., illus., cloth. Independent Publishing Co., Helena, 1900. Y-R XVI-3.

35. *Eighth Report of the Bureau of Agriculture, Labor and Industry of the State of Montana.* 733 pp., illus., cloth. Independent Publishing Co., Helena, 1902. Y-R I-15.

36. *Good Medicine* by Charles M. Russell. xii, 13–162± one leaf, illus., three-quarter blue buckram with vellum sides. Doubleday, Doran and Co., New York, 1929, words "First Edition" on copyright page. Y-R I-43. (Limited Edition of 134 copies—presented to the owners of the letters used in the book. The authors know of only two copies offered for sale in the past forty years.)

37. *The Virginian: A Horseman of the Plains* by Owen Wister. 506 pp., on Japan vellum, illus., vellum parchment and brown boards. The Macmillan Co., New York, 1911, words "Special Limited Edition, October, 1911" on copyright page. Y-R I-26a. (Limited to 100 numbered copies signed by Wister. The authors know of only three copies that have changed hands in the last forty years.)

38. *Great Adventure* by Frank H. Woodstrike. 319 pp., illus. cloth. The World Publishing Co., New York, (1937). Y-R XVI-61. (Bad poetry but a rare Russell.)

39. *Fremont and '49* by Frederick S. Dellenbaugh. 547 + (6 of advg.) pp., illus., colored illus. cloth. G. P. Putnam's Sons, New York and London, 1914. (Not in Y-R.)

40. *Charles Marion Russell, Painter of the West, 1865–1926.* Unpaged (8), illus., pic. wraps. Robert C. Vose Galleries, Boston, (1928). Y-R II-39. (The only copy known to the authors is in the Renner Collection—a number of other gal-

lery catalogs deserve ratings of very scarce to rare.)

Very Scarce to Rare

41. *Adventures with Indians and Game* (Twenty Years in the Rocky Mountains) by Dr. William A. Allen. 302 pp., illus., three-quarter calf and marbled boards. A. W. Bowen & Co., Chicago, 1903. Y-R I-16.

42. *Fifteen Thousand Miles by Stage* by Carrie Adell Strahorn. xxvii + 673 pp., 350 illus. including 85 by Russell, cloth with illus. in color on front cover. G. P. Putnam's Sons, New York, London, 1911. Y-R I-25. (Especially sought are the twelve presentation copies bound in full green morocco or any copy of the first in the original Russell illus. dust wrapper. The second edition, issued in 1915, contains one additional Russell illustration—it is much sought by Russell collectors.)

43. *I Conquered* by Harold Titus. 302 + 2 pp., frontispiece in color by Russell, cloth. Rand McNally & Company, Chicago, (1916). Y-R I-31. (Without the original d/w this is only a moderately scarce book but in the original d/w only two copies are known to the authors—so far as we know this is the only complete reproduction of the Russell illustration in color of which a detail is used as the frontispiece. The location of the original painting is unknown.)

44. *Paper Talk* (Illustrated Letters of Charles M. Russell) with introduction and commentary by Frederic G. Renner. 120 pp., illus., pic. wraps. Amon Carter Museum, Fort Worth, (1962). Y-R I-68. (The first 20 of the first issue of 1,000 copies are marked by the misspelling of the word "returning" in the text, line 3, page 14—these copies are much sought by Russell collectors.)

45. *Rawhide Rawlins Stories* by C. M. Russell. iv + 60 pp., illus. by the author, pic. wraps or cloth. Montana Newspaper Assn., Great Falls, 1921. Y-R I-36. (Reprinted several times but the first is increasingly difficult to obtain.)

46. *Bucking the Sagebrush* (The Oregon Trail in the Seventies) by Charles J. Steedman. x + 270 pp., illus., pic. cloth. G. P. Putnam's Sons, New York and London, 1904, words "Published November 1904" on copyright page. Y-R I-19. (Rated "scarce" by Adams in *The Rampaging Herd* #2153 in 1959 and now increasingly difficult to obtain.)

47. *Ranching, Sport and Travel* by Thomas Carson. 13–319 pp., illus., cloth. T. Fisher Unwin, London, Leipsic, 1911. Y-R XVI-21. (The first American edition, issued by Scribner in 1912, is scarce and the British edition is much more difficult to obtain.)

48. *Forty Years on the Frontier, the Reminiscences and Journals of Granville Stuart* edited by Paul C. Phillips. Two-volume set, 272 and 265 pp., illus., cloth. The Arthur H. Clark Company, Cleveland, 1925. Y-R XVI-37. (Long OP and reprinted in 1957, two volumes in one, by Clark.)

49. *Montana and Her Cowboy Artist.* A paper read before the Contemporary Club, Davenport, Iowa, January 30, 1950, by James W. Bollinger. 24 pp., wraps. Y-R XVII. (Small printing and long OP —reprinted by World Publishing Co., Shenandoah, Iowa, 1963, with an introduction by Otha D. Wearin.)

50. *Northern Grown Tested Seeds*

1895. 80 pp., illus., colored pic. wraps (Russell illustration). J. Ottman Lith Co., New York, for Northrup, Braslan, Goodwin Co., Minneapolis, January 1, 1895. Y-R XI-52. (An example of the elusive advertising booklets and folders using Russell illustrations—one of the two copies of this seed catalog known to the authors is in the Yost Collection.)